STRATEGIC COMMUNICATION

The focus of this book is strategic communication. Communication can be defined as strategic if its development and/or dissemination is driven by an expected outcome. These outcomes can be attitudinal, behavioral, persuasive, or knowledge-related; they can lead to change or engagement, or they can miss their mark entirely. In looking at strategic communication, one is not limited to a specific context or discipline. Many of the scholars in the volume are generating research that covers strategic communication in ways that are meaningful across fields.

This volume collects the work and ideas of scholars who cover the spectrum of strategic communication from source to message to audience to channel to effects. *Strategic Communication* offers new perspectives across contexts and is rooted firmly in the rich research traditions of persuasion and media effects. Spanning multiple disciplines and written to appeal to a large audience, this book will be found in the hands of researchers, graduate students, and students doing interdisciplinary coursework.

Anthony Dudo is an Assistant Professor at the University of Texas at Austin.

LeeAnn Kahlor is an Associate Professor at the University of Texas at Austin.

New Agendas in Communication

A Series from Routledge and the College of Communication at the University of Texas at Austin

Roderick Hart and Stephen Reese, Series Editors

This series brings together groups of emerging scholars to tackle important interdisciplinary themes that demand new scholarly attention and reach broadly across the communication field's existing courses. Each volume stakes out a key area, presents original findings, and considers the long-range implications of its "new agenda."

Recent series titles include:

Work Pressures
edited by Dawna I. Ballard and Matthew S. McGlone

Strategic Communication
edited by Anthony Dudo and LeeAnn Kahlor

Networked China: Global Dynamics of Digital Media and Civic Engagement
edited by Wenhong Chen and Stephen D. Reese

New Technologies and Civic Engagement
edited by Homero Gil de Zúñiga

The full list of series volumes is available at www.routledge.com

STRATEGIC COMMUNICATION

New Agendas in Communication

Edited by Anthony Dudo and LeeAnn Kahlor

NEW YORK AND LONDON

First published 2017
by Routledge
711 Third Avenue, New York, NY 10017

and by Routledge
2 Park Square, Milton Park, Abingdon, Oxon, OX14 4RN

Routledge is an imprint of the Taylor & Francis Group, an Informa business

© 2017 Taylor & Francis

The right of the editors to be identified as the authors of the editorial material, and of the authors for their individual chapters, has been asserted in accordance with sections 77 and 78 of the Copyright, Designs and Patents Act 1988.

All rights reserved. No part of this book may be reprinted or reproduced or utilized in any form or by any electronic, mechanical, or other means, now known or hereafter invented, including photocopying and recording, or in any information storage or retrieval system, without permission in writing from the publishers.

Trademark notice: Product or corporate names may be trademarks or registered trademarks, and are used only for identification and explanation without intent to infringe.

Library of Congress Cataloging in Publication Data
Names: Dudo, Anthony, editor. | Kahlor, LeeAnn, editor.
Title: Strategic communication : new agendas in communication / edited by Anthony Dudo and LeeAnn Kahlor.
Description: New York : Routledge, 2016. | Series: New agendas in communication | Includes bibliographical references and index.
Identifiers: LCCN 2016003435 (print) | LCCN 2016006434 (ebook) | ISBN 9781138184787 (hardback) | ISBN 9781138184794 (pbk.) | ISBN 9781315644943 (ebk.) | ISBN 9781315644943 (ebook)
Subjects: LCSH: Communication.
Classification: LCC P90 S7675 2016 (print) | LCC P90 (ebook) | DDC 302.23—dc23

ISBN: [978-1-138-18478-7] (hbk)
ISBN: [978-1-138-18479-4] (pbk)
ISBN: [978-1-315-64494-3] (ebk)

Typeset in Bembo
by Swales & Willis Ltd, Exeter, Devon, UK

CONTENTS

Contributors		*vii*
Preface		*ix*
1	A Story About Stories in Strategic Communication *Michael Dahlstrom*	1
2	Strategic Storytelling: Narrative Messaging in Entertainment and Emergent Media *Heather L. LaMarre*	20
3	The Promise of Participatory Media: Identifying the Potential Roles of Influential Content Generators in Prosocial Strategic Communication *Kajsa E. Dalrymple and Rachel Young*	42
4	The Social Nature of Online Media and Its Effects on Behaviors and Attitudes *Ashley A. Anderson*	66
5	How We Talk and Why It Matters *Myiah Hutchens*	84
6	Strategic Communication and U.S. National Security Affairs: Critical–Cultural and Rhetorical Perspectives *Hamilton Bean*	103

7 Marketer-Consumer Language Cooperation in Strategic
   Communication   125
   Ann Kronrod

8 How Marketing Communications Influence the Formation
   of Food Habits Prior to Adulthood   142
   Anna McAlister

9 Social Media and Crisis Communication: Explicating the
   Social-Mediated Crisis Communication Model   163
   Lucinda Austin and Yan Jin

Index   *187*

CONTRIBUTORS

Ashley A. Anderson (Ph.D., University of Wisconsin-Madison) is an assistant professor in Colorado State University's Department of Journalism and Media Communication. Anderson's research examines the role of communication in how people form opinions about and engage with scientific and environmental issues.

Lucinda Austin (Ph.D., University of Maryland College Park) is an assistant professor in the School of Media and Journalism at the University of North Carolina at Chapel Hill. Her research focuses on social media's influence on strategic communication initiatives, namely health and crisis communication, and explores publics' perspectives in organization-public relationship building.

Hamilton Bean (Ph.D., University of Colorado-Boulder) is Director of the International Studies Program and Associate Professor in the Department of Communication at the University of Colorado Denver, where he specializes in the study of communication and security.

Michael Dahlstrom (Ph.D., University of Wisconsin-Madison) is an associate professor in the Greenlee School of Journalism and Mass Communication at Iowa State University. Dahlstrom's research explores the use of narratives and storytelling to communicate science; ethical considerations of communicating science; and communicating beyond human scale.

Kajsa E. Dalrymple (Ph.D., University of Wisconsin-Madison) is an assistant professor in the University of Iowa School of Journalism and Mass Communication. Her research focuses on the intersection between science, strategic communication, and public policy.

Myiah Hutchens (Ph.D., Ohio State University) is an assistant professor of political communication in the Edward R. Murrow College of Communication at Washington State University. Her research focuses on exposure to counter-attitudinal views through their discussion networks and their consequences for democratic outcomes.

Ann Kronrod (Ph.D., Tel Aviv University) is an assistant professor in the Department of Advertising and Public Relations at Michigan State University. Her research brings together exploration of language use in user-generated content on social networks, pro-social marketing and the managerial aspects of marketing analytics.

Yan Jin (Ph.D., University of Missouri) is associate director of the Center for Health & Risk Communication and an associate professor in the Henry W. Grady College of Journalism and Mass Communication at the University of Georgia. Her primary research resides within the field of crisis communication and strategic conflict management and has a strong focus on how emotions influence crisis communication decision-making.

Heather L. LaMarre (Ph.D., Ohio State University) is an associate professor of Strategic Communication at Temple University School of Media and Communication where she researches the processing and effects of political and policy narratives in entertainment and emergent media.

Anna McAlister (Ph.D., University of Queensland) is an assistant professor in the Department of Advertising and Public Relations at Michigan State University. Her research focuses on consumer behavior, particularly on the application of theories of developmental psychology to the study of children's consumer socialization. McAlister's work is largely policy-oriented, with an interest in children's knowledge of food brands and their responses to food advertising.

Rachel Young (Ph.D., University of Missouri) is an assistant professor in the University of Iowa School of Journalism and Mass Communication. Young's research investigates strategic health communication and technology from many perspectives, with the goal of informing theory-based collaborations to improve health outcomes.

PREFACE

Presented in these pages is a collection of chapters, each focused on a unique aspect of strategic communication, written by new scholars who are on a journey of discovery as they carve out a niche within their respective disciplines. In these chapters, we glimpse the early stages of the research trajectories of these junior scholars and bear witness to their tremendous potential. The intended audience for this book is, no surprise, communication scholars with an interest in strategic communication, but we also edited this book with communication practitioners in mind – those who would like a sampling of current research from promising scholars.

We define strategic communication as communication that is driven by an expected outcome. That outcome can be attitudinal, behavioral, persuasive or knowledge-related; it can lead to change or engagement, or it can miss its mark entirely. In this sense, strategic communication is a thread that runs through a great deal of research produced across mass, interpersonal and rhetorical communication disciplines – including the usual suspects of advertising, public relations, and persuasive communication, but also communication studies, organizational communication, and journalism (though our j-school colleagues might be reluctant to use the term "strategic," the goal of community engagement and the harnessing of user generated content should indeed be described as strategic). Indeed, under the broad umbrella of communication research, we see strategic communication in each element of the old standby, "Who says what to whom via what channel with what effect?" Think: Source-message-channel-audience/receiver-outcome.

The collective research generated by the junior scholars featured in this book covers strategic communication in ways that are meaningful within and *across* disciplines. We emphasize this point because we often forget that well-trained scholars should be able to move easily between sub-disciplines, given that each of these sub-disciplines is drawing seamlessly from the same pool of communication theory and, at times, methods. Thus, a graduate student in advertising could gain valuable insights from the diverse perspectives emerging from scholars in rhetoric, despite the latter not being explicitly tailored to advertising-related research questions. In this way, this book is progressive in its acknowledgement that societal shifts and technology now allow for interpersonal communication to merge with mass communication, for sources to generate messages without a third party (the media), and for strategy to breach the great wall surrounding journalistic objectivity – and have that breach lead to positive audience outcomes.

When searching for junior scholars with notable new agendas to showcase in our series, we cast our net widely, which is why it was exciting to see the best chapter proposals form natural thematic clusters. These four clusters are: narrative persuasion (Dahlstrom and LaMarre), online communication and discussion (Anderson, Hutchens, and Dalrymple and Young), rhetoric (Bean and Kronrod), and strategic communication within the context of controversy (McAlister) and crisis (Austin and Jin).

These clusters signal two things. The first is that when we asked those who were most recently immersed in the canon of research that is typically covered in the world's best communication PhD programs, there was a consensus about areas that "need more work." The second is that, even with that consensus, there is always room for another scholar to carve an agenda that contributes to our understanding of the communication phenomena under study. In this sense, this book tells the story of strategic communication through the collaborative lens of the most promising junior scholars we could find.

Our book opens with a story about stories, as it were, delivered by Michael Dahlstrom (Associate Professor, Iowa State University). In his chapter, Dahlstrom uses narrative persuasion (as a narrative device) to reveal the history of narrative persuasion research, and detail the shift from a focus on message effects to the larger normative questions about when such message effects are appropriate to employ. As an opening chapter, Dahlstrom sets the stage for another chapter on narrative persuasion, this one by Heather LaMarre (Assistant Professor, Temple University). In Chapter 2, LaMarre offers a detailed examination of the fractured streams of research that currently constitute narrative persuasion. She also explores the relationship between narratives and public opinion, particularly as that relationship evolves on emergent media. Finally, she calls for a narrative messaging typology that can be used to guide empirical narrative strategy research. Together, the Dahlstrom and LaMarre chapters provide readers with a good understanding of narrative persuasion past, present, and future.

The next three chapters grapple with online communication and the role of discussion within strategic communication contexts. In Chapter 3, Kajsa Dalrymple and Rachel Young (both assistant professors at University of Iowa) review research emphasizing the importance of mobilizing social network "influentials" in prosocial campaigns. They describe characteristics of influential content generators and propose a research typology that can be used to explore how environmental and health communicators might use the affordances of social media to *listen* to users' dialogue and concerns about health and environmental issues, capitalize on user ability to *forward* messages to social networks, and *collaborate* with users to create innovative and effective campaigns.

In the book's fourth chapter, Ashley Anderson (Assistant Professor, Colorado State University) examines the extent to which different forms of online discussion and activities about scientific topics exhibit the dialogic characteristics of strategic communication. Recounting research she has conducted on formal and informal deliberation, news commenting sections, and information seeking, Anderson explores how these online communication environments engender aspects of interactivity. She then calls for research that seeks to untangle information-use habits online, particularly in terms of opinion leadership, perceptions of trust and credibility, and selective exposure. Insights emerging from that research, she argues, would help reveal how the online communication environment contributes to individuals' attitudes and behaviors.

Myiah Hutchens (Assistant Professor, Washington State University), whose research focuses on the influence of interpersonal discussion on public opinion formation about politics, authors the book's fifth chapter. Hutchens provides an overarching review of the political discussion literature and explores what she views as three key developments in this area: a clearer understanding of the cognitive processes that occur during group deliberations and the effects of deliberative events on attitudes about public policy; the use and impact of aggressive communication tactics (e.g., "flaming") in online discussions about politics; and methodological improvements in terms of how various forms of discussion are measured. Hutchens considers how her research on political discussion can help practitioners in their strategic efforts to better understand their stakeholders and facilitate more effective spaces for engagement among them.

The next two chapters highlight new agendas for strategic communication research that are based on rhetorical perspectives. In Chapter 6, Hamilton Bean (Associate Professor, University of Colorado-Denver) argues that themes related to security ought to become more central to the overall agenda of strategic communication research and establishes the need for a new research agenda that emphasizes critical-cultural and rhetorical perspectives. He maps the terrain of U.S. strategic communication research and practice and describes what critical-cultural and rhetorical communication scholarship entails and then details how his research advances the critical-cultural and rhetorical study of U.S. strategic security communication.

In Chapter 7, Ann Kronrod (Assistant Professor, Michigan State University) introduces readers to the concept of conversational cooperation as a novel framework for studying strategic communication. The framework, she contends, offers researchers a means for looking at the negotiation of persuasive communication between sender and receiver and poses the receiver as having a distinct role in the persuasive process. Kronrod describes various levels of linguistic inquiry, explicates the concept of conversational cooperation, and considers how changes in linguistic behavior due to cultural and technological changes are likely to shape the future of strategic communication.

The book's final two chapters present new agendas for strategic communication research centered on two highly salient issues: food marketing to youth, and managing crises within a rapidly shifting communication ecosystem. In Chapter 8, Anna McAlister (Assistant Professor, Michigan State University), an emerging expert in consumer behavior, explains how young people's food choices are influenced by marketing communications. She begins her chapter with a general introduction to child development then moves on to discuss children's susceptibility to persuasion. After providing this foundation, McAlister details current food and beverage marketing practices and discusses specific examples of how this knowledge of industry practices can be leveraged to help those who wish to promote healthy food and beverage choices among young people. The chapter culminates in McAlister laying out an agenda for addressing the nation's obesity epidemic through pro-social strategic communication aimed at changing family behaviors.

The final chapter centers on what has historically been the focus of much intellectual effort within the strategic communication field: how to prevent, identify, and respond to crises. Lucinda Austin (Assistant Professor, University of North Carolina) and Yan Jin (Associate Professor, University of Georgia) recently made a significant contribution to crisis communication scholarship with their Social-Mediated Crisis Communication (SMCC) model. In Chapter 9, Austin and Jin explain their model and situate it within the larger body of literature on social media and crisis communication. They also describe current and emerging issues in social media and crisis communication, provide an overview of dominant research streams and areas for special consideration, and discuss pressing areas for future research that stem from their continued refinement and application of their SMCC model.

In sum, the chapters outlined above provide readers with a sampling of new ideas emerging from promising junior scholars across a variety of communication sub-disciplines all working in the context of strategic communication. These chapters offer us a sampling of fruitful, pressing areas for strategic communication research (e.g., diversifying our research methods, exploring the online communication ecosystem, rediscovering our history in storytelling, etc.), but also point out that these areas are all works in progress – there is always room for new scholars to push the research forward. Our hope is that this compilation will serve as a catalyst, empowering readers in the development of their own new agendas in strategic communication.

1
A STORY ABOUT STORIES IN STRATEGIC COMMUNICATION

Michael Dahlstrom

Stories, more formally known as narratives in the scholarly literature, represent a format of communication describing the thoughts and actions of specific characters over time and the cause-and-effect relationships surrounding their choices. As narrative represents a general format of communication, the actual construction of particular stories varies greatly, ranging from short testimonials describing an individual's success after using a certain brand of toothpaste to great cultural literature exploring universal themes of human experience. Narratives abound in our communication environment, guiding the construction of news stories, driving the majority of entertainment media and packaging content for sharing over social media.

In addition to their ubiquity, narratives are also intrinsically persuasive. Because they present a specific experience from an individual's point of view, narratives have no need to justify the accuracy of their claims—the story itself demonstrates the claim. As such, narratives are able to assign normative values to real-world objects without the need to construct an argument—making it difficult to counter their claims (Bruner, 1991). Strategic communicators often take advantage of these persuasive aspects of narrative, using anecdotes, case studies or testimonials as evidence, or by using product placement within existing stories to infuse their brand or product with the influence of the narrative itself.

The intrinsic value of narratives to strategic communication make it particularly surprising that the scholarly examination of narrative persuasion is relatively recent. As a growing field of study, it should come as no surprise that two chapters in this volume address narratives. In this chapter, I will use narrative persuasion (as a narrative device) to reveal the history of narrative persuasion. In addition, however, I hope to portray a larger journey within this chapter—the shift from a focus on message effects to the larger normative questions about when such message effects are appropriate to employ—a journey I argue is important for both the individual scholar as well as the field itself. In Chapter 2 in this volume, LaMarre provides a detailed examination of the fractured streams of research that currently constitute narrative persuasion. Together, these two chapters should provide readers with a good understanding of narrative persuasion past, present and future.

Exposition: The Setting of Narrative Persuasion

At the turn of the previous century, the study of narrative resided in the domain of literary studies and criticism. Literary scholars from this period focused on the fictional novel to investigate the formal and functional aspects of narrative, including its internal composition, underlying meanings and differences to other forms of discourse (Kreiswirth, 2000).

Different traditions developed within this literary domain, each with a specific focus on the concept of narrative. The earliest group was the Russian formalists who stressed a distinction between a story and its discourse. Later, the American tradition focused on differences of point of view within a narrative. The French structuralists around the same time searched for a common underlying structure to all narratives (Culler, 1981). Later literary traditions also arose in Germany, the Netherlands and Israel with their own narrative foci and the eventual merging of the American tradition and French structuralism created the field of narratology (Kreiswirth, 1992). Yet, even with the subtle differences between traditions, narratives still remained within the domain of literary theory.

It wasn't until 1981 that narrative as a serious topic of study was introduced to the larger circle of scholarly discourse through a special issue of *Critical Inquiry*, titled "On Narrative" (Bruner, 1991; Kreiswirth, 1992). In contrast to its literary roots, "On Narrative" presented views of narrative outside the fictional novel, from scholars outside of the literary field, and emphasized narrative as human activity and meaning rather than its form and function (Kreiswirth, 2000). It was a shift from "what" narratives are to "how" they work and "why" they exist (Kreiswirth, 1992).

This shift in thinking led to the "narrative turn," an explosion of interest in narrative across many disciplines (Bruner, 1991). Narrative was no longer just for appreciation but had potential effects on how humans organize knowledge. Areas as diverse as economic theory and medicine that were dominated by scientific and logical approaches began to be interested in how narratives could influence their field of study (Kreiswirth, 2000). The result was the study of narrative spreading across cognitive science, pedagogy, policy analysis, sociology, experimental psychology, therapy, visual arts, music and natural sciences (Kreiswirth, 2000).

Two influential scholars helped integrate narrative within the communication and psychology fields in the 1980s. Within communication, Fisher argued that the prevailing view that people interact with the world in a rational or logical manner is false and should be replaced with a narrative paradigm, stating that people are essentially storytellers and base decisions on the coherence and probability of stories that already align with their existing beliefs and values (Fisher, 1984, 1985). Within psychology, Bruner empirically showed that narratives and rationality represent contrasting forms of cognition—a paradigmatic pathway that controls the encoding of logic-based arguments and a narrative pathway that controls the encoding of situation-based exemplars (Bruner, 1986, 1991). This division aligned with the existing distinction between semantic and episodic memory (Tulving, 1972) but began to explore the pathways that created these different forms of memory and the factors that led to the activation of one over the other.

As narratives began to gain attention from scholars in these and other disciplines, other scholars resisted the inclusion of narrative—narratives were deemed by resisters as distortions or even falsifications of the truth and thus not to be trusted as representative of anything meaningful. These anti-narrativists pointed to the fact that there are no empirical procedures of verification for narratives—a narrative based on truth does not differ in appearance or structure from one that contains no truth (Kreiswirth, 2000). Such sentiments are still voiced in certain contexts (Katz, 2013).

As a result of resistance, narratives were sometimes slow to be permitted into the canon of accepted literature across disciplines. Brock, Strange and Green note that a prominent graduate-level textbook about the psychology of attitude change published in 1993 had no mention of narrative influence (Brock, Strange, & Green, 2002; Eagly & Chaiken, 1993). Furthermore, as much of persuasion and strategic communication borrow constructs and theories from psychology, it is not surprising that persuasion was equally slow to incorporate narrative into its textbooks—as late as 2002, there was still no mention of narrative as a persuasive influence in O'Keefe's textbook of persuasion (O'Keefe, 2002).

It wasn't until Green and Brock published a seminal article in 2000 introducing the transportation-imagery model that narratives began to gain attention within persuasion (Green & Brock, 2000). The model, which is explained in more detail in LaMarre's chapter, states that the primary factor controlling narrative persuasion is the degree to which an individual becomes absorbed into the world of the narrative; the authors labeled this phenomenon "transportation." They argued that the greater the degree of transportation, the more likely the individual will accept the persuasive message embedded in the narrative. This resonated with the earlier work of Gerrig, who asserted that, when highly absorbed in the narrative (transported), individuals become so focused that they lose access to certain types of real world knowledge (Gerrig, 1993) and are thus limited in their the ability to generate counterarguments to the content being consumed. Acceptance of persuasive information was therefore described as a default state of narrative exposure, where rejection was only possible with added scrutiny afterwards (Gerrig, 1993).

These studies and others that followed supported the idea that narrative persuasion is categorically different from traditional persuasion, as many important variables of traditional persuasion models, such as motivation or personal relevance, seem to have limited significance to narrative persuasion. For example, narratives with settings or characters high in personal relevance are rarely more persuasive than narratives without (Oatley, 2002; Wheeler, Green, & Brock, 1999). This is in stark contrast to the dual processing Elaboration Likelihood Model from traditional persuasion, wherein perceived relevance is a key determinant of deeper message processing. Even need for cognition, a trait-based measure with a long history of importance in traditional persuasion, has been found to have little to no role in narrative persuasion (Appel & Richter, 2007; Green & Brock, 2000; Wheeler et al., 1999).

Instead, new variables were conceptualized to account for differences in narrative persuasion, such as identification—which is emotionally connecting to a character or situation because the narrative is perceived to be aligned with some aspect of the audience's personal history (Cohen, 2001)—and narrative realism—which is how tightly the narrative conforms to the internal rules defined by the world of the narrative itself (Busselle & Bilandzic, 2008).

One of the few situations that have been found to routinely disrupt transportation is when the persuasive intent of the narrative becomes salient (Moyer-Guse, 2008; Slater & Rouner, 2002). Such a realization draws the mind away from the narrative world causing the persuadee to begin scrutinizing the narrative information with more cognitive awareness. Many persuasive narratives, therefore, shroud their persuasive intent within the logic of the narrative world to avoid rejection based on a reaction to the intent rather than the narrative information itself.

In the last decade, the field of narrative persuasion has expanded rapidly. For example, health communication researchers began examining if narrative formats would be more persuasive in convincing individuals to engage in beneficial health practices (de Wit, Das, & Vet, 2008; Mazor et al., 2007). However, as narrative-focused research took off, inconsistencies within narrative influence soon became apparent—sometimes the research findings pointed to increased persuasion, but other times not. A meta-analysis of narrative studies within health communication specifically found no evidence that narratives had any systematic influence when compared to statistical communication, and the authors warned against the use of narrative persuasion until the phenomenon was better understood (Winterbottom, Bekker, Conner, & Mooney, 2008).

Explanations of these inconsistencies were often attributed, albeit vaguely, to a lack of "quality" in the narrative used (Green & Brock, 2000; Slater,

Rouner, & Long, 2006); the argument was that well-written narratives should be more effective than poorly written ones. However, while that is likely true, there was little discussion as to what potential variables underlie this construct of quality (Kreuter et al., 2007) and no empirical results to back up such a claim. One of the few studies that empirically examined narrative quality came from an investigation of jury deliberation that found a break in coherence or chronology of a prosecuting summary resulted in fewer guilty verdicts (Voss, Wiley, & Sandak, 1999).

In summary, narratives have expanded as a scholarly inquiry from a focus on appreciation in literary theory to effects and influences in a wide range of otherwise divergent disciplines. The field of persuasion specifically has turned to narratives as a potentially influential format for strategic communication, leading to attitude and behavior change through mechanisms that seem to circumvent many of the traditional barriers to persuasion. Yet, this enthusiasm for understanding the effects of narrative formats of communication has only emphasized their underlying complexity and current lack of predictability. In the following section, I explore what may lie behind the apparent inconsistencies in narrative effects on persuasion.

Rising Action: Addressing Internal Variance Within Narratives

One potential source for the inconsistencies in the aforementioned research is the seeming expectation of a standard narrative effect, even though there is great variety in the possible stories that can be told and how they can be constructed. Searching for a standard narrative effect seems, in hindsight, analogous to the 1930s magic-bullet conceptualization of media effects. That original conceptualization portrayed the media as a monolith that had a single effect upon all audiences; it has since been rejected in lieu of much more nuanced models of media effects (McQuail, 2010). The same pathway to understanding beckoned for narrative research. What if variables *internal* to narratives can differ in their persuasive impact? If so, then ignoring within-narrative differences would result in a scattershot of potential results, similar to what was being found in narrative persuasion research.

It was this realization that led me to pursue a research agenda focused on exploring the heterogeneous nature of narrative structure and identifying variables involved in the construction of particular narratives that may influence their persuasive impact. In other words, I agreed with Greasser and Ottati that "it is a good time for psychologists to abandon some of the weary paradigm-ridden research projects, and investigate the properties of good stories" (Graesser & Ottati, 1995). To do so, I turned to the literature of discourse psychology.

Discourse psychology explores how the mind comprehends information and creates representations of that information in memory. The underlying premise is that the mental representation of information goes beyond the information itself and, as a result, individuals do not react directly to communicated information but, rather, indirectly through the meanings that they extract from that information (Bower & Rinck, 1999). Thus it is important to understand how specific variables within communicated information influence the creation of memory representations. While the form of information examined in discourse psychology can range from product instructions (Mills, Diehl, Birkmire, & Mou, 1993) to mathematical proofs (Fletcher, Lucas, & Baron, 1999), the majority of studies examine the comprehension of narrative. This focus exists because of the assumed correspondence between narrative processing and the processing of everyday experiences—this correspondence makes the comprehension of narratives more natural than other forms of communication (Graesser, Olde, & Klettke, 2002).

Once immersed in the literature, one structural narrative variable that caught my attention was causality. The causal network model (Trabasso & Sperry, 1985) claims that causal relations represent the glue that holds narratives together (Magliano, 1999); the model has served as a basis for many of the later models of discourse psychology (Magliano, 1999; vandenBroek & Gustafson, 1999). Studies using the causal network model identify causal relations using the logical criterion of necessity (Mackie, 1980), which states that element A is considered causally related to element B if element B could not occur in the narrative without element A. It has been found that narrative statements with a greater number of causal connections are easier to recall, are recalled faster, receive higher ratings of importance to the narrative (Trabasso & Sperry, 1985) and result in faster reading times (Trabasso & Suh, 1993) than narrative statements with fewer causal connections. These causal connections can also form a causal chain, which is a linked chain of statements connected by their cause-and-effect relationships that spans the entirety of the narrative. Statements on the causal chain have similarly been found to result in greater recall and importance ratings, even after accounting for the effects of absolute number of causal connections (Trabasso & Sperry, 1985).

My growing interest in causality led me to examine if the within-narrative variance of causality (borrowed from discourse psychology) would influence persuasive outcomes and possibly improve the predictability of narrative persuasion. Because this factor had not yet been a focus within the field, I wanted to see how previous narrative stimuli had been structured with regard to causality. I therefore contacted multiple authors who had conducted research into narrative persuasion studies and asked to see their narrative stimulus materials. What I discovered was that persuasive information had been generally placed within narratives at breaks in the action, where characters could pause to discuss unrelated (and therefore easy to manipulate) persuasive statements as an aside before returning to the meaningful action of the narrative. This meant the persuasive content was often not causally relevant to the full narrative. Because the influence of the persuasive elements at these unrelated locations in the narrative had not yet been compared to their influence if they were causally relevant, I conducted and published three effects studies exploring these questions.

Study 1

The first study aimed to determine if persuasive information embedded into a narrative in such a way as to be the cause of future events differed in influence than persuasive information embedded into a narrative with no meaningful causal linkages to the story itself (Dahlstrom, 2010). In other words, would a persuasive statement's influence depend on whether or not it mattered to the plot of the story?

To explore this question, I needed to be able to compare persuasive statements in a narrative that caused plot-important events to happen to similar persuasive statements that had no meaningful impact on the causal chain of the story. To avoid confounding the specific statements used with their location relative to this causal chain, I needed a list of persuasive statements, each of which could be placed into a master narrative at either a plot-specific, causal location or a plot-indifferent, non-causal location and still make sense within the larger context of the narrative world. I could then compare the influence of a persuasive statement when it was on the causal chain in one version of the master narrative to when it was off the causal chain in an analogous version of the same narrative.

To do this, I constructed a roughly 3000-word narrative about a band of young pirates racing a more experienced group of pirates to an ultimate treasure. Being inexperienced, they carried with them a book of facts that they often consulted to help them solve challenges that they faced. The inclusion of the book served as a device to coherently insert various persuasive statements into the narrative on the causal chain causing future events to happen. Likewise, the characters would also occasionally pause to chat or read from the book between major events, which would allow statements to be inserted where they had no relevance to the causal chain of the story.

For example, in one scene that represents the causal chain, the pirates are lost in a forest without their compass and cannot find their way back to their ship. They consult the book to find a way to know where they are. The book provides an answer, which they use to continue the journey. In a later scene that represents a location off the causal chain, the pirates are sailing to a new island and waiting to arrive. One character reads out loud from the book to pass the time to which another character replies what was just said was pointless and to stop annoying him.

Two persuasive statements that were relevant to this example were (1) wild pansies rotate throughout the day to constantly face the sun and (2) berry bushes are thickest on the windward side. In one version of the narrative, the first statement about the pansies served as the clue to allow the pirates to continue their quest whereas the second statement about the berries was noted while the pirates were wasting time. In a second version of the narrative, the two were flipped—the statement about the berries provided the pirates with the answer to their problem and the statement about the pansies was mentioned later when the content was irrelevant. The master narrative contained many of these locations permitting the inclusion of 18 different persuasive statements. Participants were afterwards asked to recall facts from the story and to rate how likely each persuasive statement was to be true in the real world.

Results found that persuasive statements placed on the causal chain were both more frequently recalled and perceived as more likely to be true than when they were placed off the causal chain. These findings replicated the increased recall of casual statements from earlier research, but also introduced a persuasive effect relative to a previously overlooked structural construct present in all narratives (Dahlstrom, 2010). Thus, this first study uncovered the existence of a narrative causality effect on persuasive influence, but could not define its bounds of influence. My second effects study in this context attempted to explore these boundary conditions (Dahlstrom, 2012)

Study 2

Because many persuasive narratives attempt to influence individuals who already hold positions about an issue, exploring the interaction between the narrative causality effect and strength of pre-existing values would do much to determine when such an effect might be influential. As most people do not have strong views about pansies and berry bushes, for this study I created a new master narrative using the same manipulation structure as described previously, but employing obviously pro-environmental persuasive statements to potentially align, or oppose, with the pre-existing environmental values that many participants would bring to the study. Persuasive statements that contradict personal values would normally be met with resistance, however, the unawareness of causality as a persuasive factor may avoid such resistance.

Another boundary condition is time. Many studies measure media effects immediately after exposure, but often the duration of an effect will determine the meaningful influence on an individual. Knowing the duration of influence would also help determine when the narrative causality effect might be useful. Therefore, the study measured effects immediately after exposure and again two weeks later to capture any decay of influence over time.

Finally, understanding the mechanism underlying an effect can provide guidance in developing future research questions and linking the effect to other theoretical foundations. Because both recall and persuasive influence increased with causality in the previous study, it seemed likely that the two of them were mechanistically linked. Specifically, the narrative causality effect may be related to the availability heuristic, where causality leads to easier recall, which leads to greater persuasion because the statement retains more salience in memory. Where any interaction with pre-existing values occurs within this relationship could also suggest when the influence of causality occurs in the cognition process. To explore this, I conducted a moderated-mediation analysis to explore how these factors relate.

The results once again suggested that persuasive statements on the causal chain were more persuasive that the same statements placed off of the causal chain. Interestingly, this effect was not altered by pre-existing values. That is, while individuals with anti-environmental values agreed less with the pro-environmental statements overall, the increased acceptance of statements caused by their causal placement was no different when compared with the participants with strong pro-environmental values. Likewise, this influence remained unchanged over the two-week period of the study, suggesting that the narrative causality effect remained robust across both a diverse range of people and over time.

Furthermore, recall served as a mediator for the overall effect but there was no interaction with pre-existing values. This suggested that information placed on the causal chain gains its persuasive influence because the cause-and-effect relationship is integral to the comprehension stage of the content, resulting in acceptance prior to the activation of pre-exiting beliefs or values. That these values lacked a moderating effect suggests that the effect of narrative causality may be fairly strong in overcoming psychological resistance (Dahlstrom, 2012).

After conducting the first two studies, I began to wonder whether narrative causality would serve as a meaningful pool of variance when exploring the influence of perceived realism (of a narrative) on persuasion; this was the thrust of the third study that drove my research agenda (Dahlstrom, 2015).

Study 3

Perceived realism represents how closely a narrative aligns with an audience's perceptions of reality. It can be divided into two dimensions: the first, perceived external realism, represents how closely the events in the narrative align with perceptions of the real world; while the second, narrative realism, represents how closely the events in the narrative align with the rules of the world within the narrative (Busselle & Bilandzic, 2008). For instance, a fire-breathing dragon would be low on external realism because such beasts do not exist in the real world, but it may be high on narrative realism if the world of the story allows for dragons. However, if such a dragon began to spit chocolate instead of fire with no explanation, the rules of the narrative world would have been broken, reducing its narrative realism. While results are often inconsistent for various reasons, greater realism on both dimensions is often associated with greater persuasive influence.

To explore if there was an interaction between narrative causality and the dimensions of perceived realism, I used the same narrative and manipulation structure from the second study, but created alternative versions where either the external or narrative realism of the narrative would be perceived as high or low. The high external realism treatment portrayed the events of the story as they would occur in real life, while the low external realism treatment retained the events but replaced the characters with talking animals. The high narrative realism treatment maintained coherence with the rules of the narrative world, while the low narrative realism treatment showed characters that exhibited emotions that did not fit the situation and descriptions of characters and objects that noticeably changed over the course of the narrative with no explanation.

The results indicated that there was no interaction with narrative realism, but external realism did interact with causality, such that high external realism resulted in greater levels of persuasion, but only for persuasive statements placed on the causal chain of the narrative. In other words, the persuasive influence of external realism was only noticeable for the subset of information on the causal chain of the narrative. Therefore, accounting for narrative causality in future research on external realism could both improve its predictability and subsequent recommendations for practitioners. While external realism is just one variable used to study narrative persuasion, the results open the possibility that other common variables of narrative persuasion may benefit from considering the placement of persuasive statements relative to the causal chain. In essence, accounting for narrative causality may begin to solve a portion of the current inconsistencies within narrative persuasion research (Dahlstrom, 2015).

In total, these three studies marked the first stage of my narrative scholarship agenda; this stage was focused primarily on classic effect studies—empirical research designed to measure the effectiveness of a certain type of stimulus on a certain type of audience. While this stage was fruitful in illuminating at least one aspect of narrative persuasion, larger questions loomed, questions about the social implications of using narrative for tools of persuasion. That is, the narrative causality effect, indeed narrative persuasion in general, represents covert modes of persuasion where audiences are often being led to believe something without their knowledge of being influenced. This lack of knowledge is notable since awareness of the persuasive intent is one of the variables known to hinder narrative persuasion. It is for this reason that professions that deal in persuasion, advertising and public relations in particular, have long histories of reflection on how and when it is appropriate to use persuasive techniques. Yet, as I completed my earlier studies, it became apparent that narrative persuasion was new enough as a field that the question of ethics had yet to be discussed.

Climax: Addressing Normative Questions

As I became more interested with the larger question of when narrative persuasion tactics are not just effective, but also ethically appropriate, together with colleagues at Iowa State University, I sought seed funding to hold a series of summer symposia to address questions related to the appropriate use of communication tactics. The focus of the symposia was science communication, although the research had broader implications outside of that specific context. Within the structure of the interdisciplinary symposia, which brought together experts in science journalism and mass communication as well as normative theories of argumentation in civic controversies, it was possible to begin discussing and exploring the ethical considerations surrounding the use of narrative persuasion from a variety of perspectives. What quickly became clear was that it was important to begin this new journey with an exploration of how other persuasive tactics have been discussed normatively.

One such tactic is framing. According to Entman (1993), "to frame is to select some aspects of a perceived reality and make them more salient in a communicating text" (p. 52). Like narrative persuasion, framing can be used strategically to nudge audiences toward a particular interpretation without their knowledge of being influenced. Scholars have demonstrated that frames can strongly influence public opinions and audience interpretations of issues and events (Price, Nir, & Cappella, 2005; Price & Tewksbury, 1997; Shah, Kwak, Schmierbach, & Zubric, 2004; Shen & Edwards, 2005).

In addition to the practical utility of frames, researchers have also reflected on the social implications of framing. For example, Nisbet (2009) recommended four guiding principles for the responsible use of frames in the context of science communication—although these guidelines are likely to have utility outside of that context. He argues that (a) frames should be used "to emphasize common ground and promote dialogue" (p. 70) rather than managing information in a top-down fashion, (b) frames should clearly communicate the underlying values guiding a policy choice rather than suggesting that the facts compel a decision, (c) frames should remain accurate and not distort or exaggerate the meaning of the content, and (d) frames should not be used to typecast a particular social group or for deliberate electoral gains (Nisbet, 2009).

Frames and narratives are distinct constructs, yet both lend themselves to potentially manipulative persuasion. As a result, Nisbet's ethical framing guidelines offered valuable guidance in the construction of a similar set of guidelines for the ethical use of narratives, and for the articulation of the normative considerations that underlie the decision to use a narrative (Dahlstrom & Ho, 2012). That was the crux of the fourth article to drive my narrative research agenda. The resulting guidelines and normative considerations are detailed below.

The first consideration is to determine whether the underlying goal for using a narrative strategy is persuasion or comprehension. Within the communication of science, which was the context for the Dahlstrom and Ho (2012) project, persuasion and comprehension represent contrasting roles within society, and generally align with one of two competing models within science communication. The first is the Public Understanding of Science (PUS) model, which considers controversies about science as unnecessary and caused by a deficit in the public's understanding of key scientific facts; in this model, the role of communication is to rectify the deficit by educating the public, thereby reducing the controversy (Miller & Kimmel, 2001; Miller, Pardo, & Niwa, 1997). In contrast is the Public Engagement in Science and Technology (PEST) model, which considers controversies about science a necessary and beneficial process of aligning science with societal values. In this model, the role of communication is to engage a wider audience and increase the inclusion of science (and other considerations) within the debate, regardless of which side it is used to support (Dickson, 2001; Walker, Simmons, Irwin, & Wynne, 1999). To some extent, the PUS model aligns with persuasion in its attempt to fill a knowledge deficit with selected facts, while the PEST model aligns with comprehension in its attempt to engage as large an audience as possible with science writ large.

These two models highlight the importance of the choice that faces communicators seeking to use narratives in their communications. Ultimately, that choice is whether to use narratives to create agreement toward a preferred outcome (persuasion), or to promote personal autonomy in decision-making (comprehension). For example, a narrative aiming to persuade could exemplify the preferred side of an issue while championing a character that is rewarded for making the "right" choices. In contrast, a narrative aiming to increase comprehension could exemplify multiple sides of an issue through the eyes of a character who actively considers each of the options. Regardless of the intended outcome, deliberate reflection on the appropriate goal for the narrative should guide its creation. It is important to note here that either goal could be ethical in different circumstances.

The second consideration to guide narrative use concerns what elements within a narrative should remain "accurate" (Dahlstrom & Ho, 2012). Narratives are comprised of varied elements, including types of characters, characters' motivations and actions, settings, situations, events, cause-and-effect relationships, procedures, chronologies, and timeframes. Often, it is the case that only a few of these elements are the focus of the information that a narrative aims to communicate and therefore must remain accurate. In such a case, the other narrative elements may appropriately be fictionalized for the larger purposes of the communication, as long as the focal elements expected by the audience to be correct do retain their accuracy. For instance, if the purpose of a narrative is to show the potential causes of an action, then the cause-and-effect relationship and related events need to retain accuracy to maintain the integrity of the narrative and its message, but other elements such as the setting, specific characters and timeframes could be shaped to enhance the narrative in ways that best resonate with the audience.

Accuracy can be reflected in two levels: external realism, which is described in more detail above, and representativeness or generalizability. Representativeness is important because narratives tend to offer a specific example intended to be generalized to wider contexts; as such, the representativeness of the example used represents an important layer of accuracy. For example, selecting a worst-case scenario as the example around which to create a narrative is likely not generalizable to what is likely to occur, and is therefore representationally inaccurate. In sum, in relation to the consideration of accuracy, before crafting the narrative, one must reflect on the levels of accuracy that are appropriate for the narrative (e.g., external realism and generalizability) and on the elements of the narrative that must remain accurate for the integrity of the narrative and the message it is intended to convey.

The third and final ethical consideration asks if narratives should be used at all within a particular communication context (Dahlstrom & Ho, 2012). Two relevant pieces to this consideration are whether audiences expect narrative communication in that context and whether other communicators in that context will also employ narrative. In line with the persuasion knowledge model (Friestad & Wright, 1994), there are likely certain contexts where persuasive narratives are expected and audiences are prepared to engage with them, such as in advertising or politics. However, there are likely also contexts where narratives are not expected and the audience may be more susceptible to their influence, such as science or risk contexts. In contexts where narratives are not expected, it may be more appropriate to forgo using narrative and retain the format most expected of an audience. On the other hand, if any opposing messages being bandied about in the milieu relative to the issue being discussed are employing narratives, it may in fact be unethical *not* to use narrative because that would mean surrendering the potential benefits of this communication technique to the competition.

Along this same line of inquiry related to the socially responsible use of narratives, I also began work with a colleague from the aforementioned symposium to explore the appropriate persuasion techniques for communicating in a context *already* filled with distrust, such as that of climate change or evolution (Goodwin & Dahlstrom, 2014). Our general claim was that persuasion techniques that rely on covert means for influence, such as narrative persuasion, are more likely to backfire in contentious contexts. This is because it is in those very contexts that individuals most resistant to the message content will be more motivated to deconstruct the message—uncovering the covert persuasion technique and reacting more strongly against it. As a result, contentious contexts are better served with transparent means of persuasion, where the communicator earns trust by making himself or herself vulnerable to the scrutiny of the audience.

In hindsight, these two normative articles (Dahlstrom & Ho, 2012; Goodwin & Dahlstrom, 2014) had moved me well into the second stage of my narrative persuasion research agenda. In this stage, effect studies were no longer the end game. A deeper understanding of the techniques that make narrative communication effective eventually gave rise to questions about the appropriateness of those techniques in various contexts. Although such normative discussions have seldom surfaced in narrative communication research (at least by my estimation), such discussions fill an important, societally relevant gap that bridges research with practice in a meaningful way. And if attendance at our summer symposium series is any indication, such discussions are welcome—more than 130 scholars participated and many contributed to the proceedings volumes that resulted from the four symposia (Goodwin, 2012; Goodwin, Dahlstrom, & Priest, in press).

Denouement: The Future for Narrative Persuasion

As suggested in this chapter, our understanding of narrative persuasion is far from complete. The chapter has focused on my research journey but, undoubtedly, there are many more scholars producing relevant work that I could not include here or have personally yet to read. That is the beauty of narratives—there is always a new character ready to enter the story. I will resolve this chapter by introducing some remaining questions within narrative persuasion that future scholars could consider as entry points to the field.

One question concerns the narrative itself. There is immense variation in how specific narratives can be crafted and the potential effects of these decisions remain vastly understudied. For instance, narratives can be constructed in first, second or third person, or even a hybrid of different points of view; narratives can follow a single character or focalize through a diverse ensemble of characters; narratives can be chronological or present portions of the story out of order for effect; narratives can be constructed in text, video or interactive forms. All of these choices, and many others, result in what would be called a "narrative," but would likely influence audiences differently. Yet, most of these narrative construction factors remain obscured within the catchall and vague concept of narrative "quality."

While some studies have begun to explore such narrative construction factors, there exists no framework to explain how these choices influence audiences. In fact, this lack of a framework hinders the application of narrative persuasion by practitioners who may want to achieve narrative persuasive outcomes but are left with little guidance on the necessary choices in constructing a particular narrative. Future research needs to take a much finer-grained look at narrative construction to better account for the variance currently hidden within the narrative.

Another question concerns the audience of the narrative. Narrative persuasion generally treats audiences as passive, either being influenced by narrative stimuli in various degrees or not. Future studies should examine how an active audience engages with narrative communication in a more naturalistic setting. What expectations do audiences hold regarding narrative communication in varied contexts? When do they desire narrative formats and when are they viewed as suspect or somehow manipulative? Likewise, in most instances, a persuasive narrative merely represents one interpretation within a much larger societal discussion about the issue in question. How do persuasive narratives interact with the pre-existing and very personal narratives already guiding how individuals perceive reality? Even prior to exposure, how do audiences choose which narratives garner their precious attention within the hectic media environment?

This leads to a third and much larger question on the intersection between narratives and the new media environment. New media audiences are imbued with greater power to seek, select and share the information that interests them most. Likewise, in contrast to traditional informative reporting, blogs and other newer platforms of communication mix fact and opinion with little need to differentiate between the two (Brossard, 2013) and the new meta-content that surrounds online information, such as comments, Facebook likes or twitter mentions, can influenced the perceived quality of the content itself (Anderson, Brossard, Scheufele, Xenos, & Ladwig, 2013).

How do narratives compare to other formats of information within the new media environment? Will narratives better serve the needs of a new media audience, floating to the top of the information pool to earn greater attention and dissemination through shared personal networks? A study examining the message factors that lead to increased sharing suggests that this may be the case (Berger & Milkman, 2012). Comparing the features of the most emailed *New York Times* article to those that were not, Berger and Milkman (2012) found that the biggest predictors of sharing content with others was that the content was perceived as interesting, practical, surprising and evoked emotional reactions. Notably, these are also the characteristics of a compelling narrative.

Any influence of narratives in the new media environment is also likely to increase in the future. As the new media environment continues to increase the volume of potential messages available to audiences, and as audiences continue to morph into users who are able to select and share their media messages of choice, the competition for attention will intensify. Narratives may be recruited even more frequently in an attempt to overcome this information explosion.

This chapter represents one story within the ongoing chronicle of narrative as a focus of scholarly investigation. Within the field of strategic communication, narrative has become an increasing topic of inquiry as scholars have explored its potential persuasive benefits. As the ongoing story on narratives continues, our understanding will mature as scholars explore these open questions and identify more that have yet to be formulated in the service of strategic communication. What an exciting story it will be.

References

Anderson, A. A., Brossard, D., Scheufele, D. A., Xenos, M. A., & Ladwig, P. (2013). The "nasty effect": Online incivility and risk perceptions of emerging technologies. *Journal of Computer-Mediated Communication*, Published online before print. doi: Journal of Computer-Mediated Communication

Appel, M., & Richter, T. (2007). Persuasive effects of fictional narratives increase over time. *Media Psychology, 10*(1), 113–134. doi: 10.108/15213260701301194

Berger, J., & Milkman, K. L. (2012). What makes online content viral? *Journal of Marketing Research, 49*(2), 192–205.

Bower, G. H., & Rinck, M. (1999). Goals as generators of activation in narrative understanding. In S. R. Goldman, A. C. Graesser, & P. vandenBroek (Eds.), *Narrative comprehension, causality, and coherence: Essays in honor of Tom Trabasso* (pp. 111–134). Mahwah, NJ: Lawrence Erlbaum.

Brock, T. C., Strange, J. J., & Green, M. C. (2002). Power beyond reckoning: An introduction to narrative impact. In M. C. Green, J. J. Strange, & T. C. Brock (Eds.), *Narrative impact: Social and cognitive foundations*. Mahwah, NJ: Lawrence Erlbaum Associates.

Brossard, D. (2013). New media landscapes and the science information consumer. *Proceedings of the National Academy of Sciences of the United States of America, 110*, 14096–14101. doi: 10.1073/pnas.1212744110

Bruner, J. (1986). *Actual minds, possible worlds*. Cambridge, MA: Harvard University Press.

Bruner, J. (1991). The narrative construction of reality. *Critical Inquiry, 18*(1), 1–21. doi: 10.1086/448619

Busselle, R. W., & Bilandzic, H. (2008). Fictionality and perceived realism in experiencing stories: A model of narrative comprehension and engagement. *Communication Theory, 18*(2), 255–280. doi: 10.1111/j.1468-2885.2008.00322.x

Cohen, J. (2001). Defining identification: A theoretical look at the identification of audiences with media characters. *Mass Communication and Society, 4*(3), 245–264. doi: 10.1207/S15327825MCS0403_01

Culler, J. (1981). *The pursuit of signs—semiotics, literature, deconstruction*. Ithaca, NY: Cornell University Press.

Dahlstrom, M. F. (2010). The role of causality in information acceptance in narratives: An example from science communication. *Communication Research, 37*(6), 857–875. doi: 10.1177/0093650210362683

Dahlstrom, M. F. (2012). The persuasive influence of narrative causality: Psychological mechanism, strength in overcoming resistance, and persistence over time. *Media Psychology, 15*(3), 303–326. doi: 10.1080/15213269.2012.702604

Dahlstrom, M. F. (2015). The moderating influence of narrative causality as an untapped pool of variance for narrative persuasion. *Communication Research, 42*(6), 779–795. doi: 10.1177/0093650213487374

Dahlstrom, M. F., & Ho, S. S. (2012). Ethical considerations of using narrative to communicate science. *Science Communication, 34*(5), 592–617. doi: 10.1177/1075547012454597

de Wit, J. B. F., Das, E., & Vet, R. (2008). What works best: Objective statistics or a personal testimonial? An assessment of the persuasive effects of different types of message evidence on risk perception. *Health Psychology, 27*(1), 110–115. doi: 10.1037/0278-6133.27.1.110

Dickson, D. (2001). Weaving a social web—The Internet promises to revolutionize public engagement with science and technology. *Nature, 414*(6864), 587–587. doi: 10.1038/414587a

Eagly, A. H., & Chaiken, S. (1993). *The psychology of attitudes*. Fort Worth, TX: Harcourt Brace Jovanovich Inc.

Entman, R. M. (1993). Framing: Toward clarification of a fractured paradigm. *Journal of Communication, 43*(4), 51–58.

Fisher, W. R. (1984). Narration as a human-communication paradigm: The case of public moral argument. *Communication Monographs, 51*(1), 1–22.

Fisher, W. R. (1985). The narrative paradigm: In the beginning. *Journal of Communication, 35*(4), 74–89.

Fletcher, C. R., Lucas, S., & Baron, C. M. (1999). Comprehension of mathematical proofs. In S. R. Goldman, A. C. Graesser, & P. vandenBroek (Eds.), *Narrative comprehension, causality, and coherence: Essays in honor of Tom Trabasso*. Mahwah, NJ: Lawrence Erlbaum Associates.

Friestad, M., & Wright, P. (1994). The persuasion knowledge model: How people cope with persuasion attempts. *Journal of Consumer Research, 21*(1), 1–31.

Gerrig, R. J. (1993). *Experiencing narrative worlds: On the psychological activities of reading*. Boulder, CO: Westview Press.

Goodwin, J. (Ed.). (2012). *Between scientists and citizens: Proceedings of a symposium at Iowa State University, June 1–2, 2012*. Charleston, SC: CreateSpace.

Goodwin, J., Dahlstrom, M., & Priest, S. H. (Eds.). (in press). *Normative aspects of science communication: Proceedings of a symposium at Iowa State University, June 5–7, 2014*. Charleston, SC: CreateSpace.

Goodwin, J., & Dahlstrom, M. F. (2014). Good reasons for trusting climate science communication. *WIREs Climate Change, 5*(1), 151–160.

Graesser, A. C., Olde, B., & Klettke, B. (2002). How does the mind construct and represent stories? In M. C. Green, J. J. Strange, & T. C. Brock (Eds.), *Narrative impact: Social and cognitive foundations* (pp. 229–262). Mahwah, NJ: Lawrence Erlbaum.

Graesser, A. C., & Ottati, V. (1995). Why stories? Some evidence, questions, and challenges. In R. S. J. Wyer (Ed.), *Knowledge and memory: The real story*. HIllsdale, NJ: Lawrence Erlbaum Associates.

Green, M. C., & Brock, T. C. (2000). The role of transportation in the persuasiveness of public narratives. *Journal of Personality and Social Psychology, 79*(5), 701–721. doi: 10.1037/0022-3514.79.5.701

Katz, Y. (2013). Against storytelling of scientific results. *Nature Methods, 10*(11), 1045–1045. doi: 10.1038/nmeth.2699

Kreiswirth, M. (1992). Trusting the tale: The narrativist turn in the human sciences. *New Literary History, 23*(3), 629–657. doi: 10.2307/469223

Kreiswirth, M. (2000). Merely telling stories? Narrative and knowledge in the human sciences. *Poetics Today, 21*(2), 293–318.

Kreuter, M. W., Green, M. C., Cappella, J. N., Slater, M. D., Wise, M. E., Storey, D., . . . Woolley, S. (2007). Narrative communication in cancer prevention and control: A framework to guide research and application. *Annals of Behavioral Medicine, 33*(3), 221–235.

Mackie, J. L. (1980). *The cement of the universe*. Oxford, England: Clarendon.

Magliano, J. P. (1999). Revealing inference processes during text comprehension. In S. R. Goldman, A. C. Graesser, & P. vandenBroek (Eds.), *Narrative comprehension, causality, and coherence: Essays in honor of Tom Trabasso* (pp. 55–76). Mahwah, NJ: Lawrence Erlbaum.

Mazor, K. M., Baril, J., Dugan, E., Spencer, F., Burgwinkle, P., & Gurwitz, J. H. (2007). Patient education about anticoagulant medication: Is narrative evidence or statistical evidence more effective? *Patient Education and Counseling, 69*(1–3), 145–157. doi: 10.1016/j.pec.2007.08.010

McQuail, D. (2010). *McQuail's mass communication theory* (6th ed.). London: Sage Publications.

Miller, J. D., & Kimmel, L. (2001). *Biomedical communications: Purposes, audiences, and strategies.* New York: John Wiley.

Miller, J. D., Pardo, R., & Niwa, F. (1997). *Public perceptions of science and technology: A comparative study of the European Union, the United States, Japan, and Canada.* Chicago: Chicago Academy of Sciences.

Mills, C. B., Diehl, V. A., Birkmire, D. P., & Mou, L. (1993). Procedural text: Predictions of importance ratings and recall by models of reading comprehension. *Discourse Processes, 16,* 279–315.

Moyer-Guse, E. (2008). Toward a theory of entertainment persuasion: Explaining the persuasive effects of entertainment-education messages. *Communication Theory, 18*(3), 407–425. doi: 10.1111/j.1468-2885.2008.00328.x

Nisbet, M. C. (2009). The ethics of framing science. In B. Nerlich, B. Larson, & R. Elliott (Eds.), *Communicating biological sciences: Ethical and metaphorical dimensions* (pp. 51–73). London, UK: Ashgate.

O'Keefe, D. J. (2002). *Persuasion: Theory and research.* Thousand Oaks, CA: Sage Publications Inc.

Oatley, K. (2002). Entertainment and education and the persuasive impact of narratives. In M. C. Green, J. J. Strange, & T. C. Brock (Eds.), *Narrative impact: Social and cognitive foundations.* Mahwah, NJ: Lawrence Erlbaum.

Price, V., Nir, L., & Cappella, J. N. (2005). Framing public discussion of gay civil unions. *Public Opinion Quarterly, 69*(2), 179–212.

Price, V., & Tewksbury, D. (1997). News values and public opinion: A theoretical account of media priming and framing. In G. A. Barnett & F. J. Boster (Eds.), *Progress in communication science.* Greenwich, CN: Ablex.

Shah, D. V., Kwak, N., Schmierbach, M., & Zubric, J. (2004). The interplay of news frames on cognitive complexity. *Human Communication Research, 30*(1), 102–120.

Shen, F., & Edwards, H. H. (2005). Economic individualism, humanitarianism, and welfare reform: A value-based account of framing effects. *Journal of Communication, 55*(4), 795–809.

Slater, M. D., & Rouner, D. (2002). Entertainment-education and elaboration likelihood: Understanding the processing of narrative persuasion. *Communication Theory, 12*(2), 173–191. doi: 10.1093/ct/12.2.173

Slater, M. D., Rouner, D., & Long, M. (2006). Television dramas and support for controversial public policies: Effects and mechanisms. *Journal of Communication, 56*(2), 235–252. doi: 10.1111/j.1460-2466.2006.00017.x

Trabasso, T., & Sperry, L. L. (1985). Causal relatedness and importance of story events. *Journal of Memory and Language, 24*(5), 595–611. doi: 10.1016/0749-596X(85)90048-8

Trabasso, T., & Suh, S. (1993). Understanding text: Achieving explanatory coherence through online inferences and mental operations in working memory. *Discourse Processes, 16,* 3–34.

Tulving, E. (1972). Episodic and semantic memory. In E. Tulving & D. W. (Eds.), *Organization of memory* (pp. 381–403). New York: Academic Press.

vandenBroek, P., & Gustafson, M. (1999). Comprehension and memory for texts: Three generations of reading research. In S. R. Goldman, A. C. Graesser, & P. vandenBroek (Eds.), *Narrative comprehension, causality, and coherence: Essays in honor of Tom Trabasso* (pp. 15–34). Mahwah, NJ: Lawrence Erlbaum.

Voss, J. F., Wiley, J., & Sandak, R. (1999). On the Use of Narrative as Argument. In S. R. Goldman, A. C. Graesser, & P. vandenBroek (Eds.), *Narrative comprehension, causality, and coherence: Essays in honor of Tom Trabasso*. Mahwah, NJ: Lawrence Erlbaum Associates.

Walker, G., Simmons, P., Irwin, A., & Wynne, B. (1999). Risk communication, public participation and the Seveso II directive. *Journal of Hazardous Materials, 65*(1–2), 179–190. doi: 10.1016/s0304-3894(98)00262-3

Wheeler, S. C., Green, M. C., & Brock, T. C. (1999). Fictional narratives change beliefs: Replications of Prentice, Gerrig, and Bailis (1997) with mixed corroboration. *Psychonomic Bulletin & Review, 6*(1), 136–141.

Winterbottom, A., Bekker, H. L., Conner, M., & Mooney, A. (2008). Does narrative information bias individual's decision making? A systematic review. *Social Science & Medicine, 67*(12), 2079–2088. doi: 10.1016/j.socscimed.2008.09.037

2
STRATEGIC STORYTELLING
Narrative Messaging in Entertainment and Emergent Media

Heather L. LaMarre

Introduction

Throughout history, storytelling has played an essential role in human communication. From ancient myths, legends, and folklore to mystical plays and religious parables, narratives have shaped cultural norms, reinforced beliefs, and conveyed social expectations across time and space. The relationship between narratives and public opinion can be traced back to the beginning of democracy, demonstrating the long-held belief that stories have the power to persuade audiences, influence publics, and shape democratic outcomes. As Gottschall wrote, "We are creatures of story, and the process of changing one mind or the whole world must begin with 'Once upon a time'" (2012). Literary scholar Roland Barthes (1982) celebrated the ever presence of narratives in human culture, describing them as "present in every age, in every place, in every society" (p. 251). Landreville and LaMarre (2013) note that most conceptualizations of the narrative are grounded in the humanistic tradition of literary criticism, where scholars have long understood that stories are intrinsic to human communication (Riessman, 1993). Indeed, narratives begin with "the very history of mankind and there nowhere is nor has been a people without narrative" (Barthes, 1982, p. 251). Polkinghorne (1988) similarly articulates the importance of narrative, stating "the products of narrative schemes are ubiquitous in our lives: they fill our cultural and social environment" (p. 14).

This chapter offers a holistic view of past and emerging trends in the research on narratives—particularly narrative persuasion—and, in doing so, integrates and organizes relevant concepts and theoretical perspectives across narrative research from entertainment media to public policy. Additionally, new conceptualizations of *narrative strategy* and *strategic narrative messaging* are offered to increase organizational power and provide theoretical nuance.

Narrative strategies in emergent and hybrid media are also discussed. Finally, the chapter calls for a narrative messaging typology that can be used to guide empirical narrative strategy research.

Defining the Narrative: Two Key Perspectives

One of the issues troubling the narrative persuasion literature is a lack of conceptual and operational clarity. Generally speaking, there are several different conceptual definitions for the term *narrative,* which span many disciplines. However, two key perspectives dominate contemporary narrative persuasion scholarship (Kreuter et al., 2007; Hinyard & Kreuter, 2007). Situated at the heart of the message sender-receiver relationship, these two conceptualizations are juxtaposed as either the message sender's story or the message recipient's story. Though few scholars, if any, explicitly refer to the role of agency when offering conceptual definitions of narrative, the two prevailing definitions (detailed below) delineate themselves in terms of whether the sender or the receiver has the power to create the narrative.

Narrative as Message Sender's Story

On the one hand, a narrative can be thought of as the message sender's story. From this perspective, narratives have key elements: scene, plot, characters (e.g., protagonist and antagonist), conflict, and temporal sequencing (e.g., beginning, middle, and end) that may or may not include a message or moral to be considered (Kreuter et al., 2007; Hinyard & Kreuter, 2007; White, 1987; see also Bennett & Royle, 2014). Much of the mass communication literature draws from Kreuter and colleagues (2007), who defined a narrative as "a representation of connected events and characters that has an identifiable structure, is bounded in space and time, and contains implicit or explicit messages about the topic being addressed" (Kreuter et al., 2007, p. 222). Edutainment studies such as Moyer-Gusé, Jain, and Chung (2012, p. 1011) have also relied on Hinyard and Kreuter's (2007) conceptualization of a narrative, which defined a narrative as a "cohesive and coherent story with an identifiable beginning, middle, and end that provides information about scene, characters, and conflict" (p. 778). From the social-psychological perspective, Green (2004) defined a narrative structure as having, "a beginning, middle, and end [that] ties actions and implications together in a causal chain, rather than relying on a set of propositions that may be more or less well integrated" (p. 164).

In the public policy literature, certain structural elements are required to meet the definition of a policy narrative. For instance, Shanahan, Jones, and McBeth (2011) state that, in order to be considered a policy narrative, "the communication of interest must have at least one character and some reference to a public policy preference or stance" (p. 457). Shanahan and colleagues

(2011) conceptualize narratives as having generalizable structural elements that are evident across various contexts (e.g., setting, characters, plot, etc.) and operate at multiple levels (e.g., micro-, meso-, and macro-level influence). Generally speaking, these conceptualizations all situate the narrative from the message sender's viewpoint, broadly defining a narrative as a "story" with a unique set of structural elements that form a coherent message about a given topic (Hinyard & Kreuter, 2007; White, 1987; Bennett & Royle, 2014; Kreuter et al., 2007; see also Green, 2004).

Narrative as Message Recipient's Story

Alternatively, *narrative* has been conceptualized as the message recipient's story. Pierce (2003), along with Pierce and Kaufman (2012, p. 35), offered conceptualizations that situated narratives as consisting of two parts: the given story and the constructed story. Pierce explained:

> The given story is made up of elements actually shown, spoken, or described in a medium used for story giving (e.g., film, radio, or a children's book). The constructed story is what happens in the human mind once the story elements are received, organized, interpreted, and understood. (2003, p. 186)

Here, Pierce implies that audiences have agency over story construction, creating individualized narratives that differ from person to person. This is akin to the notion that one's perception is their reality (Pierce & Kaufman, 2012).

A stronger distinction between *story* and *narrative* has been made in consumer research literature. Van Laer, Ruyter, Visconti, and Wetzels (2014) argued, "Consumers interpret stories. Interpretation constitutes an act of consumption through which a story is converted into a narrative" (p. 799). This uncoupling of the terms *story* and *narrative*, contradicts Shankar and Goulding's (2001) contention that narratives are the just stories (p. 429), and separates the terms into distinct constructs. Contrary to Kreuter et al.'s (2007) and Pierce's (2003) conceptualizations, Van Laer and colleagues defined a narrative by stating: "In short, a narrative is a story the consumer interprets in accordance with his or her prior knowledge, attention, personality, demographics, and significant others" (p. 799). In this sense, a narrative can be thought of as a story derivative. Here, the message sender is the storyteller, but the message recipient has agency over the narrative that is created.

Clearly, the concept of *narrative* needs further explication, including inquiry into questions of agency. However, recent empirical examinations of narrative processing and effects tend to favor the former conceptualization; wherein, *narrative* is thought to be a cohesive set of events, bounded by specific structural elements (e.g., characters, plot, etc.) that have a temporal order (e.g., beginning, middle, end) and create a cohesive message (e.g., Hinyard & Kreuter, 2007; Green, 2004; Busselle, & Bilandzic, 2009; Moyer-Gusé et al., 2012).

Narrative Persuasion Theory and Application to Strategic Communication

Within strategic communication, much of the persuasion research has focused on the processing and effects of analytical messages, rhetorical arguments, and other non-narrative message formats (Ajzen & Fishbein, 1980; Bandura, 1986; Petty & Caccioppo, 1986). However, as interest in narrative messaging increases among strategic communication scholars, some sub-disciplines (e.g., health, political, advertising) have begun investigating the persuasive nature of narratively structured information (e.g., Slater, 2002a/b; Shrum, 2004). Although the totality of these studies traverse across many different research streams ranging from political entertainment to entertainment education, much of this work shares similar goals (e.g., understanding narrative processing and effects) and employs similar epistemological and methodological approaches (e.g., Green & Brock, 2000; Bandura, 2004; Sood, Menard, & Witte, 2004).

Narrative Persuasion

Although traditional persuasion theories offer some insight into how individuals process and respond to messages within entertainment media narratives, these frameworks focus on analytical persuasion techniques where messages tend to be explicit and formats are non-narrative (e.g., facts, speeches, debate, rhetorical arguments, etc.). However, much of the media that audiences, stakeholders, and key publics consume takes a narrative format, highlighting the need to understand *narrative persuasion* as a distinct construct with a unique set of antecedents and consequences (Slater, 2000a; Shrum, 2004; Bower & Morrow, 1990; Brodie, Foehr, Rideout, Baer, Miller, & Flournoy, et al., 2001; Singhal, Cody, Rogers, & Sabido, 2004).

Narrative persuasion is the process through which attitudes, opinions, behaviors, and related outcomes (e.g., policies, laws, etc.) are influenced by narrative forms of communication. Although narrative persuasion could occur through interpersonal communication (e.g., face-to-face storytelling and testimonials), empirical examinations within strategic communication mainly focus on mediated narratives (e.g., film, television, social media, etc.). Here, the discussion of narrative persuasion is limited to mass-mediated narratives, which influence attitudes, opinions, behaviors, and related socio-political outcomes. As opposed to the relatively more overt messages found in rhetorical and analytical messages, persuasive arguments found in narratives tend to be less explicit. Dahlstrom (2012) refers to narrative persuasion as a "covert mode of persuasion, where information is generally accepted first and only scrutinized later" (p. 502). Van Laer and colleagues explain, "narrative persuasion refers to attitudes and intentions developed from processing narrative messages that are not overtly persuasive, such as novels, movies, or video games" (Van Laer et al., 2014, p. 800).

Dominant Theories of Narrative Persuasion

Several theoretical frameworks have been developed to explain (and test) narrative persuasion processes and effects (e.g., The Extended Elaboration Likelihood Model [E-ELM], Slater, 2002a/b; The Transportation Imagery Model [TIM], Green & Brock, 2000). However, use of these theories has remained somewhat limited in strategic communication research. Much of the literature continues to draw upon traditional, analytical persuasion and learning models such as the theory of reasoned action and theory of planned behavior (Ajzen & Fishbein, 1980), the Elaboration Likelihood Model (ELM) (Petty & Cacioppo, 1986), and social cognitive theory (Bandura, 2002, 2004). Among these, social cognitive theory has been applied most often in entertainment education research (Sood et al., 2004). Additionally, the ELM has been extended to entertainment narratives in an attempt to account for the unique experience narratives induce (e.g., media engagement and character identification) (Slater & Rouner, 2002). These, along with the Transportation Imagery Model (TIM) (Green & Brock, 2000) and the Entertainment Overcoming Reactance Model (EROM) (Moyer-Gusé, 2008) are detailed below.

Social Cognitive Theory (SCT)

Entertainment education (EE) research has relied heavily on social cognitive theory (SCT) to explain how, when, and under what conditions individuals learn from entertainment media (Bandura, 2004; Sood et al., 2004). SCT outlines how social learning occurs from experience and observation, including behavioral models found in mediated forms (e.g., television shows) (Bandura, 1986). Specific to entertainment, the SCT proposition that attractiveness or perceived similarity can increase social learning has been extended to fictional characters in entertainment media (Bandura, 2002, 2004). Here, SCT overlaps with Cohen's (2001) character identification theory, suggesting that stronger character identification will motivate individuals to attend to, observe, and imitate behaviors of fictional characters. Sood (2002) also examined audience involvement in EE, finding that involvement in the fictional narrative increased one's learning from entertainment. From the SCT perspective, character identification and story involvement are thought to increase one's motivation to attend to, retain, and produce the behavior models found in entertainment. Although EE focuses on pro-social (positive) behaviors, SCT dictates that people select which behaviors they observe, model, and perform. Thus, it is possible that negative behaviors could also be learned from entertainment-based narratives (Bandura, 2002, 2004).

Transportation Imagery Model

The Transportation Imagery Model (TIM) (Green & Brock, 2000; Green, Brock, & Kaufman, 2004) stems from a psychological perspective in which narratives are thought to have distinct features that encourage audiences to become transported into the story. The term *transportation* was originally developed by Gerrig (1993) to encapsulate the key difference audiences experienced in response to narrative and non-narrative communications. Gerrig (1993), along with Green and Brock (2000), contends that narratives induce a unique state in which individuals' thoughts, emotions, and visualizations take them into the narrative world. Green and Brock (2000) explained that narrative transportation includes "emotional reactions, mental imagery, and a loss of access to real-world information" (p. 703). From this conceptualization, narrative transportation is similar to other media engagement concepts found in entertainment psychology including, *flow* (Csikszentmihalyi, 1990), *simulation* (Oatley, 1999), *involvement* (Wirth, 2006), and *engagement* (Slater, Rouner, & Long, 2006).

The TIM is operationalized using the transportation scale developed by Green and Brock (2000, 2005), and has been employed as the theoretical framework in a variety of strategic communication research (e.g., Green, 2006). The TIM (commonly referred to as transportation theory) is often situated as, "the primary mechanism that underlies the effect of narrative message (or stories)" (Banerjee & Green, 2012, p. 565). There is a growing body of research supporting transportation as a key determinant in narrative persuasion, including studies in health (e.g., Dunlop, Wakefield, & Kashima, 2010; Braverman, 2008), policy (e.g., LaMarre & Landreville, 2009); and advertising (e.g., Escalas, 2004) contexts. However, there have also been concerns that the transportation scale does not properly measure the distinct psychological state it conceptualizes. Rather, it merely draws from several other psychological constructs (e.g., attention, involvement, empathy, affective disposition, etc.), making it difficult to delineate between the various mechanisms.

Extended Elaboration Likelihood Model (E-ELM)

The Extended Elaboration Likelihood Model (E-ELM) draws upon Petty and Cacioppo's ELM (1986) by situating entertainment media as having the ability to reduce message scrutiny and counterarguing. According to the ELM, one's likelihood to elaborate (in the form of message scrutiny or counterargumentation) influences how deeply one processes the message such that relatively less elaboration leads to the peripheral route and relatively more elaboration leads to the central route (Petty & Cacioppo, 1986). Reduced counterarguing, induced by entertainment narratives, suggests that audiences think less about the messages they receive in entertainment, and in turn, are more influenced by the heuristic cues in the entertainment media (Slater, 2002a/b; Slater & Rouner, 2002; see LaMarre, Landreville, Young, & Gilkerson, 2014 for an in-depth analysis of this theoretical perspective in strategic political narratives). From the E-ELM perspective, the likelihood of thinking critically about entertainment-based messages depends on how engaged one becomes with the story and how much one identifies with the characters. Here again, transportation and character identification play key roles in the processing framework set forth by the E-ELM.

Past research demonstrates that increased narrative transportation reduces counterarguing and increases persuasion (e.g., Green & Brock, 2000; Knowles & Linn, 2004; Slater & Rouner, 2002; Slater, Rouner, & Long, 2006; see also Appel & Richter, 2007). Cohen (2001) suggests that when an individual highly identifies with a fictional character they engage in perspective taking and are less likely to be critical of the character. This could, in turn, lead to less critical thinking about the character's actions and behaviors. However, Slater and Rouner's (2002) conceptualization of character identification is somewhat circumspect. The E-ELM defined identification as a process "in which an individual perceives another person as similar or at least as a person with whom they might have a social relationship" (Slater & Rouner, 2002, p. 178). This definition overlaps with Cohen's (2001) character identification theory and Rubin, Perse, and Powell's (1985) para-social relationship theory, as well as several other psychological constructs (e.g., social identity, homophily, empathy, etc.). The lack of conceptual clarity makes it difficult to test the role of character identification within the model. As with the TIM, overlapping constructs and non-distinct conceptualizations trouble the E-ELM framework. Still, recent applications of the ELM to political narratives support the notion that entertainment media reduces one's propensity to think critically about the embedded messages (e.g., LaMarre & Walther, 2013; Young, 2008). However, these studies pointed to mechanisms other than transportation and character identification as being responsible for the reduced message scrutiny, suggesting the need for further testing of mechanisms affecting narrative message processing.

Entertainment Overcoming Reactance Model (EROM)

Although for different reasons, the TIM and the E-ELM both situate entertainment narratives as reducing one's ability and/or motivation to think critically about the messages portrayed in the story. Moreover, all three frameworks (SCT, TIM, E-ELM) focus on psychological mechanisms thought to draw one into the story (e.g., identification, transportation), thereby altering cognitive and affective reactions to the narrative messages. Alternatively, the Entertainment Overcoming Reactance Model (EORM) focuses on entertainment's disarming quality.

Moyer-Gusé and colleagues (2012) explain that an entertainment-based narrative "obscures its persuasive intent compared with a more explicit persuasive message and therefore does not induce reactance in the way that an overtly persuasive message would" (p. 62). From this perspective, narrative messaging is thought to be less overt than expository and rhetorical forms of persuasion (Moyer-Gusé, 2008). Here, the premise of narrative persuasion lies in the belief that when someone is not aware of persuasive intent, they are less resistant to persuasion. This view stems from psychological reactance theory, which posits that individuals seek the freedom to form their own attitudes (Brehm, 1966).

Reactance theory suggests that perceived attempts at persuasion will result in defensive reactions referred to as *reactance* (Brehm, 1966; Brehm & Brehm, 1981). The EORM posits that entertainment media, which conveys subtle messages embedded in storylines and conveyed through characters and events, is unlikely to trigger reactance. Therefore, individuals who consume entertainment-based narrative messages will elicit less resistance to persuasion than those who consume similar messages in non-entertainment formats (Moyer-Gusé, 2008). There is some literature to support the EORM. Weinstein, Grubb, and Vautier (1986) demonstrated that once individuals become aware of the persuasive intent narrative persuasion is reduced, and conversely, less explicit attempts are more influential. Moyer-Gusé et al. (2012) tested the use of explicit appeals at the end of entertainment programs, but didn't find a reactance effect.

The question then becomes whether the entertainment was so powerful that it mitigated reactance to the explicit persuasive appeal, or if reactance is less of a concern than previously thought. Landreville and LaMarre (2013) examined the intertexuality between fictional political film and real political news, finding that narrative engagement did influence how audiences cognitively responded to the news article. Although the authors were not examining the EORM model, their findings do lend support to Moyer-Gusé's (2008) contention that entertainment has the ability to mitigate resistance to persuasion.

Narrative Messaging in Entertainment, Emergent, and Hybrid Media

Interestingly, the key theoretical perspectives used in this line of research primarily focus on entertainment-based narratives, which has largely bound narrative persuasion research to entertainment-based messaging contexts. For instance, Moyer-Gusé (2008) specifically applied the concept of using entertainment to overcome reactance to entertainment-education (EE), which she defined as, "pro-social messages that are embedded into popular *entertainment* media content" (p. 408, emphasis added). From the EE perspective, entertainment-based narratives don't require persuasive intent. Rather, educational messages can also be added to story lines for dramatic or comedic appeal. Nonetheless, EE messages are said to result in a variety of persuasive outcomes including attitude and behavior change at the micro-, meso-, or macro-level (Singhal et al., 2004; Collins, Elliott, Berry, Kanouse, & Hunter, 2003).

In this sense, entertainment media are seen as vehicles for disseminating persuasive messages (albeit sometimes unintentionally), and by extension, key entertainment constructs are thought to significantly influence observable narrative effects (Bandura, 2004; Slater, 2002a/b; Green & Brock, 2000). Although entertainment media and related constructs (e.g., transportation, character identification, engagement) remain central to narrative processing and effects research, new research is expanding the boundaries of entertainment-specific messaging contexts to include digital and social media narratives (e.g., Housholder & LaMarre, 2014, 2015; Neiderdeppe, Shapiro, Kim, Bartolo, & Porticello, 2013; Igartua & Barrios, 2012). In the wired age, narrative messaging has become prevalent in entertainment and non-entertainment media, prompting researchers to examine the express role of entertainment in producing narrative effects (e.g., LaMarre, 2013; Landreville & LaMarre, 2013).

Entertainment Media Narratives

Within the narrative persuasion literature, entertainment media are considered in two important ways. Namely, entertainment media are examined as a vehicle for disseminating persuasive narratives (e.g., films, music, and television programs with persuasive storylines) (e.g., Collins et al., 2003; Deighton, Romer, & McQueen, 1989; Landreville & LaMarre, 2011). Alternatively, entertainment media constructs (e.g., media engagement, perceived realism, character identification, etc.) are examined as mechanisms thought to influence narrative processing (e.g., Busselle, & Bilandzic, 2009; Cho, Lijian, & Wilson, 2012; LaMarre & Landreville, 2009; see also Van Laer et al., 2014). Vorderer, Klimmt, and Ritterfeld (2004) argued that entertainment is essentially a physiological, cognitive, and affective experience.

With regard to its persuasive nature, the *entertainment experience* has been said to disarm message recipients (e.g., Landreville & LaMarre, 2013; Dahlstrom, 2012), reduce one's propensity to scrutinize embedded messages (e.g., LaMarre & Walther, 2013); reallocate cognitive resources away from message processing (e.g., LaMarre et al., 2014; Young, 2008); prime prior attitudes (e.g., Moy, Xenos, & Hess, 2006); bias message processing (e.g., LaMarre et al., 2009); reduce counterarguing (e.g., Green & Brock, 2005), and reduce psychological reactance (e.g., Moyer-Gusé, 2008). Taken together, these studies support conceptualizations of narrative persuasion as a more subtle form of persuasion that uses less overt messages, generally resulting in less cognitive focus on the entertainment-based messages and more heuristic processing (e.g., Dahlstrom, 2010, 2012; Van Laer et al., 2014).

Recognizing that entertainment is not a monolith, researchers have unpacked the affective and cognitive dimensions of the entertainment experience, focusing on the specific underlying processes and mechanisms leading to known entertainment consumption goals such as enjoyment and appreciation (Zillmann, 1991, 1996; Raney, 2003, 2004). This line of research originated in entertainment psychology and was developed to understand a host of entertainment effects (apart from narrative persuasion) such as enjoyment (Raney, 2004), mood management (Zillmann, 1996), and para-social interaction (Rubin et al., 1985). Drawing from entertainment and media psychology, extant literature has identified several processing mechanisms that play a central and significant role in narrative persuasion, including character identification (Cohen, 2001), para-social relationships (Rubin et al., 1985), perceived realism (Busselle & Bilandzic, 2008; Pouliot & Cowen, 2007), affective disposition (Raney, 2003), media engagement (Busselle & Bilandzic, 2009), narrative transportation (Green & Brock, 2000; Gerrig, 1993), and enjoyment (Raney, 2004). Among these, narrative transportation and character identification have received significant attention (Slater & Rouner, 2002; Green, Brock, & Kaufman, 2004). As outlined above, the dominant narrative persuasion frameworks overlap in their belief that "transportation, or engagement with the narrative, as well as identification with characters serve to increase persuasive impact" (Dahlstrom, 2012, p. 502).

Non-Entertainment Narratives

Special attention is often paid to entertainment-based narratives. However, the term *narrative* is certainly not synonymous with *entertainment*. Prior research has also demonstrated the significant role non-entertainment narratives play in shaping attitudes and opinions (e.g., Braverman, 2008; Niederdeppe et al., 2013; de Wit, Das, & Vet, 2008). Many types of narratives have little to do with entertaining audiences. For instance, personal testimony (a narrative form in which the narrator conveys a personal account from their own experience) is used in many areas of strategic communication, especially behavior change campaigns (e.g., Braverman, 2008; Housten et al., 2011; Greene & Brinn, 2003). Recent work has examined the influence of online and emergent media narratives in shaping support for obesity-related health policies (e.g., Niederdeppe, Kim, Lundell, Fazili, & Frazier, 2012), changing attitudes toward tanning bed usage (e.g., Greene, Campo, & Banerjee, 2010), and affecting climate change opinion (e.g., McComas & Shanahan, 1999). Still, these studies draw upon the same set of constructs (e.g., character identification, narrative transportation) found in entertainment-based research; all of which stem from entertainment and media psychology (Zillmann, 1991, 1996; Raney, 2003, 2004; Vorderer et al., 2004). Though entertainment and non-entertainment media narratives are theoretically similar and utilize overlapping constructs, strategic communication researchers' propensity to self-identify as context experts (i.e., health communication, political communication, advertising, PR, etc.) or by media type (i.e., social media, entertainment media, hybrid media) has created gaps in strategic narrative research that appear to be widening.

The Need for Theoretical Integration

Within strategic communication, narrative persuasion research remains fractured as it struggles to find its place among well-established rhetorical and expository persuasion theories. Researchers tend to favor dominant discipline-specific effects theories such as the theory of planned behavior in health (Ajzen & Fishbein, 1980) or framing theory in political communication (Iyengar & Kinder, 1987). Additionally, classic persuasion and attitude theories (e.g., ELM) offer researchers well-established systematic models for testing narrative processing and effects. However, entertainment theory has repeatedly demonstrated a unique set of constructs that significantly influence narrative processing (Cohen, 2001; Green & Brock, 2000). As such, recent calls for the integration of entertainment psychology and narrative persuasion approaches into a cohesive, theoretical framework for strategic narrative processing and effects have emerged (LaMarre & Landreville, 2009; Landreville & LaMarre, 2011).

In their recent examination of political film narratives, Landreville and LaMarre (2013) argue that limiting political narrative perspectives "to only include the 'political' and all but ignore the 'entertainment' variables and theories fails to recognize the truly unique nature of this media form" (p. 348). Likewise, narrative persuasion studies in health (e.g., Green, 2006), public policy (e.g., LaMarre & Landreville, 2009), and advertising (e.g., Zheng & Phelps, 2012) contexts have touted the importance of integrating entertainment psychology as a means of developing stronger theoretical models.

Alternatively, LaMarre and Walther (2013) formally extended the Elaboration Likelihood Model (ELM) (Petty & Cacioppo, 1986) to the study of entertainment media messages in late-night comedy shows, demonstrating that the narrative format was more influential than the expository format on audience attitudes and opinions. Though the authors employed a classic persuasion theory to test their assertions, LaMarre and Walther (2013) acknowledged that important differences between narrative and non-narrative formats limited the usefulness of the ELM and echoed earlier calls for the development of stronger narrative-specific processing and effects frameworks (e.g., Slater, 2002a, 2002b; Moyer-Gusé, 2008). Moreover, researchers interested in narrative messaging effects recognize the need to bridge gaps between discipline-specific and entertainment psychology approaches to narrative persuasion, as well as create more nuanced understandings of key concepts.

Narratives and Strategic Messaging

EE research maintains that persuasive intent is not a requirement for narrative-based learning (Sood et al., 2004). However, strategic communicators are especially interested in developing and testing communication models that can be used to formulate effective message strategies across multiple contexts in support of specific organizational goals, social agendas, or democratic aims. Not only does this imply persuasive intent, but it also demands that narrative persuasion models are scalable, replicable, and generalizable. Thus, narrative persuasion research within strategic communication contexts may well examine non-purposive narratives (created without specific intent) to better understand their processing and effects; however, such an endeavor must be undertaken with the aim of developing empirically tested, theory-based purposive narratives (created with specific intent). As such, theoretical development demands that narrative strategy research become more discerning between non-purposive and purposive narratives. Likewise, it is incumbent upon scholars interested in narrative messaging to conceptually and operationally define said differences. To this end, a first definition of the purposive narrative (referred to herein as *strategic narrative*) is offered below.

Defining the Strategic Narrative

A *strategic narrative* is conceptualized as purposive, narratively structured information that seeks to intentionally influence audiences at the micro-, meso-, or macro-level in support of organizational, socio-political, or policy goals. As opposed to entertainment education narratives that have been described as either intentionally or unintentionally influencing audiences (Slater & Rouner, 2002), strategic narratives are developed with specific intent. The terms "narrative strategy" and "strategic narrative" are used to differentiate this form of messaging from "narrative persuasion" or "persuasive narratives" because these purposive narratives extend beyond persuasive acts. While persuasive narratives can be strategic in their aims, not all strategic narratives are developed to persuade. Rather, strategic narratives can be constructed to serve other messaging goals including information dissemination, stakeholder engagement, agenda building, coalition building, etc. Still, persuasion is often a primary or secondary aim in one's overall narrative strategy. Additionally, strategic narratives are not limited to entertainment media. Although entertainment and media psychology play important roles in the development of purposive narratives, they can take many different forms, ranging from feature films and television programs to online testimonials and socially mediated stories (LaMarre, 2013; Landreville & LaMarre, 2013).

Climate change narratives and political satire offer two excellent examples to consider. Climate change narratives, ranging from feature films (e.g., Disney's *Earth*) and documentaries (e.g., *An Inconvenient Truth*) to online personal stories (e.g., social media testimonials), generally have an underlying goal of increasing public support for climate change policy (Jones, 2014). However, using the narrative format to engage audiences, they often differ in whether policy support serves as the primary (e.g., *An Inconvenient Truth*) or secondary goal (e.g., Disney's *Earth*) (LaMarre & Landreville, 2009; see also Holbert, 2005).

Alternatively, political satire almost always has a primary goal of entertaining audiences (LaMarre, Landreville, & Beam, 2009; Young, 2008). Yet, embedded political messages often carry a secondary goal of influencing audience attitudes regarding the joke target (LaMarre, 2013; LaMarre et al., 2014).

Still, one might argue that Hollywood film studios and political comedians are not strategic communicators; in this way, strategic narratives need not be limited to professional strategic communications developed for the sole purpose of supporting a strategic campaign (e.g., advertising narratives, see Zheng & Phelps, 2012). Rather, strategic narratives cover a broad range of entertainment and non-entertainment narratives that can have singular purpose (e.g., increase brand favorability) or multiple purposes (e.g., entertain audiences while shaping public opinion). Additionally, strategic narratives can be consumed in multiple formats, channels, and outlets, and can be combined with non-narrative information (e.g., explicit appeals following an entertainment show, see Moyer-Gusé et al., 2012). A key distinction between general narratives and strategic narratives is specific intent. Although both narrative forms influence audiences, strategic narratives are developed in support of strategic communication goals, designed with specific aims, and calculated to influence audiences in specific ways.

Within several areas of strategic communication, researchers have sought to develop and test strategic narratives, including health (e.g., Neiderdeppe et al., 2013), risk (e.g., Green, 2006), science (e.g., Jones, 2014), political (e.g., Igartua & Barrios, 2012), and advertising (e.g., Phillips & McQuarrie, 2010). However, with the exception of LaMarre (2013; see also above in this chapter for formal definition), scholars have yet to explicitly invoke the term *strategic narrative*, opting instead to talk about persuasive narratives with ubiquitous terms such as infotainment, digital story-telling, and political entertainment or context-specific titles such as health narratives, science stories and patient-storytelling. Using this myriad of terms creates two problems. First, context-specific labels (e.g., science stories, health narratives) indicate narrow applications of the research, which unnecessarily divides strategic narrative research into silos and impedes theory-development at the broader level. Second, ubiquitous terms (e.g., infotainment, digital storytelling, political entertainment) signal larger research domains, largely dominated by non-narrative paradigms that employ a host of methodological and theoretical frameworks. Alternatively, developing a common conceptualization for *strategic narratives* can integrate theoretical and methodological developments from context-specific research streams and provide a focused, systematic approach to strategic narrative processing and effects research within strategic communication.

Creating Organizational Power: Toward a Narrative Typology

Narratively structured messages can be presented in a variety of formats with differing levels of information, entertainment, and persuasive intent. Differentiating between entertainment and non-entertainment based formats, as well as between purposive and non-purposive intent, provides researchers some ability to parse and test the effectiveness of different types of narratives. Still, the narrative messaging literature generally lacks organizational power. Presently, narrative persuasion research within strategic communication tends to be categorized by context of study. This discipline-specific approach leads to fractured concepts, duplicative research streams, and the lack of theoretical integration. Alternatively, a typology for narratives that moves beyond context and focuses on inherent factors can encourage theory building that transcends cognate areas within the field. An organized structure typified by universal characteristics or inherent factors creates shared knowledge across the various sub-fields and formalizes an empirical approach to testing strategic narrative processing and effects. Drawing from the literature, it is possible to identify some of the inherent factors conducive for creating a narrative typology. Here, two dimensions are offered for initial consideration: agency and intentionality.

Agency

Recalling that narratives can be defined as either the sender's story or the recipient's story, agency is clearly an inherent factor to consider (Kreuter et al., 2007; Hinyard & Kreuter, 2007; Pierce, 2003). A sender's story gives relatively more agency to the individual, group, or organization developing and delivering the narrative, while a recipient's story allows audiences to maintain relatively more control over how one processes the narrative. Recent work in political entertainment narratives provides empirical evidence that relative differences in agency have consequential effects on how audiences process and respond to narratives (LaMarre et al., 2014).

Equally as important, LaMarre and colleagues (2014) note that narrative elements (e.g., tone and style) signal different processing mechanisms through which agency is affected. Put differently, message senders might have the ability to design narratives such that audiences are more likely to interpret them as planned; thereby giving the sender dominion over the story and maintaining relatively more control over audience response. This would be ideal for those interested in narrative strategy. Still, there are many situations in which audiences selectively attend to and interpret narratively structured information, giving relatively more control to the message recipients (LaMarre, 2013; LaMarre et al., 2014). Research grounded in motivated cognition theory has also demonstrated the role of audience agency in narrative processing. For example, LaMarre et al. (2009) found evidence of biased message processing among late-night political comedy viewers, suggesting that audience agency significantly influenced how individuals processed and responded to the political narratives.

On the whole, there is still much to be learned regarding how, when, and under what conditions a narrative becomes a sender's story versus a recipient's story.

34 Heather L. LaMarre

Nonetheless, questions of agency (which also trouble the definition of narrative) are critical to narrative processing and effects. For organizational clarity, narratives can be thought of as points on an agency continuum that ranges from a message sender story to a message recipient story (see Figure 2.1). Still, it is incumbent on future researchers to explicate these concepts and provide clear guidance regarding how to operationalize, measure, and test relative differences in narratives along the agency continuum.

Intentionality

Another important factor in typing narratives is whether the message intends to influence audiences, as well as whether such intent is primary or secondary. Holbert's (2005) political entertainment television typology delineated between programs that had politics as either the primary or secondary focus and political messages as ranging from explicit to implicit. In a similar manner, it is helpful to think about the goal of the narrative. Narratives with a primary or secondary goal of influencing audiences in support of specific aims should be thought of as strategic narratives, while narratives that unintentionally influence audiences are considered non-strategic narratives. Although strategic communicators are likely more interested in developing strategic narratives, non-strategic narratives have also been shown to influence audiences (Sood, 2002; Slater & Rouner, 2002). As such, strategic messaging scholars are necessarily interested in examining both types of narratives.

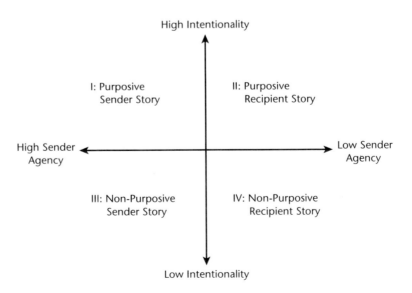

FIGURE 2.1 Narrative Typology

In terms of organizing narratives for future research, it makes sense to conceptualize narratives as ranging from 'primary intent' to influence audiences to 'no intent' to influence audiences (see Figure 2.1). For instance, a science documentary about global climate change developed to specifically influence public opinion (e.g., *An Inconvenient Truth*) exemplifies primary persuasive intent. Satirical sketch comedy (e.g., *Saturday Night Live*) ridiculing a public policy issue offers an example of secondary persuasive intent. Alternatively, a fictional television show designed to entertain audiences that features likable characters with poor health habits might influence viewers' health behaviors (e.g., characters on *The Simpsons*). Because influencing health behaviors was not part of the creators' intent, such a show would not be classified as having persuasive intent. As with the message sender-message recipient definitions of narrative, there is little evidence to support clear operational definitions for specific levels of intentionality. Rather, infinite permutations might exist wherein complex storylines, media formats, and narrative elements create differing degrees of explicit/implicit intentionality. Until more work can be done to identify and categorize narratives by primary, secondary, etc. intent to influence audiences, it makes more sense to conceptualize a continuum of intentionality (Figure 2.1).

Taken together, agency and intentionality represent two key dimensions of narratives (Figure 2.1). Thinking of these along an XY axis, four domains (or categories) appear. Namely, narratives can be categorized into the following four quadrants: (I) Purposive sender stories; (II) Purposive recipient stories; (III) Non-purposive sender stories; and (IV) Non-purposive recipient stories. Within this organizational framework, purposive sender (quadrant I) and purposive recipient (quadrant II) stories would be considered strategic narratives, while non-purposive sender and recipient stories would be considered non-strategic narratives (Figure 2.1). Still, this only offers a preliminary way of organizing narratives. Future research needs to fully explicate each domain with a focus on developing clear conceptual and operational definitions for types of narratives that fall into each quadrant.

Concluding Remarks

Although there is much more to consider before a narrative typology can be fully validated, this initial four-domain typology suggests the potential to develop an organizing framework for researching narratively structured messages. As discussed herein, narrative persuasion holds great promise for strategic communication. Early research suggests that narratively structured information is more readily accepted (Moyer-Gusé, 2008), less scrutinized (LaMarre et al., 2014; Young, 2008), and potentially more persuasive than expository and rhetorical forms of persuasion (LaMarre & Walther, 2013). Additionally, elements unique to narratives have demonstrated increased persuasive effects such as transportation (Green & Brock, 2000) and character identification (Cohen, 2001). Still, the context-specific research streams that rely heavily on dominant theories within their respective disciplines impede theoretical integration. Presently, there is no organizing framework for categorizing narratives beyond context area. Thus, a typology is needed to guide systematic, empirical testing of narrative processing mechanisms.

Moving forward, researchers can use a narrative typology to examine differential effects between narrative types, as well as test the role of mediating and moderating variables across the quadrants. For instance, recipient-based stories that give relatively more agency to the sender during message processing (i.e., types I & III, see Figure 2.1) are likely to be interpreted differently than those offering more agency to the receiver (i.e., types II & IV). Past work has demonstrated that receiver agency levels affect one's motivation to think about the message (LaMarre et al., 2014) and that vague or complex narrative-based messages lead to more biased processing (e.g., LaMarre et al., 2009). Thus, research focusing on recipient-based narratives might be well informed by theories of motivated cognition and biased processing. Hence, the typology offers a sort of theoretical guidance for future work.

Similarly, future work can explore potential differences along the intentionality continuum (Y-axis, see Figure 2.1). By using the quadrants to categorize purposive and non-purposive stories, research can begin to examine the conditions under which narratives reduce reactance versus invoking it. Thinking about the mixed results found in recent EORM research (Moyer-Gusé et al., 2012), it is possible that intentionality plays a significant role in reactance. While non-purposive entertainment narratives might leave viewers less guarded, it is reasonable to suspect that blatant attempts to persuade audiences could actually promote reactance. Researchers can use the typology coupled with prior research to guide investigations of these and related suppositions. Additionally, there may be interactions between perceptions of the sender's intention and differing levels of agency. Likewise, character liking, engagement, transportation, and related constructs could yield differing effects across the quadrants. Perhaps a recipient-based story with low perceived intentionality promotes transportation and increases persuasion, while a sender-based story with high intentionality impedes transportation and reduces persuasion. These and related questions become more manageable with a typology to guide research. Additionally, the organizational framework allows future research to study more nuanced processes and build stronger theoretical models.

Moreover, narratives serve as powerful messaging systems. Professional communicators can invoke strategic storytelling as a means of achieving specific organizational or societal goals such as informing, persuading, and engaging audiences. Still, research in this area remains fragmented and somewhat contradictory. To better understand how, when, and why narratively structured messages influence audiences, we need more organizational power and stronger theoretical integration. The narrative typology offers a first step in this direction, providing future research with a systematic framework for building and testing effective narrative strategy models. Once explicated and validated, the typology can also serve as a focusing point for narrative-based research across different context areas and sub-disciplines. Moving forward, we should focus on theoretical integration as a means of developing more refined models and nuanced understandings of power narratives hold.

References

Appel, M., & Richter, T. (2007). Persuasive effects of fictional narratives increase over time. *Media Psychology, 10*, 113–134. doi: 10.108/15213260701301194

Ajzen, I., & Fishbein, M. (1980). *Understanding attitudes and predicting social behavior.* Englewood Cliffs, NJ: Prentice Hall.

Banerjee, S. C., & Greene, K. (2012). Role of transportation in the persuasion process: Cognitive and affective responses to antidrug narratives. *Journal of Health Communication, 17*(5), 564–581.

Bandura, A. (1986). *Social foundations of thought and action: A social cognitive theory.* Englewood Cliffs, NJ: Prentice-Hall.

Bandura, A. (2002). Social cognitive theory of mass communication. In J. Bryant & D. Zillmann (Eds.), *Media effects: Advances in theory and research* (pp. 121–154). Mahwah, NJ: Lawrence Erlbaum.

Bandura, A. (2004). Social cognitive theory for personal and social change by enabling media. In A. Singhal, M. J. Cody, E. M. Rogers, & M. Sabido (Eds.), *Entertainment-education and social change: History, research, and practice* (pp. 75–96). Mahwah, NJ: Lawrence Erlbaum.

Barthes, R. (1982). Introduction to the structural analysis of narratives. In S. Songtag (Ed.), *A Barthes Reader* (pp. 251–295). New York: Macmillan.

Bennett, A. & Royle, N. (2014). *An introduction to literature, criticism, and theory* (4th ed.). New York: Routledge.

Bower, G. H., & Morrow, D. G. (1990). Mental models in narrative comprehension. *Science, 247*(4938), 44–48. doi: 10.1126/science.2403694

Braverman, J. (2008). Testimonials versus informational persuasive messages: The moderating effect of delivery mode and personal involvement. *Communication Research, 35,* 666–694.

Brehm, J. (1966). *A theory of psychological reactance.* New York: Academic Press.

Brehm, S. S., & Brehm, J. W. (1981). *Psychological reactance: A theory of freedom and control.* San Diego, CA: Academic.

Brodie, M., Foehr, U., Rideout, V., Baer, N., Miller, C., Flournoy, R., et al. (2001). Communicating health information through the entertainment media: A study of the television drama ER lends support to the notion that Americans pick up information while being entertained. *Health Affairs, 20,* 192–199.

Busselle, R. W., & Bilandzic, H. (2008). Fictionality and perceived realism in experiencing stories: A model of narrative comprehension and engagement. *Communication Theory, 18,* 255–280. doi: 10.1111/j.1468-2885.2008.00322.x

Busselle, R., & Bilandzic, H. (2009). Measuring narrative engagement. *Media Psychology, 12*(4), 321–347. doi: 10.1080/15213260903287259

Cho, H., Lijian, S., & Wilson, K. (2012). Perceived realism: Dimensions and roles in narrative persuasion. *Communication Research, 40*(6). doi: 10.1177/0093650212450585.

Cohen, J. (2001). Defining identification: A theoretical look at the identification of audiences with media characters. *Mass Communication & Society, 4,* 245–264.

Collins, R. L., Elliott, M. N., Berry, S. H., Kanouse, E. E., & Hunter, S. B. (2003). Entertainment television as a healthy sex educator: The impact of condom efficacy information in an episode of Friends. *Pediatrics, 112,* 1115–1121.

Csikszentmihalyi, M. (1990). *Flow: The psychology of optimal experience.* New York, NY: Harper and Row.

Dahlstrom, M. F. (2010). The role of causality in information acceptance in narratives: An example from science communication. *Communication Research, 37,* 857–875. doi: 10.1177/0093650210362683

Dahlstrom, M. F. (2012). The persuasive influence of narrative causality: Psychological mechanism, strength in overcoming resistance, and persistence over time. *Media Psychology, 15*(3), 303–326. doi: 10.1080/15213269.2012.702604

Deighton, J., Romer, D., & McQueen, J. (1989). Using drama to persuade. *Journal of Consumer Research, 16,* 335–343.

de Wit, J. B. F., Das, E., & Vet, R. (2008). What works best: Objective statistics or a personal testimonial? An assessment of the persuasive effects of different types of message evidence on risk perception. *Health Psychology, 27,* 110–115. doi: 10.1037/0278-6133.27.1.110

Dunlop, S. M., Wakefield, M., & Kashima, Y. (2010). Pathways to persuasion: Cognitive and experiential responses to health-promoting mass media messages. *Communication Research, 37,* 133–164.

Escalas, J. E. (2004). Imagine yourself in the product: Mental stimulation, narrative transportation, and persuasion. *Journal of Advertising, 33,* 37–48.

Gerrig. R. (1993). *Experiencing narrative worlds: On the psychological activities of reading.* New Haven, CT: Yale University Press.

Gottschall, J. (2012, May 2). *Why storytelling is the ultimate weapon.* Fastcocreate.com. Downloaded February 2, 2014 from http://www.fastcocreate.com/1680581/why-storytelling-is-the-ultimate-weapon

Green, M. C. (2004). Transportation into narrative worlds: The role of prior knowledge and perceived realism. *Discourse Processes, 38,* 247–266.

Green, M. C. (2006). Narratives and cancer communication. *Journal of Communication, 56*S163-S183. doi: 10.1111/j.1460-2466.2006.00288.x

Green, M. C., & Brock, T. C. (2000). The role of transportation in the persuasiveness of public narratives. *Journal of Personality and Social Psychology, 79,* 701–721.

Green, M. C., & Brock, T. C. (2005). Persuasiveness of narratives. In T. C. Brock & M. C. Green (Eds.), *Persuasion: Psychological insights and perspectives* (2nd ed., pp. 117–142). Thousand Oaks, CA: Sage.

Green, M. C., Brock, T. C., & Kaufman, G. F. (2004). Understanding media enjoyment: The role of transportation into narrative worlds. *Communication Theory, 14,* 311–327.

Greene, K., & Brinn, L. (2003). Messages influencing college women's tanning bed use: Statistical versus narrative evidence format and a self-assessment to increase perceived susceptibility. *Journal of Health Communication, 8,* 443–461.

Greene, K., Campo, S., & Banerjee, S. C. (2010). Comparing normative, anecdotal, and scientific risk evidence to discourage tanning bed use. *Communication Quarterly, 58,* 111–132.

Hinyard. L. J., & Kreuter, M.W. (2007). Using narrative communication as a tool for health behavior change: A conceptual, theoretical, and empirical overview. *Health Education and Behavior, 34,* 777–792.

Holbert, R. L. (2005). A typology for the study of entertainment television and politics. *American Behavioral Scientist, 49*, 436–453.

Housholder, E., & LaMarre, H. L. (2015). Political social media engagement: Comparing campaign goals with voter behavior. *Public Relations Review, 41*(1), 138–140. doi: 10.1016/j.pubrev.2014.10.007

Housholder, E., & LaMarre, H. L. (2014) Facebook politics: Toward a process model for achieving political source credibility through social media. *Journal of Information Technology & Politics, 11*(4), 368–382. doi: 10.1080/19331681.2014.951753

Houston, T. K., Cherrington, A., Coley, H. L., Robinson, K. M., Trobaugh, J. A., Williams, J. H., & Allison, J. J. (2011). The art and science of patient storytelling-harnessing narrative communication for behavioral interventions: The ACCE project. *Journal of Health Communication, 16*(7), 686–697. doi: 10.1080/10810730.2011.551997

Igartua, J., & Barrios, I. (2012). Changing real-world beliefs with controversial movies: Processes and mechanisms of narrative persuasion. *Journal of Communication, 62*(3), 514–531. doi: 10.1111/j.1460-2466.2012.01640.x

Iyengar, S., & Kinder, D. (1987). *News that matters: Television and American opinion*. Chicago: University of Chicago Press.

Jones, M. (2014). Cultural characters and climate change: How heroes shape our perception of climate science. *Social Science Quarterly, 95*, 1–39. doi: 10.1111/ssqu.12043

Kreuter, M. W., Green, M. C., Cappella, J. N., Slater, M. D., Wise, M. E., Storey, D., . . . Woolley, S. (2007). Narrative communication in cancer prevention and control: A framework to guide research and application. *Annals of Behavioral Medicine, 33*, 221–235.

Knowles, E. S., & Linn, J. A. (2004). The importance of resistance to persuasion. In E. S. Knowles & J. A. Linn (Eds.), *Resistance and persuasion* (pp. 3–11). Mahwah, NJ: Lawrence Erlbaum.

LaMarre, H. L. (2013). When parody and reality collide: Examining the effects of Colbert's Super PAC satire on issue knowledge and policy engagement across media formats. *International Journal of Communication, 7*, 394–413. doi: 19328036=20130005

LaMarre, H. L., & Landreville, K. D. (2009). When is fiction as good as fact? Comparing the influence of documentary and historical reenactment films on engagement, affect, issue interest, and learning. *Mass Communication & Society, 12*(4), 537–555. doi: 10.1080/15205430903237915

LaMarre, H. L., & Walther, W. (2013). Ability matters: Testing the differential effects of political news and late-night political comedy on cognitive responses and the role of ability in micro-level opinion formation. *International Journal of Public Opinion Research*. Advance online publication. doi: 10.1093/ijpor/edt008

LaMarre, H. L., Landreville, K. D., & Beam, M. A. (2009). The irony of satire: Political ideology and the motivation to see what you want to see in The Colbert Report. *International Journal of Press Politics, 14*, 212–231.

LaMarre, H. L., Landreville, K. D., Young, D., & Gilkerson, N. (2014). Humor works in funny ways: Humorous tone as a key determinant in political humor message processing. *Mass Communication and Society, 17*(3), 400–423. doi: 10.1080/15205436.2014.891137

Landreville, K., & LaMarre, H. (2013) Examining the intertextuality of fictional political comedy and real-world political news. *Media Psychology, 16*(3), 347–369. doi: 10.1080/15213269.2013.796585

Landreville, K. D., & LaMarre, H. L. (2011). Working through political entertainment: How negative emotion and narrative engagement encourage political discussion intent in young Americans. *Communication Quarterly*, 59(2), 200–220. doi: 10.1080/01463373.2011.563441

McComas, K., & Shanahan, J. (1999). Telling stories about global climate change: Measuring the impact of narratives on issue cycles. *Communication Research*, 26, 30–57. doi: 10.1177/009365099026001003

Moy, P., Xenos, M. A., & Hess, V. K. (2006). Priming effects of late-night comedy. *International Journal of Public Opinion Research*, 18, 198–210. doi: 10.1093/ijpor/edh092

Moyer-Gusé, E. (2008). Toward a theory of entertainment persuasion: Explaining the persuasive effects of entertainment-education messages. *Communication Theory*, 18, 407–425. doi: 10.1111/j.1468-2885.2008.00328.x

Moyer-Gusé, E., Jain, P., & Chung, A. H. (2012). Reinforcement or reactance? Examining the effect of an explicit persuasive appeal following an entertainment-education narrative. *Journal of Communication*, 62(6), 1010–1027. doi: 10.1111/j.1460-2466.2012.01680.x

Niederdeppe, J., Kim, H. K., Lundell, H., Fazili, F., & Frazier, B. (2012). Beyond counterarguing: Simple elaboration, complex integration, and counter-elaboration in response to variations in narrative focus and sidedness. *Journal of Communication*, 62(5), 758–777.

Niederdeppe, J., Shapiro, M., Kim, H. K., Bartolo, D., & Porticella, N. (2013). Narrative persuasion, causality, complex integration, and support for social policy. *Health Communication*, 29(5): 431–444. doi: 10.1080/10410236.2012.761805.

Oatley, K. (1999). Meeting of minds: Dialogue, sympathy and identification in reading fiction. *Poetics: Journal of Empirical Research on Literature, Media and the Arts*, 26, 439–454. doi: 10.1016/S0304-422X(99)00011-X

Petty, R. E., & Cacioppo, J. T. (1986). *Communication and persuasion: Central and peripheral routes to attitude change*. New York: Springer-Verlag.

Pierce, D. L. (2003). *Rhetorical criticism and theory in practice*. New York: McGraw-Hill.

Pierce, D. L., & Kaufman, K. (2012). Visual persuasion tactics in narrative development: An analysis of the Matrix. *Visual Communication Quarterly*, 19(1), 33–47. doi: 10.1080/15551393.2012.656063

Phillips, B. J., & Mcquarrie, E. F. (2010). Narrative and persuasion in fashion advertising. *Journal of Consumer Research*, 37(3), 368–392.

Polkinghorne, D. (1988). *Narrative knowing and the human science*. New York: State University of New York Press.

Pouliot, L., & Cowen, P. S. (2007). Does perceived realism really matter in media effects? *Media Psychology*, 9, 241–259.

Raney, A. A. (2003). Disposition-based theories of enjoyment. In J. Bryant, D. Roskos-Ewoldsen, & J. Cantor (Eds.), *Communication and emotion: Essays in honor of Dolf Zillmann* (pp. 61–84). Mahwah, NJ: Lawrence Erlbaum Associates.

Raney, A. A. (2004). Expanding disposition theory: Reconsidering character liking, moral evaluations, and enjoyment. *Communication Theory*, 14, 348–369.

Riessman, C. (1993). *Narrative analysis*. New York: Sage.

Rubin, A. M., Perse, E. M., & Powell, R. A. (1985). Loneliness, parasocial interaction, and local television news viewing. *Human Communication Research*, 12, 155–180.

Shanahan, E., Jones, M. D., & McBeth, M. K. (2011). Policy narratives and policy processes. *The Policy Studies Journal*, 39, 535–561.

Shankar, A., & Goulding, C. (2001). Interpretive consumer research: Two more contributions to theory and practice. *Qualitative Market Research*, 4(1), 7–16.

Shrum, L. J. (Ed.). (2004). *The psychology of entertainment media: Blurring the lines between entertainment and persuasion*. Mahwah, NJ: Lawrence Erlbaum.

Singhal, A., Cody, M. J., Rogers, E. M., & Sabido, M. (2004). *Entertainment-education and social change: History, research, and practice*. Mahwah, NJ: Lawrence Erlbaum.

Slater, M. D. (2002a). Entertainment education and the persuasive impact of narratives. In M. C. Green, J. J. Strange, & T. C. Brock (Eds.), *Narrative impact: Social and cognitive foundations* (pp. 157–182). Mahwah, NJ: Lawrence Erlbaum.

Slater, M. D. (2002b). Involvement as goal-directed strategic processing: Extending the elaboration likelihood model. In J. P. Dillard & M. Pfau (Eds.), *The persuasion handbook: Developments in theory and practice* (pp. 175–194). Thousand Oaks, CA: Sage.

Slater, M. D., & Rouner, D. (2002). Entertainment-education and elaboration likelihood: Understanding the processing of narrative persuasion. *Communication Theory, 12*, 173–191.

Slater, M. D., Rouner, D., & Long, M. (2006). Television dramas and support for controversial public policies: Effects and mechanisms. *Journal of Communication, 56*, 235–252. doi: 10.1111/j.1460-2466.2006.00017.x

Sood, S. (2002). Audience involvement and entertainment-education. *Communication Theory, 12*, 153–172.

Sood, S., Menard, T., & Witte, K. (2004). The theory behind entertainment-education. In A. Singhal, M. J. Cody, E. M. Rogers, & M. Sabido (Eds.), *Entertainment-education and social change: History, research, and practice* (pp. 117–145). Mahwah, NJ: Lawrence Erlbaum.

Van Laer, T., Ruyter, K., Visconti, L. M., & Wetzels, M. (2014). The Extended Transportation-Imagery Model: A meta-analysis of the antecedents and consequences of consumers' narrative transportation. *Journal of Consumer Research, 40*(5), 797–817. doi: 10.1086/673383

Vorderer, P., Klimmt, C., & Ritterfeld, U. (2004). Enjoyment: At the heart of media entertainment. *Communication Theory, 14*, 388–408.

Weinstein, N. D., Grubb, P. D., and Vautier, J. S. (1986). Increasing automobile seat belt use: An intervention emphasizing risk susceptibility. *Journal of Applied Psychology, 71*, 285–290.

White, H. (1987). *The content of the form: Narrative discourse and historical representation*. Baltimore, MD: Johns Hopkins University Press.

Wirth, W. (2006). Involvement. In J. Bryant & P. Vorderer (Eds.), *Psychology of entertainment* (pp. 199–214). Mahwah, NJ: Erlbaum.

Young, D. G. (2008). The privileged role of the late-night joke: Exploring humor's role in disrupting argument scrutiny. *Media Psychology, 11*, 119–142. doi: 10.1080/15213260701837073

Zheng, L., & Phelps, J. E. (2012). Working toward an understanding of persuasion via engaging narrative advertising: Refining the Transportation-Imagery Model. In S. Rodgers & E. Thorson (Eds.), *Advertising theory* (pp. 255–268). New York: Routledge.

Zillmann, D. (1996). The psychology of suspense in dramatic exposition. In P. Vorderer, H. J. Wulff, & M. Friedrichsen (Eds.), *Suspense: Conceptualizations, theoretical analyses, and empirical explorations* (pp. 199–232). Mahwah, NJ: Erlbaum.

Zillmann, D. (1991). Empathy: Affect from bearing witness to the emotions of others. In J. Bryant & D. Zillmann (Eds.), *Responding to the screen: Reception and reaction processes* (pp. 135–167). Hillsdale, NJ: Lawrence Erlbaum Associates.

3

THE PROMISE OF PARTICIPATORY MEDIA

Identifying the Potential Roles of Influential Content Generators in Prosocial Strategic Communication

Kajsa E. Dalrymple and Rachel Young

Participatory media platforms have created new opportunities for individuals to connect and communicate through channels unbound by time and space. Interpersonal interactions may be mediated rather than just face-to-face, group deliberation may occur in virtual hangout rooms, and sharing information with an entire social network can happen at the click of a button. Connected media users are not only gaining access to new sources of knowledge, but they may also participate in the creation and distribution of information. These days, anyone with Internet access can publish content online and claim expertise in a topic area based on personal experience and anecdotal evidence. As a result, participatory online media have displaced some of the power that has traditionally been held by politicians, journalists, and other experts.

Participatory Media and Product Marketing

As our daily communication routines have evolved, marketers have been forced to react quickly and adopt new strategies for attracting consumers and converting them into customers. The traditional one-way strategic communication approach has been replaced with a "multi-way" approach that focuses on involving the consumer in the marketing process (e.g., Kabani, 2013; Kerpen, 2011). Successful marketers recognize that user-generated content can greatly influence public perceptions about a product. Whether through a tweet about poor restaurant service, or a thorough review of a product on Amazon, consumers are gaining increased influence over the behaviors of other consumers (e.g., Chevalier & Mayzlin, 2006).

Scholars have identified these types of consumers as content generators—users who both create and disseminate content (e.g., Armstrong & Hagel, 2000; Deuze, 2001; Jenkins, 2006; Walther & Jang, 2012). Content generated by these consumers often includes responses to proprietor content or to other user-generated messages on a proprietor's site (see Walther & Jang, 2012, for differences between user-generated and proprietor content). As content generators have gained access to more platforms online, website proprietors have also ceded power over messaging. Ten years ago an anecdote about a surly waiter may have reached a few close friends and acquaintances. Now, that same story can reach hundreds of potential customers both inside and outside of the disgruntled customer's network of offline friends via social media sites operated by the business owners.

As the number of content generators continues to grow online, some contributors gain more influence than others. Drawing from research in the fields of political, health, science, organizational and environmental communication, we know that there are individuals in our lives whom we rely on for information, advice, and behavioral cues (Bode & Dalrymple, 2014; Brosius & Weimann, 1996; Dalrymple, Shaw, & Brossard, 2013a, 2013b; Katz, 1957; Katz & Lazarsfeld, 1955; Norris & Curtice, 2008; Weimann, 1982). Similar to groups offline, online social networks are composed of individuals with varying levels of influence. Marketers have long understood the importance of content creators and the persuasive power that social network influentials can have on customer behaviors. By publishing or highlighting information produced by influential content generators (ICGs), organizations can help empower these individuals, who in turn help increase credibility of the product, and strengthen relationships between customers and the company.

However, where corporate marketers have successfully utilized ICGs, prosocial marketers have fallen behind. Although most environmental and health scholars have recognized the increasingly important role that social media play in engaging large public groups, limited research has explored the potential effect that ICGs can have on influencing positive environmental and health-related social change. Existing research regarding prosocial health and environmental campaigns has focused on how discussion develops online, and whether user-generated content on health or environmental topics contradicts or threatens expert knowledge (e.g., Mythen, 2009). Less is known about what characteristics are associated with prosocial content producers, and what types of individuals are most influential in encouraging change. In order to address these issues, the following chapter will review research emphasizing the importance of mobilizing social network influentials in prosocial campaigns, describe characteristics of ICGs, and propose a research typology that can be used to explore how environmental and health communicators might use the affordances of social media to *listen* to users' dialogue and concerns about health and environmental issues, capitalize on user ability to *forward* messages to social networks, and *collaborate* with users to create innovative and effective campaigns.

Marketing a Social Good: A Review of Relevant Literature

Prosocial marketing applies marketing techniques to the promotion of socially beneficial ideas and causes instead of products and services in the commercial sense (Fox & Kotler, 1980). The origins of prosocial marketing are grounded in the informational approach, where campaign goals are primarily focused on increasing awareness of a social issue or cause. Over time, campaign strategists recognized that in order to encourage social change, campaigns must focus on more than disseminating information—they also needed to persuade. As socially conscious organizations witnessed the effectiveness of prosocial campaigning they began to consider its potential for changing public attitudes and behavior. Now, prosocial marketing involves extensive marketing research, audience analysis, product development, incentives, and well-constructed infrastructure to ensure the sustainability and success of a campaign. Properly designed, these campaigns have the potential to shape public attitudes and encourage better behaviors among social groups.

Drawing From Theory

In order to be successful, prosocial campaigns must first understand how individuals develop attitudes, and identify what factors lead to changes in their behaviors (Fishbein & Cappella, 2006). Based on our current understanding of human behavior, we know that a behavior is guided by existing beliefs. Several well-tested theories map the relationships between cognitions and behavior. For example, the theory of planned behavior suggests that behavioral intention is guided by three important beliefs: (1) beliefs about the behavior and the potential outcomes of adopting that behavior (attitudes toward the behavior); (2) perceived social norms regarding compliance with the behavior (subjective norms); (3) perceived self-efficacy and perceptions of barriers that may impede the performance of the behavior (perceived behavioral control). Together, these beliefs influence the formation of behavioral intention, which mediates the relationship between attitude and action. For instance a behavior like converting your home to an environmentally conscious standard of living would be guided by beliefs about whether adopting those standards is an effective means of reducing use of non-renewable energy, whether you believe that others think you should adopt those standards, and whether that adoption is an affordable and otherwise feasible behavior for you to perform.

Similarly, the health belief model proposes additional variables to explain an individual's likelihood to engage in a health-promoting behavior (Rosenstock, 1974). This model is based on the argument that individuals' health behaviors are primarily driven by (1) their desire to avoid illness and (2) their belief that a specific action will help them prevent or avoid illness. Building on this hypothesis, the health belief model proposes several factors that contribute to an individual's decision to adopt a positive health behavior: perceived severity of a health problem, perceived susceptibility to developing that health problem, perceived benefits of and barriers to taking action, perceived self-efficacy, and the presence of a cue to action (Carpenter, 2010; Glanz, Rimer, & Viswanath, 2008; Janz & Becker, 1984; Rosenstock, 1974).

A significant body of research has used the theory of planned behavior and the health belief model to successfully explain and predict health behaviors (Noar & Zimmerman, 2005; Fishbein & Cappella, 2006). Additionally, studies have also used these models to explain and predict a range of ecological behaviors such as recycling (Kaiser & Gutscher, 2003; Oom Do Valle, Rebelo, Reis, & Menezes, 2005; Shaul & Katz-Gerro, 2006), purchasing environmentally friendly products (Chan & Lau, 2001), improving riparian areas (Corbett, 2002), encouraging lower carbon modes of transportation (Wall, Devine-Wright, & Mill, 2007), and using energy-saving light bulbs (Harland, Staats, & Wilke, 1999).

According to these theories, personal values and beliefs are likely to vary across different audiences (Fishbein & Ajzen, 1975; Fishbein & Cappella, 2006). As a result, strategic messages that target specific group and individual existing beliefs (for instance about the outcomes related to a specific pro-environmental behavior) may be more effective in producing behavior change. In order to engage specific social groups, many prosocial campaigns rely on the media as a tool for informing the public and encouraging behavior change.

Traditional One-Way Communication Efforts

Past prosocial campaign efforts have utilized traditional media outlets to influence public attitudes prior to the development of negative behaviors. This approach highlights the traditional top-down method that prosocial campaigns have relied on for decades, where campaign teams establish what prosocial behaviors should be and then disseminate persuasive messages about those behaviors to the public to better inform future decision making. In this model, campaign managers conduct extensive audience analyses that determine the current attitudes, behaviors, and beliefs of the target audience (Fishbein & Cappella, 2006).

Recent efforts have turned to the Internet as a way of increasing interaction with audiences. For example, Bass et al. (2006) discovered that newly diagnosed cancer patients seeking information from the National Cancer Institute's Cancer Information Center found the Internet to be a powerful source of information that helped increase their confidence in participating in treatment decisions, asking physicians questions, and sharing feelings of concern (i.e., self-efficacy). Similarly, a meta-analysis of 22 articles concluded that web-based interventions are more likely than traditional media to positively influence patients' likelihood to chat with others online about their health concerns, change diet, and participate in health care (i.e., both self-efficacy and participation: Wantland, Portillo, Holzemer, Slaughter, & McGhee, 2004). Such findings point to the potential of the Internet in encouraging self-efficacy and the adoption of more positive health and environmental behaviors.

Other research highlights the potential for interpersonal interaction online to increase engagement with campaign messages. Hornik (2002) suggests that interpersonal dialogue about campaign messages and meanings is more influential than merely attending to health communication campaigns. In addition to offering prosocial campaign managers new avenues for communicating with their audiences, the Internet also allows individuals to interact with campaign information and one another in ways that may enhance the effectiveness of campaign messages.

Adopting a Multi-way Approach

Social scientific theories like the theory of planned behavior (see Ajzen, 1985, 1988, 1991, 2002), health belief model (see, Rosenstock, 1974), diffusion of innovations (see Rogers, 2003; Rogers & Shoemaker, 1971), and social cognitive theory[1] (see Bandura, 1986, 2001) also emphasize the importance of social influence on the development of attitudes and adoption of prosocial behaviors. Specifically, research shows that we often rely on our perceptions of others as a way to determine whether we will engage in a particular behavior. This trend has been highlighted in much health and environmental research investigating the importance of subjective norms in encouraging prosocial behaviors. For instance campaigns encouraging behaviors like maintaining a healthier diet (Lytle et al., 2003), using condoms to prevent sexually transmitted diseases (Fishbein, von Haeften, & Appleyard, 2001), and recycling (Terry, Hogg, & White, 1999) have successfully mobilized group leaders and encouraged change through social norms.

Despite the fact that mass media are widely recognized as important sources for health and environmental information and powerful instruments in shaping our attitudes toward many social issues (Allum, Sturgis, Tabourazi, & Brunton-Smith, 2008; Brossard & Shanahan, 2003; Priest, 2001), interpersonal communication can be a more powerful factor in shaping public behaviors. In fact, it is often the interaction with the informed and active members of one's social network that can be most influential when making behavioral decisions (e.g., Hornik, 2002). This is also highlighted by additional theories that predict the role of other individuals in modeling behavior. For instance, social cognitive theory suggests we learn about behaviors and their consequences by observing the behaviors of influential or socially similar others (Bandura, 1977, 2001).

Research investigating social influence often focuses on the role of opinion leaders, or social network influentials, in shaping social norms, informing fellow citizens, and altering behavior (Asch, 1956; Bode & Dalrymple, 2014; Cialdini, 2001; Crutchfield, 1955; Dalrymple, Shaw, & Brossard, 2013a, 2013b; Keller & Berry, 2003; Lakin & Chartrand, 2003; Mackie, 1987). Such research shows that there are individuals in society who become more involved in the issues than others (Keller & Berry, 2003). These individuals tend to fill the important role of passing along information to their social networks and upholding social norms. Subsequently these individuals are more persuasive in convincing others whether or not to adopt certain opinions and behaviors (Katz & Lazarsfeld, 1955; Keller & Berry, 2003). Diffusions of innovations, which Rogers (2003) developed to explain the rate of behavioral adoption across social groups, suggests that while opinion leaders may not be recognized as individuals of power within their communities, they can still serve as champions for change. Additionally, the influence of these individuals may occur unknowingly when they are conducting daily behaviors such as offering advice or recommendations, participating in local forums or discussions, or engaging in debates about various opinions and behaviors. As a result, these social network influentials can aid in the encouragement of prosocial behaviors while remaining unaware of their influence on others (Nisbet & Kotcher, 2009; Weimann, 1994).

Incorporating social network influentials into prosocial campaign efforts can help develop more sophisticated and effective campaigns. Research has consistently demonstrated that when people are unsure about what to do in a particular behavioral domain, they are especially likely to look toward others for evidence of how to act (Cialdini & Goldstein, 2004; Griskevivius, Tybur, & Van den Bergh, 2008; Shaw, 2010). They are also likely to pay attention to trusted sources that have a position of authority in their community (Kelly et al., 1992). Social network influentials can, therefore, serve as strategic vectors in communicating with the public about prosocial issues and are likely to be more successful at persuading audiences to adopt new behaviors.

In addition to relying on trustworthy members of our social groups to direct our behaviors, our natural tendency to conform can also impact the success of a prosocial campaign (Cialdini & Goldstein, 2004; Chartrand & Bargh, 1999). As a result, individuals are likely to adapt their behaviors to others' because it often leads to more informed decision making when facing unfamiliar topics, interactions, or situations (Cialdini, 2001; Crutchfield, 1955; Mackie, 1987). More importantly, conforming to another person's beliefs or behaviors often tends to produce a positive interaction between individuals, which helps accomplish the goal of affiliation or popularity. This normative influence can be especially powerful because of the common perception that individuals who deviate from the norm are more likely to be rejected by other group members (Janes & Olseon, 2000; Kruglanski & Webster, 1991). For example, in the classic Asch (1956) psychological experiments, participants were more likely to conform to the group due to a concern of being singled out, as opposed to believing that the consensus of the group reflected the correct answer. Similarly, when people have a heightened desire to affiliate with a group, conformity tends to increase (e.g., Lakin & Chartrand, 2003).

Both health and environmental research supports these arguments with consistent findings pointing to the importance of social norms in encouraging positive behavior change or compliance. For instance, research investigating AIDS risk reduction shows that discussions with "trendsetting" individuals (i.e., social network influentials) were more effective in encouraging protected sexual interactions than standard AIDS education programs (Kelly et al., 1992). Analysis of data from long-term projects such as the Framingham Heart Study demonstrate that health outcomes such as obesity and behaviors such as smoking are more commonly shared among friends who are connected within social networks than among neighbors, people who live near each other but who may not be within the same social circles. Christakis and Fowler (2013) argue one explanation for this trend is that health behaviors are contagious: interactions with and observations of others within our social networks construct the norms that guide our behaviors. Additionally, in the context of environmental issues and products, Griskevivius, Tyburg, and Van den Bergh (2010) discovered that the reputational benefits of purchasing "green" environmentally conscious products outweighed the fact that such products are often of lower quality, convenience and performance. Oakley and Salam (2014) also show that the sense of responsibility that an individual feels about their environment is strongly impacted by ICGs within their computer mediated social networks who both create and send messages that activate awareness and a sense of caring for the environment.

The number of individuals participating in online discussions about health and the environment is continuing to grow, as is evidence that the norms constructed within interpersonal interactions guide social behaviors. With that growth comes a number of new opportunities for prosocial marketers to mobilize social network influentials online. As social media continue to upend the traditional top-down relationship between the marketer and the individual, these media can enable marketers to bring audience members into their campaigns and engage them in content creation, distribution, and evaluation. We argue that a crucial next step for prosocial marketers is in identifying the source characteristics of content generators most likely to exercise outsize influence within their online social networks.

Identifying Influential Content Generators (ICGs)

As described above, theory suggests that interpersonal sources can be influential in determining whether behaviors are adopted, but not all interpersonal sources are equal in their influence. Our understanding of when and how social network sources are influential is bolstered by basic research studies that attempt to define which source characteristics distinguish ICGs from other content generators (see Table 3.1). Literature thus far has identified the importance of rethinking credibility and expertise in relation to ICG content and in recognizing the significance of perceived similarity.

Though expertise enhances the credibility of health care provider or scientist sources, for ICG content, perception of expertise might actually work

TABLE 3.1 Definitions From Past Literature Referencing Social Network Influentials

Term	Definition	Relevant Literature
Opinion Leader	Sociable individuals who have contact with relevant information supplied to them from the media outside of their immediate social networks.	Katz & Lazarsfeld, 1955; Rogers, 2003
Influentials	Individuals who have a strong personality and are more socially connected within their networks and can, therefore, influence opinion formation.	Garceau, 1951; Keller & Berry, 2003
Key Informants	Individuals with social positions that give them specialist or expert knowledge about an issue, related individuals and social processes.	Tremblay, 1957
Strategic Informants	Individuals interested in the behaviors of those in their social networks, who observe the development of culture and speculate about both.	Sjoberg & Nett, 1968
"Marginal" Innovators	Individuals who are rich in weak ties and therefore enhance the diffusion process.	Granovetter, 1973
Prosumer	People who produce some of the goods and services that they also consume.	Toffler, 1980
Stakeholder	Any group or individual who can affect or is affected by the achievement of an organization's objective.	Freeman, 2010
Policy Entrepreneurs	Policy actors who are most often responsible for the infusion of new ideas into the policy environment.	Kingdon, 1970; Baumgartner & Jones, 1993
Produser	People who are collaborating to produce and create content.	Bruns, 2008
Free Agent	Individuals who are fluent in social media and passionate about a social cause, but are working outside of a nonprofit organization to organize, mobilize, raise money, and engage with others.	Kanter & Fine, 2010

against perceptions of similarity because expertise conveys social distance. Wang, Walther, Pingree, & Hawkins (2008) endorse this argument, stating that "heterophily connoted for most users by a source with great medical expertise may compete with homophily one may experience through interactive or observational communication with peers in discussion groups" (p. 359). Others suggest that a lot of similarity and a little bit of expertise might be the optimal mix (McCroskey, Hamilton, & Weiner, 1974). Rogers and Shoemaker (1971) define this ideal characteristic as "optimal heterophily," which refers to a source who shares our perspective but with the addition of expertise or experience within the relevant domain.

To determine how source expertise influences perception of similarity of peer sources, Young (2013) manipulated cues indicating sources did or did not share attitudes and demographic characteristics to research participants and were experts in health and medicine. Overall, sources who were defined as similar were considered more credible than sources who were dissimilar. However, similar sources who were also high in expertise were considered less credible than dissimilar sources with high expertise. In line with the idea of optimal heterophily this finding echoes the contention that the ideal peer source is highly similar in ways that are salient to the message recipient and only a bit of an expert in the relevant domain, since too much expertise might in fact counter perception of similarity. Instead, indications that a source was very similar seemed to call into question the veracity of that source's expertise. In a study testing the optimal heterophily concept among bloggers, Yamamoto and Matsumura (2009) found that people communicated online with others who were slightly more knowledgeable or influential compared to those with the same or a lot more knowledge or influence. The authors argue that many "grassroots influentials," rather than a few "super influentials," perpetuate diffusion of electronic word-of-mouth (e-WOM), providing support to the decentralized model of idea dissemination proposed by diffusion of innovation theory (Rogers, 2003).

Other research also suggests that credibility assessment is more complex than the way it is sometimes modeled in communications research. In addition to determining source credibility heuristically rather than systematically, Internet users often consider endorsements of other users in determining which sites or messages are worthy of being believed. In fact, Metzger, Flanagin, and Medders (2010) state that social factors are perhaps the most influential in assessing credibility of Internet sources. It behooves prosocial marketers to accept that social endorsement of content is a major factor in determining the credibility of online information. As corporate marketers have done, they can then begin to determine how to best parlay this phenomenon into content that is relevant and useful to target audiences.

Perceived similarity (i.e., characteristics of similarity established by the individual that often extend beyond general demographic characteristics) is another source variable that online users look for in a social network influential. For example, ICG sources might be considered influential insofar as they are perceived as similar to the message recipient. In an experiment, Wang et al. (2008) found that perceived similarity mediated the relationship between message and behavioral intentions for messages from both health web sites and health discussion boards. Perceived similarity has also been suggested as one potential mechanism through which entertainment media and messages incorporating social norms alter or reinforce attitudes. One experiment investigating norms-based health messages found that perceived similarity to the exemplar in the message narrative predicted message effectiveness (Andsager, Bemker, Choi, & Torwel, 2006). Critical analysis of norms-based messages found that messages communicating norms through base-rate information affected normative statistical judgments, or the amount that participants believed their peers performed a behavior, but not attitudes related to that behavior (Campo et al., 2003; Campo, Cameron, Brossard, & Frazer, 2004). One proposed explanation for this discrepancy is that prototypical behavior is not as relevant to message recipients as the behavior of friends or close peers, those perceived as more interpersonally similar (Campo et al., 2003). This and other research demonstrates that not all peer or network sources are equally resonant and underscores the value in considering which specific source characteristics influence whether a social network source is perceived as influential.

Online ICGs are likely to be perceived as trustworthy by those in their social networks (Granovetter, 1973; Keller & Berry, 2003). They are looked to as a source of information as they are likely to consume a lot of news about the issues that they believe to be most important. In addition to source-level characteristics such as perceived expertise or similarity, features of networks and descriptions of behavior, such as the size of an individual's social network, how often their content is forwarded, and the frequency of their content creation, can help marketers recognize who has influence within their social network and observe how others behave in response to those ICGs.

The task of identifying ICGs and partnering with them to disseminate prosocial content is complicated by the intricate nature of health and environmental information and decision-making. For a corporate marketer, deputizing a social network influential via social media is as simple as searching Tweets for a positive product mention, and then either forwarding that message or engaging the ICG in a conversation witnessed by followers (much like change agents can encourage diffusion by encouraging an opinion leader to adopt or reject an innovation; see Rogers, 2003). However, a strategic communicator with the goal of promoting a health behavior, such as vaccination for the seasonal flu, has to ensure that any content co-created with ICGs is scientifically sound and must also contend with divergent messages from other ICGs that are not just hostile or critical but potentially dangerous in their couching of opinion and anecdote as scientific fact. Health and scientific experts may fear that their credibility will be damaged by inadvertent associations with inaccurate content or, worse, that perceived endorsement of inaccurate ICG content may lead to poor decisions. Partnerships with ICGs are potentially hindered by the fact that non-experts cannot always provide information that's perceived as complete and of high quality. While ICGs may be *likely* to be believed, they are not often *worthy* of being believed.

Blurring of anecdote or emotion and expert opinion is a factor in many health and environmental issues, including vaccination, genetically modified foods, and climate change. One way to resolve this justifiable concern is to clearly delineate between scientific experts and ICGs and to define what constitutes credibility and expertise among ICGs. While ICGs should not supplant experts as sources in areas that require expert knowledge, surveys suggest that the public can be nuanced in their opinions about which sources are credible in different situations. For health, a Pew survey suggests that the preferred source depends on the information need (Fox & Duggan, 2013). While nearly all respondents agree that professional medical sources like doctors and nurses are most helpful when seeking a medical diagnosis (91%) or information about medications (85%), they also agree that peers are most helpful when the need is emotional support for dealing with a health issue (59%) or a quick remedy for an everyday health problem (51%). Peers and professionals are equally helpful when respondents need practical advice for coping with everyday health situations (45% named peers as most helpful, and 46% said professionals).

Examining the potential impact of co-created content will provide unique insight as to the possible influence of "non-experts," or lay-expertise, on the way individuals think and talk about broader societal issues related to public health and our environment. However, there are several possible reasons why prosocial campaigns have been timid in their exploration of the potential impact of ICG content in health and environmental initiatives. First, information regarding these two topic areas is often driven by experts. Therefore, collaborating with ICGs may also be perceived as relinquishing control over information quality. Second, both health and environmental initiatives often prioritize behavior change in the context of complicated social and structural factors. The influence of multilevel factors, and the complexities of prosocial behavioral change create communication challenges distinct from those faced by corporate marketers. Third, many prosocial health and environmental campaigns focus on communities that may still lack home computers and broadband internet access. Thus, the individuals who are most crucial to reach with relevant and accurate health and environmental risk information may also be those without easy access to information or interventions that require reliable access to a computer.

Although we recognize these challenges, ICGs are creating health and environmental content online daily (Oakley & Salam, 2014; Sarasohn-Kahn, 2008;

Vance, Howe, & Dellavalle, 2009). These individuals have increasing influence over their social networks and are currently underutilized in campaign efforts. Developing a deeper understanding of the source characteristics and behaviors of ICGs, including conceputalizations of expertise and credibility in the context of the participatory web, will only lead to more innovative and effective future collaborations.

Listening, Forwarding, Collaborating: A Typology

Decades of research have demonstrated the influence of social network sources on health and environmental attitudes and behaviors as well as the characteristics that influence whether a network source is likely to be believed. In addition to recognizing research that outlines the characteristics of ICGs, it is also important to examine how campaigns have utilized ICGs online to influence environmental and health attitudes and behaviors. In reviewing these campaigns, we can categorize prosocial marketing campaigns into three broad categories: campaigns that employ listening, forwarding, and/or collaborative strategies. The following typology of research on ICGs in prosocial campaigns, will describe these categories with particular focus on efforts that actively engage ICGs in creation and dissemination of prosocial content (see Table 3.2). Examining research according to these three categorizations will not only provide scholars with a novel method of comparing and contrasting campaigns, but will also allow future researchers to more efficiently identify positive contributions or critical drawbacks of past and existing prosocial campaign strategies.

Listening

Prosocial campaigns that hope to empower ICGs in future campaigns must build from the models of past campaigns while being aware of the nuance of online co-creation. First, campaign designers must practice listening. In corporate marketing, social listening refers to the process of investigating what is being said about a product or company online to better inform future strategic messages and campaigns. Health and environmental communicators should continue to prioritize prosocial listening on a range of online legacy and social media platforms. Fine-grained, theoretically based descriptive studies of ICG health and environmental content can serve as a foundation for prosocial content co-creation. Understanding extant online interactions around specific health topics can inform environmental and health communicators about the tenor and nature of the public conversation.

A wealth of studies have described the content and interactions on health and environmental message boards (e.g., Macias, Lewis, & Smith, 2005; Nimrod, 2009) or on social media sites (e.g., Prochaska, Pechmann, Kim, & Leonhardt,

TABLE 3.2 Application of Typology to Existing Research

Campaign Category	Definition	Sample Citations
Listening	The process of investigating what is being said about a health or environmental topic on participatory web platforms to develop an understanding of baseline knowledge and attitudes and to inform future strategic messages and campaigns	*Forums/message boards*: Macias, Lewis, & Smith, 2005; Nimrod, 2010; Zhao et al., 2014 *Social media platforms*: Oakley & Salam, 2014; Prochaska, Pechmann, Kim, & Leonhardt, 2011; Young & Miles, 2014; Zhang et al., 2013
Forwarding	Either (1) identifying user-generated messages aligned with campaign goals and disseminating them via an organization's social media platforms; or (2) constructing online content designed to be disseminated by publics within their own individual online social networks	*Campaigns meant to be forwarded*: Mackert, Kim, Guadagno, & Donovan-Kicken, 2012 *Predictors of forwarding/virality*: Alhabash & McAlister, 2014
Collaborating	Partnering with influential online content generators to construct and disseminate health and environmental messages within online social networks	*Beneficial effects of collaboration*: Namkoong et al., 2010; Dalrymple, Shaw, & Brossard, 2013a; Kreuter & McClure, 2004

2011). Other studies examine public use of online tools that encourage prosocial behaviors (Wicks, Vaughan, Massagli, & Heywood, 2011). Some innovative studies go beyond description and large-scale analysis of health message board content to examine the linguistic determinants of source influence in peer-to-peer online interactions (Zhao et al., 2014) or to understand how user characteristics moderate effects from reading and posting messages (Namkoong et al., 2010). As long as researchers are sensitive to the particular ethical concerns involved in studying messages that blur lines between private and public (Vayena, Mastroianni, & Kahn, 2012), listening to ICGs can provide descriptions of how peers interact online and can also provide insight into how particular interactions unfold and how these interactions influence readers and writers of online messages.

Because online data are both vast and messy, well-structured prosocial listening studies will ideally be conducted with goals for application in mind. Young and Miles (2014) investigated aggressive online interactions on ask.fm, a social media platform mostly unknown to adults but a favorite among young adolescents. While concern about online aggression and cyberbullying have increased, few studies have taken advantage of Internet affordances to examine how site users aggress, how victims respond, and how bystanders intervene. On ask.fm, victims used a range of rhetorical strategies to address aggressors, including counterattack, nonchalance, sarcasm, or interrogating the aggressor's motives. Supportive bystanders inserted themselves by attacking the aggressors or using second- or third-person language to support the victim and argue against any negative characterizations voiced by the aggressor. Interventions designed to address cyberbullying will benefit from a catalogue of key words and phrases that recur frequently in aggressive encounters as well as an understanding of common rhetorical strategies used by victims and bystanders that may successfully turn the tables on online aggressors. And this same strategy could serve other contexts as well. Use of relevant language may be one way of culturally tailoring messages (Kreuter & McClure, 2004). Persuasive messages that use the rhetorical strategies preferred by target populations may be perceived as more relevant because they sound authentic.

Forwarding

In addition to listening, prosocial campaigns employ the strategy of forwarding or content sharing via participatory media. We use the term forwarding to refer to the practice of (1) constructing online content designed to be disseminated by publics within their own individual online social networks, the process described by the term virality, as well as (2) identifying user-generated messages aligned with campaign goals and disseminating them via an organization's social media platforms. Virality is an example of the potential impact of forwarding on the adoption of new behaviors and uptake of new information (Eckler & Rodgers, 2014; Alhabash & McAlister, 2014). Successful prosocial campaigns already attempt to harness the power of networked publics to disseminate persuasive messages, or to encourage virality. For instance, health organizations have capitalized on the connections among networked users by designing Facebook applications that enable message forwarding or take advantage of the linked-network affordance in persuasive communication. One example from the New York City Department of Health and Mental Hygeine, is the e-condom app allowing Facebook users to forward friends an image of a condom with a message promoting protection (Chan, 2009). Similarly, Cervical Cancer-Free Kentucky created the Cause the Movement campaign that involved message forwarding as well as a graphic that used images from a specific friend network to illutrate potential deaths from cervical cancer (http://www.cervicalcancerfreeky.org/ctm).

These campaigns engage our tendency to give more credence to sources we already know to attract attention to their behavior goal: condom use or HPV vaccination. However, the likelihood that messages will be forwarded likely depends on their perceived relevance and the norms for use on social media sites (Mackert et al., 2012). In two studies of the virality of prosocial messages, Alhabash and McAlister (2014) found that participants' forwarding behavior varied by platform: liking prosocial posts on Facebook was more common than commenting or reposting/forwarding, while retweeting on Twitter was more common than favoriting or responding. They suggest that intent to forward might vary as a function of cognitive demand, which also varies by platform affordances and norms of use. A clearer understanding of the motivations for forwarding health and environmental messages and of the characteristics that influence whether content is forwarded will help in crafting messages that are more likely to be endorsed and passed along within online social networks. In addition, research should investigate whether the practice of identifying and forwarding relevant user-generated content via organization sites can be another effective method of reaching publics.

Collaborating

While listening and forwarding are crucial steps toward understanding the phenomenon of prosocial ICG communication online, the richest relationship between prosocial marketing and ICGs will come from true collaboration. Critical analysis of health and environmental communication has levied charges of paternalism at unidirectional mass mediated campaigns that tell people how to behave without a clear understanding of public understanding, sentiment, and behavioral constraints. The affordances of the Internet allow prosocial marketers to engage directly with publics. We can listen to how people are already talking about health and environmental issues, identify how and when ICGs forward and comment on existing content, and, most importantly, propose collaborations either offline or online that then levy existing networked publics to spread culturally relevant messages.

The idea of harnessing the audiences of internet users to influence those within their social networks already has an analog in health and environmental practices, through the use of peer counselors or community leaders. These lay experts are individuals from a community who work within a community to promote individual and community health or environmental preservation (e.g., Witmer, Seifer, Finocchio, Leslie, & O'Neil, 1995). The community may be defined spatially, as in a neighborhood; economically; by age; or by national, racial, or ethnic background; or by connection online. Future prosocial marketing campaigns should look to this literature for ideas on how to collaborate with community leaders in promoting health or environmental outcomes. While some community interventions use lay leaders as mouthpieces for existing messages, the principles of community-based participatory research insist that communities be not just messengers but also active participants in setting goals, planning communication, and creating messages. Community collaborations could bridge offline discussion with online message dissemination to reach a broader audience.

Future collaborations can be informed by community goals as well as by an understanding of which types of messages are most relevant when coming from ICG sources. Credibility may be considered not only as a concrete attribute of a source, but also as the fit between a message or a source and the goal for use (Hilligoss & Rieh, 2008). Information is not necessarily credible because it represents truth or expert opinion but because it is what is needed within that situation. By this definition, information from a socially proximal source may be considered credible in constructing perceived norms of behavior or in determining which health beliefs and behaviors are socially sanctioned. Prosocial campaigns that capitalize in some way on ICG content and connections should consider how situational and social assessment of credibility informs how audiences will respond to messages. Tips about saving water in a drought-stricken area or advice on dealing with cravings during dietary changes might be equally or even more credible coming from someone coping with the same issues than from an expert.

Another example of how online collaborators may help in changing behavior is as instrumental support in setting or reaching goals. People seeking to reach a goal or change a behavior encounter roadblocks and develop strategies to address them. In the goal-setting literature, the a priori performance of this process, anticipating roadblocks and developing solutions in advance, is called implementation intention. A test using construal level theory found that participants who read health messages from socially proximal others were likely to list barriers or roadblocks to performing a specific health beahvior (Young, 2015). Thus, messages from socially proximal others might be one way to spark consideration of feasiblity concerns that can be addressed through implementation intention or other theoretically based faciliations. With physical activity, for example, a barrier may be a busy work schedule, and the solution may be exercising during the lunch hour. Meta-analyses have shown that considering barriers and solutions in advance is effective in promoting goal achievement (Gollwitzer & Sheeran, 2006). Interactions that address feasibility concerns are also a hallmark of patient-led counseling tactics, such as motivational interviewing (Outlaw et al., 2010).

In addition, successful collaborations among prosocial communications and ICGs may result in positive changes not just for audiences but for the ICGs themselves. Pingree's (2007) bidirectional model of message effects suggests that creating content and also disseminating content to an audience online should have effects on the creator. One documented effect of producing and disseminating content online is an increase in self-efficacy related to that topic; studies of health message boards have found that positive effects of producing content in an online community are mediated by self-efficacy (Namkoong et al., 2010). In a controlled experiment, Young and Wise (2012) found that student participants who wrote brief messages about exercise had a greater positive change in exercise-related self-efficacy from baseline than did those in a control group. In addition, for participants who wrote exercise-related messages, an increase in self-efficacy mediated increased behavioral intention to exercise in the next week. Research has shown that an individual's perceived self-efficacy is a powerful factor that influences the likelihood of an influential to contribute to prosocial causes, and subsequently influence their social group (Dalrymple, Shaw, & Brossard, 2013a). In fact, researchers exploring potential explanations for behavior change/compliance agree that an individual's beliefs about any barriers that may interfere with the performance of a behavior tend to influence the likelihood of accepting that behavior (see Ajzen, 1985; Bandura, 1977; Rimal, 2001; Witte, 1992, 1994). Consequently, individuals who believe that they can execute a behavior are much more likely to discuss that behavior and encourage their social networks to follow their lead.

Finally, despite historical disparities in access to home computers and the Internet, adoption of Internet-enabled smartphones and high rates of social network site use among racial and ethnic minority populations suggests ICG collaborations might be beneficial in these communities as well (Gibbons et al., 2011). Though microblogging sites such as Twitter are already used to disseminate messages during natural disasters, not all members of affected communities are likely to follow the relevant government agencies online. Messages from online influentials within a social network could prompt action during natural disasters or other environmental events, such as the need for water conservation during droughts. These and other ICG collaborations would also benefit from the perspective of cultural insiders (Kreuter & McClure, 2004).

Where Do We Go From Here?

The listening, forwarding, and collaborating typology describes an iterative process in which research in one domain informs and improves research and practice in another. A clear sense of the norms and syntax used in discussing health or environmental messages on social network sites will lead to clearer conceptualizations of culturally relevant collaborations. Collaborations with cultural insiders will lead to prosocial messages from similar sources that perhaps feel more engaging and more relevant and are thus more likely to be forwarded. A key assumption of this feedback loop is the assumption that the public has tacit knowledge about health and environmental behaviors that's worthy of being understood and that true collaborations that grant agency to communities will lead to better, more inclusive communication.

Applying our typology to existing and future campaigns will not only help evaluate the success of prosocial messages, but will also identify areas where strategic efforts are lacking. For instance, in reviewing recent studies examining the effects of various prosocial campaigns, we recognize a paucity of research investigating the potential effect of forwarding ICG messages about environmental issues (see Table 3.2). Additionally, we recognize that there is a clear need for strategists to engage ICGs and emphasize collaboration in future campaigns. Approaching the development of future research with our typology in mind will therefore help avoid repetition in scholarship and encourage innovative research that contributes to the development of strategic communication theory.

Considering the original definition of prosocial marketing, we believe it is time to embrace new trends in communication technologies and work to apply current trends in marketing to the promotion of prosocial ideas. Corporate marketers have successfully adapted to these new consumer environments, executing strategic plans on social media platforms with ease and precision. Now, prosocial marketers have an opportunity to move beyond the listening stage and recognize the importance of forwarding and collaborating with online influential ICGs. Encouraging better relationships between prosocial strategic communicators and online ICGs will not only benefit those developing the campaign, but also may encourage agency within social networks. Getting ICGs involved at the ground level can inspire confidence and help address concerns about important social issues at the source. As ICGs gain self-efficacy during a campaign it will encourage further participation, creation, and distribution of strategic messages. Ideally, these effects will spread throughout an ICG's social network and affect agency among others online. In short, collaborating with ICGs online will not only benefit society through the promotion of prosocial behaviors, but also by increasing public discussion and empowering citizens to focus on a greater good.

Note

1 Social cognitive theory, first called social learning theory, assumes an agentic perspective where individuals learn (1) by experiencing the effects of their actions, and (2) through the practice of social modeling. Bandura explains social modeling, or vicarious learning, as a short cut to experiential learning where we learn behaviors based on our exposure to the successes and mistakes of others (see Bandura, 1986, 2001).

References

Ajzen, I. (1985). From intentions to actions: A theory of planned behavior. In J. Kuhl & J. Beckmann (Eds.), *Action control: From cognition to behavior* (pp. 11–39). Berlin, Germany: Springer.

Ajzen, I. (1988). *Attitudes, personality, and behavior.* Chicago: The Dorsey Press.

Ajzen, I. (1991). The theory of planned behavior. *Organizational Behavior and Human Decision Processes, 50*, 179–211.

Ajzen, I. (2002). Perceived behavioral control, self-efficacy, locus of control, and the theory of planned behavior. *Journal of Applied Social Psychology, 32*(4), 665–683.

Ajzen, I. (2008). Consumer attitudes and behavior. In C. P. Haugtvedt, P. M. Herr, & F. R. Kardes (Eds.), *The handbook of social psychology* (pp. 525–548). New York: Lawrence Erlbaum Associates.

Alhabash, S., & McAlister, A. (2014). Redefining virality in less broad strokes: Predicting viral behavioral intentions from motivations and uses of Facebook and Twitter. *New Media & Society*. Published online February 24, 2014. doi: 10.1177/1461444814523726

Allum, N., Sturgis, P., Tabourazi, D., & Brunton-Smith, I. (2008). Science knowledge and attitudes across cultures: A meta-analysis. *Public Understanding of Science, 17*(1), 35–54.

Andsager, J. L., Bemker, V., Choi, H.-L., & Torwel, V. (2006). Perceived similarity of exemplar traits and behavior: Effects on message evaluation. *Communication Research, 33*, 3–18.

Armstrong, A., & Hagel, J. (2000). The real value of online communities. In E. Lessor, M. A. Fontaine, & J. A. Lusher (Eds.), *Knowledge and Communities* (pp. 85–95). Boston: Butterworth.

Asch, S. E. (1956). Studies of independence and conformity: I. A minority of one against a unanimous majority. *Psychological Monographs: General and Applied, 70*(9), 1.

Bandura, A. (1977). *Social learning theory*. Englewood Cliffs, NJ: Prentice-Hall.

Bandura, A. (1986). *Social foundations of thought and action: A social cognitive theory*. Englewood Cliffs, NJ: Prentice-Hall.

Bandura, A. (2001). Social cognitive theory: An agentic perspective. *Annual Review of Psychology, 52*(1), 1–26.

Bass, S. B., Ruzek, S. B., Gordon, T. F., Fleisher, L., McKeown-Conn, N., & Moore, D. (2006). Relationship of Internet health information use with patient behavior and self-efficacy: Experiences of newly diagnosed cancer patients who contact the National Cancer Institute's Cancer Information Service. *Journal of Health Communication, 11*(2), 219–236.

Baumgartner, F. R., & Jones, B. D. (1993). *Agendas and instability in American politics*. Chicago: University of Chicago Press.

Bode, L., & Dalrymple, K. E. (2014). Politics in 140 characters or less: Campaign communication, network interaction, and political participation on Twitter. *Journal of Political Marketing*. doi: 10.1080/15377857.2014.959686

Brosius, H. B., & Weimann, G. (1996). Who sets the agenda: Agenda-setting as a two-step flow. *Communication Research, 23*(5), 561–580.

Brossard, D., & Shanahan, J. (2003). Do citizens want to have their say? Media, agricultural biotechnology, and authoritarian views of democratic processes in science. *Mass Communication, 3*, 47–63.

Bruns, A. (2008). *Blogs, Wikipedia, Second Life, and beyond: From production to produsage*. New York: Peter Lang.

Campo, S., Cameron, K. A., Brossard, D., & Frazer, M. S. (2004). Social norms and expectancy violation theories: Assessing the effectiveness of health communication campaigns. *Communication Monographs, 71*(4), 448–470.

Campo, S., Brossard, D., Frazer, M. S., Marchell, T., Lewis, D., & Talbot, J. (2003). Are social norms campaigns really magic bullets? Assessing the effects of students' misperceptions on drinking behavior. *Health Communication, 15*(4), 481–497.

Carpenter, C. J. (2010). A meta-analysis of the effectiveness of health belief model variables in predicting behavior. *Health Communication, 25*(8), 661–669.

Chan, R. Y. K., & Lau, L. B. Y. (2001). Explaining green purchasing behavior: A cross-cultural study on American and Chinese consumers. *Journal of International Consumer Marketing, 14,* 9–40.

Chan, S. (2009). City unveils Facebook page to encourage condom use. *New York Times.* Retrieved from http://www.nytimes.com/2009/02/12/nyregion/12econdom.html

Chartrand, T. L., & Bargh, J. A. (1999). The chameleon effect: The perception-behavior link and social interaction. *Journal of Personality and Social Psychology, 76,* 893–910.

Chevalier, J., & Mayzlin, D. (2006). The effect of word of mouth on sales: Online book reviews. *Journal of Marketing Research, 43*(3), 345–354.

Christakis, N. A., & Fowler, J. H. (2013). Social contagion theory: Examining dynamic social networks and human behavior. *Statistics in Medicine, 32*(4), 556–577.

Cialdini, R. B. (2001). *Influence: Science and practice* (4th ed.). New York: Allyn & Bacon.

Cialdini, R. B., & Goldstein, N. J. (2004). Social influence: Compliance and conformity. *Annual Review of Psychology, 55,* 591–621.

Corbett, J. B. (2002). Motivations to participate in riparian improvement programs: Applying the Theory of Planned Behavior. *Science Communication, 23,* 243–263.

Crutchfield, R. S. (1955). Conformity and character. *American Psychologist, 10*(5), 191–198.

Dalrymple, K. E., Shaw, B. R., & Brossard, D. (2013a, June). Making waves: Mass media, opinion leaders, and the campaign for environmental change. Paper presented at the annual convention of the International Communication Association, London.

Dalrymple, K. E., Shaw, B. R., & Brossard, D. (2013b). Following the leader: Using opinion leaders in environmental strategic communication. *Journal of Society and Natural Resources, 26*(12), 1438–1453. doi: 10.1080/08941920.2013.820812

Deuze, M. (2001). Online journalism: Modelling the first generation of news media on the World Wide Web. *First Monday, 6*(10). Retrieved from http://firstmonday.org/ojs/index.php/fm/article/view/893/802

Eckler, P., & Rodgers, S. (2014). Viral advertising: A conceptualization. In H. Cheng (Ed.), *The handbook of international advertising research* (pp. 139–160). Chichester, UK: John Wiley & Sons.

Fishbein, M., & Ajzen, I. (1975). *Belief, attitude, intention, and behavior: An introduction to theory and research.* Reading, MA: Addison-Wesley.

Fishbein, M., & Cappella, J. N. (2006). The role of theory in developing effective health communications. *Journal of Communication, 56,* S1–S17.

Fishbein, M., von Haeften, I., & Appleyard, J. (2001). The role of theory in developing effective interventions: Implications from Project SAFER. *Psychology, Health & Medicine, 6,* 223–238.

Fox, K. F., & Kotler, P. (1980). The marketing of social causes: The first 10 years. *The Journal of Marketing,* 24–33.

Fox, S., & Duggan, M. (2013). Health Online 2013. Pew Internet & American Life Project, January 15, 2013. http://www.pewinternet.org/files/old-media//Files/Reports/PIP_HealthOnline.pdf

Freeman, R. E. (2010). *Strategic management: A stakeholder approach.* Cambridge: Cambridge University Press.

Garceau, O. (1951). Research in the political process. *American Political Science Review, 45*(1), 69–85.

Gibbons, M. C., Fleisher, L., Slamon, R. E., Bass, S., Kandadai, V., & Beck, J. R. (2011). Exploring the potential of Web 2.0 to address health disparities. *Journal of Health Communication, 16*(sup1), 77–89.

Glanz, K., Rimer, B. K., & Viswanath, K. (Eds.). (2008). *Health behavior and health education: Theory, research, and practice.* John Wiley & Sons.

Gollwitzer, P. M., & Sheeran, P. (2006). Implementation intentions and goal achievement: A metaanalysis of effects and processes. *Advances in Experimental Social Psychology, 38,* 69–119.

Granovetter, M. (1973). The strength of weak ties. *American Journal of Sociology, 78*(6), 1.

Griskevivius, V., Tybur, J. M., & Van den Bergh, B. (2010). Going green to be seen: Status, reputation, and conspicuous conservation. *Journal of Personality and Social Psychology, 98*(3), 392–404.

Harland, P., Staats, H., & Wilke, H. A. (1999). Explaining proenvironmental intention and behavior by personal norms and the Theory of Planned Behavior. *Journal of Applied Social Psychology, 29,* 2505–2528.

Hilligoss, B., & Rieh, S. Y. (2008). Developing a unifying framework of credibility assessment: Construct, heuristics, and interaction in context. *Information Processing & Management, 44*(4), 1467–1484.

Hornik, R. C. (2002). Public health communication: Making sense of contradictory evidence. In R. C. Hornik (Ed.), *Public health communication: Evidence for behavior change.* Hillsdale, NJ: Lawrence Erlbaum.

Janes, L. M., & Olson, J. M. (2000). Jeer pressure: The behavioral effects of observing ridicule of others. *Personality and Social Psychology Bulletin, 26*(4), 474–485.

Janz, N. K., & Becker, M. H. (1984). The health belief model: A decade later. *Health Education & Behavior, 11*(1), 1–47.

Jenkins, H. (2006). *Fans, bloggers, and gamers: Exploring participatory culture.* New York: New York University Press.

Kabani, S. (2013). *The zen of social media marketing: An easier way to build credibility, generate buzz, and increase revenue.* Dallas, TX: BenBellaBooks.

Kaiser, F. G., & Gutscher, H. (2003). The proposition of a general version of the theory of planned behavior: Predicting ecological behavior. *The Journal of Applied Social Psychology, 33,* 586–603.

Kanter, B., & Fine, A. H. (2010). *The networked nonprofit: Connecting with social media to drive change.* San Fransisco: Jossey-Bass.

Katz, E. (1957). The two-step flow of communication: An up-to-date report on an hypothesis. *Public Opinion Quarterly, 21*(1), 61–78.

Katz, E., & Lazarsfeld, P. F. (1955). *Personal influence: The part played by people in the flow of mass communications.* New Brunswick, NJ: Transaction Publishers

Keller, E. B., & Berry, J. L (2003). *The influentials: One American in ten tells the other nine how to vote, where to eat, and what to buy.* New York: Simon & Schuster.

Kelly, J. A., St. Lawrence, J. S., Stevenson, L. Y., Hauth, A. C., Kalichman, S. C., Diaz, Y.E., et al. (1992). Community AIDS/HIV risk reduction: The effects of endorsements by popular people in three cities. *American Journal of Public Health, 82,* 1483–1489.

Kerpen, D. (2011). *Likeable social media: How to delight your customers, create an irresistible brand, and be generally amazing on Facebook (and other social networks).* New York, NY: McGraw-Hill.

Kingdon, J. W. (1970). Opinion leaders in the electorate. *Public Opinion Quarterly, 34,* 256–261.

Kreuter, M. W., & McClure, S. M. (2004). The role of culture in health communication. *Annual Review of Public Health, 25,* 439–455.

Kruglanski, A. W., & Webster, D. M. (2991). Group members' reactions to opinion deviates and conformists at varying degrees of proximity to decision deadline and of environmental noise. *Journal of Personality and Social Psychology, 61*(2), 212–225.

Lakin, J. L., & Chartrand, T. L. (2003). Using nonconscious behavioral mimicry to create affiliation and rapport. *Psychological Science, 14*(4), 334–339.

Lytle, L., Varnell, S., Murray, D., Story, M., Perry, C., Birnbaum, A., & Kubik, M. (2003). Predicting adolescents' intake of fruits and vegetables. *Journal of Nutrition Education and Behavior, 35*(4), 170–178.

Macias, M., Lewis, L. S., & Smith, T. L. (2005). Health-related message boards/chat rooms on the web: Discussion content and implications for pharmaceutical sponsorships. *Journal of Health Communication, 10*(3), 209–223.

Mackert, M., Kim, E., Guadagmo, M., & Donovan-Kicken, E. (2012). Using Twitter for prenatal health promotion: Encouraging a multivitamin habit among college-aged females. In A. C. Smith (Ed.), *Global telehealth 2012: Delivering quality healthcare anywhere through telehealth* (Vol. 182) (pp. 93–103). Amsterdam: IOS.

Mackie, D. M. (1987). Systematic and nonsystematic processing of majority and minority persuasive communications. *Journal of Personality and Social Psychology, 53*(1), 41–52.

McCroskey, J. C., Hamilton, P. R., & Weiner, A. N. (1974). The effect of interaction behavior on source credibility, homophily, and interpersonal attraction. *Human Communication Research, 1*(1), 42–52.

Metzger, M. J., Flanagin, A. J., & Medders, R. B. (2010). Social and heuristic approaches to credibility evaluation online. *Journal of Communication, 60*(3), 413–439.

Mythen, G. (2009). Reframing risk? Citizen journalism and the transformation of news. *Journal of Risk Research, 13*(1), 45–58.

Namkoong, K., Shah, D., Han, J. Y., Kim, S. C., Yoo, W., Fan, D., McTavish, F. M., & Gustafson, D. (2010). Expression and reception of treatment information in breast cancer support groups: How health self-efficacy moderates effects on emotional well-being. *Patient Education and Counseling, 81S*, S41–S47.

Nimrod, G. (2010). Seniors' online communities: A quantitative content analysis. *The Gerontologist, 50*(3), 382–392.

Nisbet, M. C., & Kotcher, J. E. (2009). A two-step flow of influence? Opinion-leader campaigns on climate change. *Science Communication, 30*, 328–354.

Noar, S., & Zimmerman, R. S. (2005). Health behavior theory and cumulative knowledge regarding health behaviors: Are we moving in the right direction? *Health Education Research, 20*(3), 275–290.

Norris, P., & Curtice, J. (2008). Getting the message out: A two-step model of the role of the internet in campaign communication flows during the 2005 British general election. *Journal of Information Technology & Politics, 4*(4), 3–13.

Oakley, R. L., & Salam, A. F. (2014). Examining the impact of computer-mediated social networks on individual consumerism environmental behaviors. *Computers in Human Behavior, 35*, 516–526.

Oom Do Valle, P., Rebelo, E., Reis, E., & Menezes, J. (2005). Combining behavioral theories to predict recycling involvement. *Environment and Behavior, 37*(3), 364–396.

Ostman, R. E., & Parker, J. L. (1987). Impact of education, age, newspapers, and television on environmental knowledge, concerns, and behaviors. *Journal of Environmental Education, 19*(1), 3–9.

Perloff, R. (2008). *The dynamics of persuasion: Communication and attitudes in the 21st century* (3rd ed.). New York: Lawrence Erlbaum Associates.

Pingree, R. J. (2007). How messages affect their senders: A more general model of message effects and implications for deliberation. *Communication Theory, 17*, 439–461.

Priest, S. H. (2001). *A grain of truth: The media, the public, and biotechnology.* Lanham, MD: Rowman & Littlefield.

Prochaska, J. J., Pechmann, C., Kim, R., & Leonhardt, J. M. (2011). Twitter = quitter? An analysis of Twitter quit smoking social networks. *Tobacco Control, 21,* 447–449.

Rimal, R.N. (2001). Perceived risk and self-efficacy as motivators: Understanding individuals' long-term use of health information. *Journal of Communication, 51*(4), 633–654.

Rogers, E. M. (2003). *Diffusion of innovations* (5th ed.). New York: Free Press.

Rogers, E. M., & Shoemaker, F. F. (1971). *Communication of innovations: A cross-cultural approach.* New York: Free Press.

Rosenstock, I. M. (1974). Historical origins of the health belief model. *Health Education & Behavior, 2*(4), 328–335.

Sarasohn-Kahn, J. (2008). *The wisdom of patients: Health care meets online social media.* Oakland, CA: California Health Care Foundation.

Shaul, O., & Katz-Gerro, T. (2006). Predicting proenvironmental behavior cross-nationally: Values, the theory of planned behavior, and value-belief-norm theory. *Environment and Behavior, 38,* 462–483.

Shaw, B. (2010). Using temporally oriented social science models and audience segmentation to influence environmental behaviors. In L. Kahlor & P. Stout (Eds.), *New agendas in science communication* (pp. 109–130). Mahwah, NJ: Lawrence Erlbaum Associates.

Sjoberg, G., & Nett, R. (1968). *A methodology for social research.* New York: Harper & Row.

Terry, D., Hogg, M., & White, K. (1999). The theory of planned behaviour: Self-identity, social identity and group norms. *British Journal of Social Psychology, 38,* 225–244

Toffler, A. (1980). The rise of the prosumer. In *The third wave: The classic study of tomorrow* (pp. 265–288). New York: William Morrow and Co.

Tremblay, M. A. (1957). The key informant technique: A nonethnographic application. *American Anthropologist, 59*(4), 688–701.

Vayena, E., Mastroianni, A., & Kahn, J. (2012). Ethical issues in health research with novel online sources. *American Journal of Public Health, 102*(12), 2225–2230.

Vance, K., Howe, W., & Dellavalle, R. P. (2009). Social internet sites as a source of public health information. *Dermatologic Clinics, 27,* 133–136.

Wall, R., Devine-Wright, P., & Mill, G. A. (2007). Comparing and combining theories to explain proenvironmental intentions: The case of commuting mode-choice. *Environment and Behavior, 39,* 731–753.

Walther, J. B., & Jang, J.-W. (2012). Communication processes in participatory websites. *Journal of Computer-Mediated Communication, 18,* 2–15.

Wang, Z., Walther, J. B., Pingree, S., & Hawkins, R. P. (2008). Health information, credibility, homophily, and influence on the internet: Web sites versus discussion groups. *Health Communication, 23,* 358–368.

Wantland, D. J., Portillo, C. J., Holzemer, W. L., Slaughter, R., & McGhee, E. (2004). The effectiveness of web-based vs. non-web-based interventions: A meta-analysis of behavioral change outcomes. *Journal of Medical Internet Research, 6*(4), e40.

Weimann, G. (1982). On the importance of marginality: One more step into the two-step flow of communication. *American Sociological Review, 47*(6), 764–773.

Weimann, G. (1994). *The influential: People who influence people.* Albany, NY: State University of New York Press.

Wicks, P., Vaughan, T. E., Massagli, M. P., & Heywood, J. (2011). Accelerated clinical discovery using self-reported patient data collected online and a patient-matching algorithm. *Nature Biotechnology, 29*(5), 411–414.

Witmer, A., Seifer, S. D., Finocchio, L., Leslie, J., & O'Neil, E. H. (1995). Community health workers: Integral members of the health care work force. *American Journal of Public Health, 85*(8Pt1), 1055–1058.

Witte, K. (1992). Putting the fear back into fear appeals: The extended parallel process model. *Communication Monographs, 59*, 225–249.

Witte, K. (1994). Fear control and danger control: A test of the Extended Parallel Process Model (EPPM). *Communication Monographs, 61*, 113–134.

Yamamoto, H., & Matsumura, N. (2009, March). Optimal heterophily for word-of-mouth diffusion. In *Third International AAAI Conference on Weblogs and Social Media*. http://www.aaai.org/ocs/index.php/ICWSM/09/paper/view/164/488

Young, R. (2013). Social proximity and user-generated health content: An experimental test of perceived source similarity and construal level theory. Ph.D. dissertation. University of Missouri.

Young, R. (2015). Source similarity and social media health messages: Extending construal level theory to message sources. *Cyberpsychology, Social Networking, and Behavior, 18*, 547–551.

Young, R., & Miles, S. (2014). Status negotiation and cyberbullying on a social media site: A content analysis of posts from aggressors, profile owners, and supportive bystanders. Accepted to the Kentucky Conference on Health Communication; Lexington, KY; April 2014.

Young, R., & Wise, K. (2012, August). Fitter with Twitter? The direct and efficacy-mediated effects of reading, writing, and Tweeting health messages online. Paper presented at the Association for Education in Journalism & Mass Communication Annual Meeting, Communicating Science, Environment, and Risk Division, Chicago, IL.

Zhang, N., Campo, S., Janz, K. F., et al. (2013). Electronic word of mouth on Twitter about physical activity in the United States: Exploratory infodemiology study. *Journal of Medical Internet Research, 15*, e261. doi: 10.2196/jmir.2870.

Zhao, K., Yen, J., Greer, G., Qiu, B., Mitra, P., & Portier, K. (2014). Finding influential users of online health communities: A new metric based on sentiment influence. *Journal of the American Medical Informatics Association*, e212–e218. doi: http://dx.doi.org/10.1136/amiajnl-2013-002282

4

THE SOCIAL NATURE OF ONLINE MEDIA AND ITS EFFECTS ON BEHAVIORS AND ATTITUDES

Ashley A. Anderson

In 2015, *PLOS*, a well-known peer reviewed scientific journal, announced it would have opportunities for anyone to converse with its published authors on reddit, a website that features commenting forums among its community members (Costello, 2015). Reddit is known for its "Ask Me Anything (AMA)" series, in which people will answer any question posed to them. The series has featured several celebrities, including U.S. President Barack Obama, famous actors, and well-known scientists like Bill Nye the Science Guy and Buzz Aldrin. Therefore, the site provides a setting for back-and-forth dialogue among lay audiences and experts who may also represent organizations and institutions. The series is exemplary of computer-mediated communication in user-generated websites, where dialogue occurs among people who would not normally interact with each other.

Online media is characterized and distinguished from other forms of media through its social nature. How people engage with and form opinions about issues is embedded within conversations happening in user-generated media, such as social media and online comments, which occur directly alongside news media, entertainment media, and advertisements.

In this chapter, I examine how different types of online activities fit a dialogic or interactive framework of mediated communication. Using science communication as the issue area of focus, I review literature about social communication online, including research I have conducted in the communication spaces of formal deliberation, news commenting sections, and online information gathering. I explore how these online communication environments engender aspects of dialogic models of communication: audience predispositions and interaction. Finally, I will present future directions of strategic communication research on social communication that happens online.

Dialogic Approaches in Strategic Communication

The field of strategic communication has emphasized a dialogic approach toward understanding attitude formation. This approach considers how organizations or institutions and members of various publics work together to develop, discuss, and engage with various social and public issues. Thus, the dialogic framework focuses on how publics create meaning and make sense of issues in mediated communication contexts (Botan & Taylor, 2004). Older models of communication examine the flow of communication as uni-directional from message producer (who creates the meaning) to the audience (who interprets the meaning). Dialogic models, on the other hand, emphasize a relational approach, where individuals and organizations engage in dialogue with each other, or interaction. Dialogic models also take into account how audience members' cognitive processes, existing attitudes, and the values they hold impact the meaning of the messages. In other words, it is not simply a matter of the sender creating the meaning, which is then received by the audience member, but also audience predispositions that impact what meaning individuals derive from a message. Here, I discuss how different forms of online discussions and activities fit into dialogic approaches of communication within the context of science communication.

In the field of science communication, scholars have focused on dialogic models of communication that consider how citizens, scientists, funders, journalists, and policymakers contribute to public understanding of science. In practice, this is portrayed in several ways. For instance, communication practitioners might take into account attitudes of members of specific publics when targeting an informational campaign. Or, lay audiences might be invited to a public forum with scientists or other experts on an emerging scientific topic. While the predominant models of science communication are specific to the topical areas of scientific issues, they often reflect similar frameworks in communication scholarship more broadly (Trench, 2012). Therefore, the science issue context is appropriate for examining trends in strategic communication more broadly.

In this chapter, I first describe a move from a one-way transmission model toward an interactive perspective within science communication scholarship that is reflective of a similar trend toward dialogue in strategic communication scholarship. Science communication has been concerned with shifting away from top-down communication models toward perspectives that involve information exchanges of multiple parties (e.g., the public forum that engages lay audiences and scientists in discussions about policy surrounding scientific research and development). Dialogic approaches of communication in the science context fall within different models, including the public participation and contextual models of science communication (Lewenstein, 2003). These frameworks were developed in response to the deficit model, which assumes a one-way top-down approach to science communication. In short, the deficit model is based on the idea that public appreciation and support for science can be bolstered via the transmission of accurate scientific information and consequent 'improvement' of laypersons' science literacy (for a review, see Bauer, Allum, & Miller, 2007). Yet, little empirical evidence exists for this model (Miller, 2001). Instead, scholars have turned to other models such as the contextual or public participation models to understand how individuals form opinions about science.

The contextual model of science communication recognizes that individuals approach messages they encounter in media with an existing set of cognitive schema, value predispositions, and cultural perspectives (e.g., Brossard, Scheufele, Kim, & Lewenstein, 2009; Scheufele & Lewenstein, 2005; Sturgis & Allum, 2004). These prior frameworks are employed when an individual selects, processes, interprets, and acts upon a media message. Researchers have used this to understand how different publics interpret a variety of science issues. For instance, people may know little about an issue like nanotechnology, so they rely upon their religiosity or their attitudes about other science topics when forming judgments about it (e.g., Brossard et al., 2009). Or, people rely on their political affiliations when they encounter messages about climate change (e.g., Dunlap & McCright, 2008). As a result, communication practitioners may take these audience predispositions into account when crafting media messages in order to reach different audiences. The contextual model goes beyond the deficit model by not assuming members of the public will automatically "learn" media messages broadly via transmission. Instead, it recognizes that different audiences have different ways they will interpret and act upon a message. Thus, based on the contextual model, we know that one attribute of dialogic communication is the activation of predispositions when people interpret media messages.

Moving beyond the contextual model, the public participation model of science communication aims to integrate citizens into active debate and the policymaking process itself (see Rowe & Frewer, 2000). Examples of communication within the public participation framework are consensus conferences and science cafes. In these forms of interpersonal communication, members of lay publics engage in discussions with other citizens, with scientific experts, or with policymakers under the goal of either informing public judgments about science or policy about science (e.g., Einsiedel & Eastlick, 2000). Citizen panels is a broad moniker for deliberations among citizens that are informed by expert knowledge (Brown, 2006). For instance, in consensus conferences, members of the public discuss scientific issues with experts and with each other to write policy recommendations about the scientific issue under debate (Joss & Durant, 1995). Science cafes are organized in a public space, such as a coffeehouse or a pub, and feature informal conversations between scientists and members of the public about a particular scientific topic (Powell & Colin, 2009). In these forms of communication, lay publics have direct interaction and dialogue with experts, and vice versa. Thus, based on models of public participation, we know that another attribute of dialogic models is interaction.

These two attributes identified here—audience predispositions and interaction—are the dialogic model attributes I will focus on in this chapter as I discuss how different online communication activities fit the dialogic framework.

Where Online Activities Fit in Dialogic Models

There are different types of online activities that reflect different forms of communication. One space for interaction are formal deliberations in which people engage in discussions with other individuals, policymakers, and experts, often with the goal of informing policy or producing more informed opinion (Joss & Durant, 1995). Starting in the 1990s, there was a surge of these types of formal deliberation mechanisms (e.g., Luskin, Fishkin, & Jowell, 2002). Deliberation scholars and practitioners also began to focus on the Internet as a space for realizing deliberative outcomes (e.g., Froomkin, 2004). This scholarship focuses on both formal deliberation, where people engage in synchronous real-time discussion in chatrooms, as well as informal spaces of deliberation, such as wikis or collaborative tools that allow for asynchronous spaces of dialogue that also involve other forms of feedback and filtering. For instance, a feedback mechanism might be as simple as a number of individuals pushing certain comments to the top of commenting sections by evaluating it positively, or as complex as Wikipedia edits that remove non-relevant information on a subject area. In other words, communication on the Internet characterizes as participatory when various users—both proprietors of websites and traditional editors, as well as other everyday users—contribute to a loose order of intake, filtering, and synthesis that focuses attention on informational sources that would not obtain attention in more traditional media arenas, such as popular magazines or newspapers (Benkler, 2006). Although the majority of websites will not be linked to, a lesser-known site can be pulled into mainstream attention if a well-known website links to it (Benkler, 2006). This is considered to be an inclusive form of communication because it provides space for anyone to participate in public debates and not just a small number of professional media organizations or editors. A pioneering study by Barabasi and Albert (1999) demonstrated that how websites are hyperlinked to each other is representative of this structure. Their research revealed that the distribution of hyperlinks into and out of nodes, or websites, in the network of websites they studied follows a power law, which means that there is a very low probability any node (website) in the network is highly connected to many others (Barabasi & Albert, 1999). Alternatively, there is a large probability that a very large number of nodes are connected only loosely, or not at all (Barabasi & Albert, 1999). As a result, new nodes will preferentially attach to other already well-attached nodes (Barabasi & Albert, 1999). Subsequent research has identified power law distributions in not only websites (Broder, et al., 2000), but also within other online networks, such as the number of votes a story receives on Digg (Huberman, 2008), and the structure of replies among participants in Usenet newsgroups (Himelboim, 2008).

In summary, there are spaces within online communication that allow for both formal and informal deliberation. These discussions happen alongside information-seeking and consumption behaviors to round out common online activities. Next, I provide an example of how each type of online communication—formal and informal discussions and information-seeking behaviors—displays different characteristics of dialogic models of communication, and ultimately how they shape attitudes and behaviors.

Formal Discussions Online

A formal deliberation model is one where the discussions among participants are organized by a third party, such as a local governmental planning board, a news organization, or a university-based scholar, to occur at a set time in a specific place. Organizers of this type of public fora often combine in-person discussions with online communication. One common goal of conducting an online discussion is to engage larger, more heterogeneous, more geographically representative groups of individuals in the discussion process. In 2008, my colleagues and I facilitated the local site of a nationwide deliberation project about nanotechnology that involved both in-person discussions (i.e. face-to-face discussions), as well as online discussions (Anderson, Delborne, & Kleinman, 2012a; Delborne, Anderson, Kleinman, Colin, & Powell, 2009; Kleinman, Delborne, & Anderson, 2011; Powell, Colin, Lee Kleinman, Delborne, & Anderson, 2011; Powell, Delborne, & Colin, 2011). The in-person discussions were held among small groups of individuals locally and bookended online discussions over the course of four weeks that involved all individuals from six sites from around the United States. One of our core research objectives was to examine how individuals use sources of mediated information alongside their involvement in formal interpersonal communication discussions that occur in deliberative settings. This question is particularly relevant considering the time individuals spend online with easy access to search engines while engaged in the online portion of the deliberation. People naturally gravitate toward their own information searches as their thoughts about the issue deepen while they participate in online discussion sessions.

We found that people had several motivations for seeking out their own information sources during the formal in-person and online discussions

(Anderson et al., 2012a). Forum participants used their information seeking to learn more, verify claims made by the forum experts, understand what aspects of the technology are currently available, and evaluate the potential personal impacts of the technology. Therefore, the outside information seeking helped them navigate and make an otherwise abstract issue like nanotechnology more concrete. As a result, the informal information seeking online that occurred alongside more formal deliberations played an important role in how forum participants created meaning around the discussions. The everyday information-seeking habits people bring with them are among existing predispositions that participants use to engage in the interaction and dialogue with others. Thus, the two aspects of dialogic models mentioned earlier—interaction and predispositions—are an important part of formal deliberation models of communication online.

Despite the potential for online communication to encourage more involvement in formal deliberations, we know that a small percentage of the population actually participates in such activities (Scheufele, 2011). Therefore, in this next section, I discuss a more common type of online discussion: the informal conversation.

Informal Discussions Online

Informal discussions about important social issues are the spontaneous interactions that occur among friends, family, or colleagues, and even strangers (Eveland, Morey, & Hutchens, 2011). In the online environment, these interactions are mediated and make up a range of activities from social media interactions among friends who normally engage in discussions in person, or offline, to reading a comment from an anonymous stranger.

One concern social scientists and communication practitioners have over user-generated comments is the tendency for people to be rude and uncivil when they write them (Coe, Kenski, & Rains, 2014; Meltzer, 2014). The impersonal nature of computer-mediated communication, alongside a lack of non-verbal cues, can lead to caustic communication exchanges in online media (Dutton, 1996; Papacharissi, 2002). When an individual writes a nasty comment in online spaces, they often do not experience the same consequences they would normally experience in more traditional face-to-face settings. Other characteristics of computer-mediated communication, such as the absence of authority and the tendency to imagine conversations in their minds rather than in-person, can lead to a disinhibition effect whereby individuals are more likely to be hostile (Suler, 2004). Indeed, early research of online discussions examining conversations in online media, such as Usenet newsgroups or online discussion forums to assess how people discuss politics online, often revealed the presence of incivility (Benson, 1996; Kayany, 1998; Papacharissi, 2004).

In one research project, my colleagues and I examined how exposure to uncivil comments in informal online discussions impacted attitudes (Anderson, Brossard, Scheufele, Xenos, & Ladwig, 2014). We conducted an experiment using a nationally representative sample of the American public and examined how they responded to uncivil comments in the context of an emerging technology issue, nanotechnology. Because nanotechnology is an emerging issue, people tend to rely on pre-existing values or their opinions about other scientific issues to form judgments about it (Scheufele & Lewenstein, 2005). Consistent with the contextual model of science communication, we know that people's interpretation about a variety of scientific issues can be based on their existing judgments and values. Therefore, in our study, we looked at how these existing values and opinions can interact with the messages they encounter in online user-generated content. Specifically, we looked at how their initial attitudes about nanotechnology and their religious involvement influenced their interpretation of the messages about nanotechnology when they were contained within uncivil comments. We found that by simply changing the tone about either the risks or the benefits of nanotechnology incivility polarized individuals' attitude formation about nanotechnology. For individuals with pre-existing unfavorable opinions about nanotechnology and for those who were highly religious, incivility made them perceive nanotechnology as being more risky. People who saw civil comments, on the other hand, were no more or less likely to perceive nanotechnology as risky regardless of their existing attitudes and values.

Thus, we concluded that the degree of (in)civility in online conversations can influence how individuals shape their perceptions of social issues within those communication spaces. Our evidence points to the negative nature of those attitudes. We dubbed the ability of uncivil comments to shape perceptions of news and news content the "nasty effect" (Anderson et al., 2014). In short, both the interactive nature of online comments, as well as the predispositions people rely on to interpret those messages, are important for how people shape attitudes in the context of informal conversations online.

Information Seeking

Traditional Media vs. Online Media

The advancement of publishing platforms provided by the Internet, such as blogs, online video sites, and social media sites, that are accessible by anyone with the most basic technical know-how has led to a proliferation of user-generated media. This shift is fundamentally altering which individuals and institutions can effectively filter information onto the public agenda. Gatekeeping is an inherent part of journalism; the process by which all available messages are filtered, selected, and covered in mass media (Shoemaker, 1997). Editors create the overall structure of the news based on a number of factors, including newsworthiness and available space, as well as factors beyond editorial control, including institutional structures and market pressures (Shoemaker, Eichholz, Kim, & Wrigley, 2001). Thus, editorial control by a select group of media professionals influences what issues reach the news agenda and, ultimately, audiences. Yet, gatekeepers are shifting in spaces of online media (Meraz, 2009; Mitchelstein & Boczkowski, 2009).

Initial perspectives regarding online media platforms expected the process of gatekeeping in online journalism to be quite similar to that of traditional journalism. Boczkowski (2004), for example, noted that online newspapers produce "shovelware," or content produced for the traditional print outlet merely shoveled onto the website in the same version (p. 55). However, more recent analyses of different types of user-generated online communication point to key divergences from traditional media sources relative to issue salience. Research on a range of user-generated media sites (e.g., blogs, crowdsourced informational sites, etc.) has demonstrated how online media can differ from more traditional forms of media in determining public issue agendas (Anderson, Brossard, & Scheufele, 2012; Meraz & Papacharissi, 2013).

Downs' (1972) issue-attention cycle is one common model for identifying how public attention to certain issues rises and falls. The model predicts that issues, and particularly scientific issues, gain traction in media coverage when they enter an overtly political realm, then decline in coverage when they transition to a more technical realm. One study by my colleagues and me, however, found evidence that blogs are not bound to the classic Downsian issue-attention cycle (Anderson et al., 2012b). Our study examined one story about nanoparticle-related deaths of Chinese factory workers that exemplified characteristics—specifically, novelty and controversy—that would typically increase its coverage in traditional print media. Yet, we found that the story was ten times more likely to be covered in online media sources (e.g., blog posts from sites such as 2020science.org or a blog on the Center for Disease Control's website) than it was in traditional print media sources (e.g., the *Guardian* or the *Belfast Telegraph*) (Anderson et al., 2012b). Furthermore, the volume of online media coverage endured longer than it did in print media (Anderson et al., 2012b). We concluded that complex issues like nanotechnology that tend to garner limited media coverage when they reside in the technical arena do not necessarily follow a similar issue attention cycle in user-generated online media, such as blogs. Indeed, other related research has provided evidence that blog coverage of an emerging technologies differs from its print counterpart, with blog coverage continuing to rise while print coverage declines (Cacciatore et al., 2012). Additionally, recent evidence suggests that online sources include more diverse discussions of themes related to nanotechnology than traditional print media coverage (Cacciatore et al., 2012). Overall, research points to important gatekeepers outside of traditional media and editors that are setting public agendas around scientific issues.

In sum, our research has helped to empirically demonstrate how online, non-traditional media are playing important roles filtering messages and information about technology in ways that differ from traditional media platforms. Alongside those shifting gatekeeping roles from traditional editors toward opinion leaders who tap into user-generated content platforms, such as bloggers, are changes in how individuals access and consume information, the topic to which I turn next.

Google

The Internet provides a range of ways to seek out and obtain information, with the predominant information-seeking platform being Google. For specific science issues in particular, more than 60% of people reported they would go online to find information (Science & Engineering Indicators, 2014). Early research on science information consumption provides evidence that search engines like Google are the primary source for 90% of people who do go online to find out more about a scientific issue (Horrigan, 2006). Online media use for scientific news and information is particularly prevalent among younger generations (Su, Akin, Brossard, Scheufele, & Xenos, 2015). Thus, understanding how platforms such as Google portray information provides important insights into the media environment for scientific issues. Yet, the way Google portrays information is bound within behavior patterns from information consumers, as well as Google's search algorithm. Here, I will highlight several studies that my colleagues and I undertook to examine the interplay of information-seeking habits in the platform of Google and the patterns of content areas in top sources featured in Google.

In one study, my colleagues and I examined how the top websites returned in Google search results portrayed nanotechnology (Anderson, Brossard, & Scheufele, 2010). We found that certain topics, such as health and business issues, were the most predominant in the search results. However, when we looked at different types of websites featured in the top Google search results—government websites and nano-specific and non-nano-specific blogs and websites—we found important differences. For instance, while health and environmental dimensions of nanotechnology were highly covered on websites not specific to nanotechnology, websites focused primarily on nanotechnology were more focused on business dimensions. Blogs dedicated to nanotechnology topics were more likely to focus on environmental or national security issues, while the non-nanotechnology-specific blogs were more likely to focus on health issues. We also examined the top keyword searches related to nanotechnology, and found them to be nanobots, health, definitions, applications, and future. These analyses unearthed evidence suggesting a degree of consonance between the most common content themes in websites and individuals' most common information searches.

Our research also points to a symbiotic relationship between what individuals search for and what search engines display in shaping the information people encounter online. For instance, when we compared top keyword searches in Google and the top categories of content within common searches for nanotechnology, we found evidence that Google predominantly displays one theme surrounding the issue: health (Ladwig, Anderson, Brossard, Scheufele, & Shaw, 2010). Over time, people's most common keyword searches started to align with the most commonly featured Google content. We took this to suggest a reinforcing spiral of information among keyword searches, content, and suggestions, with Google largely determining the most salient issues. This outcome highlights the diversity and complexity of information people encounter is limited when using Google as a portal for information.

In a follow-up study, we found that content about nanotechnology portrayed in the web pages of the top ten results of Google (i.e., the first page of search results) was substantively different from the content within web pages found in search results listed later (i.e., those listed after the first page) (Li, Anderson, Brossard, & Scheufele, 2014). For instance, the top content focused on environmental themes related to nanotechnology, while content in later search results focused more on health themes before transitioning to environmental themes. We concluded that the difference in themes portrayed most prominently in early search results from later search results is empirical evidence of concerns about Google's power over the information people encounter in online spaces. Research suggests that people rely heavily on the first page of Google search results in their online information seeking (Eysenbach & Köhler, 2002). If those pages are different from other pages, this speaks to the potential for Google to limit what information-seekers see. Ultimately, these studies demonstrate how individuals' information-seeking habits via search engines—particularly Google—have the potential to shape how individuals perceive and engage with social issues.

In summary, I have examined how different online communication activities, including formal deliberations, informal conversations, and information-seeking habits, engender different aspects of dialogic frameworks of communication. I emphasized that people who engage in online formal deliberative settings use their predispositional information-seeking habits to engage in interactions with other forum participants. In addition, people who encounter interactive messages online that are created in a more informal discursive setting—such as newspaper comments—rely on their predispositions to interpret and respond to those comments. Finally, in their online information-seeking habits, individuals have (1) access to dialogic content through the advent of user-generated content (e.g., blogs) and (2) information searches that are shaped (i.e., constrained) by algorithmic search engines like Google. In other words, information consumers shape the current and future content they receive when their past information behaviors—a type of predisposition—interact with the algorithms they encounter in search engines and social media sites, among other online communication sources. Thus, each type of online communication activity at least partially uses or relies upon the two aspects of dialogic communication—audience predispositions and interactions—discussed here. Yet, how they engage each aspect and the depth of each aspect varies.

Future Directions for Strategic Communication Research

The goal of this chapter was to evaluate how different forms of online discussion and activities fit into a dialogic framework of strategic communication. Future research in the field of strategic communication should continue to focus on how different activities in networked information environments (e.g., engaging in conversations among different publics in social media sites or online commenting spaces) do or do not engender aspects of dialogic frameworks for communication.

Our modern, online information ecosystem is growing ever more social in its architecture and functionality. News organizations increasingly embed social cues in their online platforms, such as most viewed or most emailed articles or comment sections. Companies now interact directly with customers through social media platforms, like Twitter and Facebook. And people share content with their networks almost effortlessly via these same social media sites. Indeed, more than three in ten Internet users in the United States report they have posted comments to an online news group, website, blog or photo site, and 65% of online Americans report using an online social networking site, such as Facebook (Purcell, Rainie, Mitchell, Rosenstiel, & Olmstead, 2010). Nearly 20% of adults have participated in online discussions in the form of posting a comment on a news story or blog post about a political or social issue (Smith, 2013). In addition, people are exposed to news items during online activities, such as Facebook consumption, even when they were not intending to consume news (Pew Research Center, 2013a).

Untangling behaviors such as information seeking or news consumption—both incidental and purposeful—from algorithmic influences is challenging. The news and information environment is rife with social cues and is also highly personalized. Broad patterns and trends among prominent information sources, such as Facebook or Google, are observable but are also somewhat more elusive, depending upon how much information these major information platforms provide about their choices to portray certain types of content over other types. For instance, we have general information about how Google arrives at the content it displays, but understanding or predicting what it will specifically display is not possible without details about its algorithms. Furthermore, understanding these broad patterns within the context of information platforms that constantly tailor to the individual consumer is a challenge to being able to generalize research findings to other settings. Nonetheless, information-use habits can be observed through access to behavior data, as well as self-reported data. Below, I comment on three different areas of scholarship related to information-use habits particularly relevant to the social context of online media.

Opinion Leadership

The concept of opinion leadership is more than a half-century old and is based in the two-step flow of communication, recognizing that specific individuals are central nodes in their social networks, acting as key information sources for the remainder of individuals within the network who are more peripheral (Katz, 1957; Watts & Dodd, 2007). An opinion leader, in short, is traditionally thought of as a person who uses some form of interpersonal communication to engage others with information about issues.

Opinion leaders also exist in the online media environment. A lesser-known blog, for example, will receive more attention once a well-known media source, such as the Huffington Post, links to the blog from its more prominent (i.e., central) Internet location. People who are not major media entities, however, also lead opinion in social media platforms. Research shows that individuals who post on spaces such as Twitter are not representative of Internet users more broadly (Pew Research Center, 2013b), which indicates they may turn to the social media platform to spread innovative ideas. Furthermore, research provides evidence that Facebook use does contribute to the feeling that one is an opinion leader (Vraga, Anderson, Kotcher, Maibach, & Leiserowitz, 2015). Future research should make connections between opinion leaders such as these and the types of content they are sharing to understand how social cues in the online environment are shaping attitudes and behaviors among broader populations.

Trust and Credibility

Exploring how individuals perceive trust and credibility in the online environment is an important factor in understanding information use patterns online (e.g., Metzger, 2007; Thorson, Vraga, & Ekdale, 2010; Westerman, Spence, & Van Der Heide, 2014). Online media that include social discussions among media consumers, such as comments in news stories, provide a new context for news audiences to construct meaning about scientific issues. Thus, understanding the impact of those social conversations on notions of expertise (lay and technical) and trust for information about science will be crucial for understanding how the changing nature of individuals' information environments are shaping information habits and perceptions of scientific issues.

Selective Exposure

Several scholars have expressed concern over the polarizing and isolating nature of Internet communication on society. One of the main concerns within this perspective is that Internet communication provides individuals more opportunities to selectively expose themselves to information that matches their existing attitudes and perspectives on issues (Bennett & Iyengar, 2008; Sunstein, 2007; Tewksbury, 2005). Individuals already pay closer attention to and engage more with information within their existing perspectives (Hart et al., 2009; Lazarsfeld, Berelson, & Gaudet, 1944), and the Internet gives individuals more control to avoid viewpoints that do not match their own by choosing like-minded sources and following like-minded others within social networking sites. In so doing, individuals are less frequently exposed to the range of perspectives that many consider requisite for civic participation in a democratic society (Bennett & Iyengar, 2008). Yet, empirical evidence for this is mixed, with evidence also pointing toward the use of sources that are discrepant from one's existing attitudes (Garrett, Carnahan, & Lynch, 2013).

Investigating how individuals respond to like-minded individuals in social media platforms and how they select information that aligns with their existing perspectives is important for future strategic communication research. What other factors, such as issue involvement, play a role in information selection? For instance, does depth of previous thoughts about an issue override a tendency toward selecting information already congruent with one's views? Does the effect of one's issue involvement differ based on whether the congruent view comes from a known acquaintance (e.g., a social media friend)? Understanding how these different predispositions play a role in information selection in various information platforms is an important part of understanding how individuals' information habits interact with social contexts in online communication.

Conclusion

In this chapter, I set out to review how different online forms of communication contain two key attributes of dialogic models of strategic communication. Using the setting of science communication in particular, I explored to what extent formal discussions, commenting sections, and information seeking that happens online engender two key components of dialogic models: audience predispositions and interactions.

In a review of work conducted by myself and colleagues, as well as other researchers, I show that there are differing levels of these two components in each type of online activity. Some online communication spaces (e.g., formal deliberations) produce obvious opportunities for interaction between scientists and lay audiences. Reddit's "Ask Me Anything" series featuring scientists is an example of high interaction, in which people can easily access and discuss issues with experts. There are other communication spaces (e.g., Google) in which the interactions are more opaque. In a search engine, the interactions that contribute to what information people obtain and use are the result of aggregate search habits informing what sources of information are ranked higher in search results. In addition, how audience predispositions matter for meaning-making in online communication varies. For instance, predispositions that matter for how one interprets a message can exaggerate individuals' judgments about a topic when they encounter the uncivil user comments common in online discussions. Predispositions are a part of formal discussions, as they determine how individuals enter the discussion. Yet, the component of dialogic models most prevalent in a formal discussion is the interaction. In the example of reddit AMAs introduced earlier, predispositions matter for how individuals introduce their questions, as well as for how they interpret others' comments.

With the rising importance of social communication settings online, the information environment is changing how individuals are encountering media messages. Understanding how individuals respond to all types of user-generated content is key to understanding how they shape their attitudes and act upon messages in the online communication environment.

References

Anderson, A. A., Brossard, D., & Scheufele, D. A. (2010). The changing information environment for nanotechnology: Online audiences and content. *Journal of Nanoparticle Research*, *12*(4), 1083–1094. doi: 10.1007/s11051-010-9860-2

Anderson, A. A., Brossard, D., & Scheufele, D. A. (2012b). News coverage of controversial emerging technologies. *Politics and the Life Sciences*, *31*(1–2), 87–96. doi:10.2990/31_1-2_87

Anderson, A. A., Brossard, D., Scheufele, D. A., Xenos, M. A., & Ladwig, P. (2014). The "Nasty Effect": Online incivility and risk perceptions of emerging technologies: Crude comments and concern. *Journal of Computer-Mediated Communication*, *19*(3), 373–387. http://doi.org/10.1111/jcc4.12009

Anderson, A. A., Delborne, J., & Kleinman, D. L. (2012a). Information beyond the forum: Motivations, strategies, and impacts of citizen participants seeking information during a consensus conference. *Public Understanding of Science*. doi: 10.1177/0963662512447173

Barabasi, A. L., & Albert, R. (1999). Emergence of scaling in random networks. *Science*, *286*(5439), 509–512. doi: 10.1126/science.286.5439.509

Bauer, M. W., Allum, N., & Miller, S. (2007). What can we learn from 25 years of PUS survey research? Liberating and expanding the agenda. *Public Understanding of Science*, *16*(1), 79–95. doi: 10.1177/0963662506071287

Benkler, Y. (2006). *Wealth of networks: How social production transforms markets and freedom.* New Haven, CT: Yale University Press.

Benson, T. W. (1996). Rhetoric, civility, and community: Political debate on computer bulletin boards. *Communication Quarterly*, *44*(3), 359–378. doi: 10.1080/01463379609370023

Bennett, W. L., & Iyengar, S. (2008). A new era of minimal effects? The changing foundations of political communication. *Journal of Communication*, *58*(4), 707–731. doi: 10.1111/j.1460-2466.2008.00410.x

Boczkowski, P. (2004). *Digitizing the news: Innovation in online newspapers.* Cambridge, MA: The MIT Press.

Botan, C. H., & Taylor, M. (2004). Public relations: State of the field. *Journal of Communication*, *54*(4), 645–661. doi: 10.1111/j.1460-2466.2004.tb02649.x

Broder, A., Kumar, R., Maghoul, F., Raghavan, P., Rajagopalan, S., Stata, R., et al. (2000). Graph structure in the web. *Computer Networks, 33*, 309–320. doi: 10.1016/S1389-1286(00)00083-9

Brossard, D., Scheufele, D. A., Kim, E., & Lewenstein, B. V. (2009). Religiosity as a perceptual filter: Examining processes of opinion formation about nanotechnology. *Public Understanding of Science, 18*(5), 546–558. doi: 10.1177/0963662507087304

Brown, M. B. (2006). Survey article: Citizen panels and the concept of representation*. *Journal of Political Philosophy, 14*(2), 203–225. doi: 10.1111/j.1467-9760.2006.00245.x

Cacciatore, M. A., Anderson, A. A., Choi, D.-H., Brossard, D., Scheufele, D. A., Liang, X., ... Dudo, A. (2012). Coverage of emerging technologies: A comparison between print and online media. *New Media & Society, 14*(6), 1039–1059. doi: 10.1177/1461444812439061

Coe, K., Kenski, K., & Rains, S. A. (2014). Online and uncivil? Patterns and determinants of incivility in newspaper website comments. *Journal of Communication*. doi: 10.1111/jcom.12104

Costello, V. (2015). Ask our authors anything: New PLOS "AMA" series debuts on redditscience. Retrieved from http://blogs.plos.org/plos/2015/04/plos/

Delborne, J. A., Anderson, A. A., Kleinman, D. L., Colin, M., & Powell, M. (2009). Virtual deliberation? Prospects and challenges for integrating the Internet in consensus conferences. *Public Understanding of Science, 20*(3), 367–384. doi: 10.1177/0963662509347138

Downs, A. (1972). Up and down with ecology—the "issue-attention cycle." *Public Interest, 28*, 38–50.

Dunlap, R. E., & McCright, A. M. (2008). A widening gap: Republican and Democratic views on climate change. *Environment: Science and Policy for Sustainable Development, 50*(5), 26–35. doi: 10.3200/ENVT.50.5.26-35

Dutton, W. H. (1996). Network rules of order: Regulating speech in public electronic fora. *Media Culture & Society, 18*(2), 269–290. doi: 10.1177/016344396018002006

Einsiedel, E. F., & Eastlick, D. L. (2000). Consensus conferences as deliberative democracy: A communications perspective. *Science Communication, 21*(4), 323–343. doi: 10.1177/1075547000021004001

Eveland, W. P., Morey, A. C., & Hutchens, M. J. (2011). Beyond deliberation: New directions for the study of informal political conversation from a communication perspective. *Journal of Communication, 61*(6), 1082–1103. doi: 10.1111/j.1460-2466.2011.01598.x

Eysenbach, G., & Köhler, C. (2002). How do consumers search for and appraise health information on the world wide web? Qualitative study using focus groups, usability tests, and in-depth interviews. *BMJ, 324*(7337), 573–577. doi: 10.1136/bmj.324.7337.573

Froomkin, A. M. (2004). Technologies for democracy. *Democracy Online: The Prospects for Political Renewal through the Internet, 3*, 12–15.

Garrett, R. K., Carnahan, D., & Lynch, E. K. (2013). A turn toward avoidance? Selective exposure to online political information, 2004–2008. *Political Behavior, 35*(1), 113–134. http://doi.org/10.1007/s11109-011-9185-6

Hart, W., Albarracín, D., Eagly, A. H., Brechan, I., Lindberg, M. J., & Merrill, L. (2009). Feeling validated versus being correct: A meta-analysis of selective exposure to information. *Psychological Bulletin, 135*(4), 555–588. doi: 10.1037/a0015701

Himelboim, I. (2008). Reply distribution in online discussions: A comparative network analysis of political and health newsgroups. *Journal of Computer-Mediated Communication, 14*(1), 156–177.

Horrigan, J. (2006). *The internet as a resource for news and information about science*. Retrieved from http://www.pewinternet.org/Reports/2006/The-Internet-as-a-Resource-for-News-and-Information-about-Science.aspx

Huberman, B. A. (2008). Crowdsourcing and attention. *Computer, 41*(11), 103–105. doi: 10.1109/MC.2008.450

Joss, S., & Durant, J. (Eds.) (1995). *Public participation in science: The role of consensus conferences in Europe*. London: Science Museum.

Katz, E. (1957). The two-step flow of communication: An up-to-date report on an hypothesis. *Public Opinion Quarterly, 21*, 61–78. doi: 10.1086/266687

Kayany, J. M. (1998). Contexts of uninhibited online behavior: Flaming in social newsgroups on Usenet. *Journal of the American Society for Information Science, 49*(12), 1135–1141.

Kleinman, D. L., Delborne, J. A., & Anderson, A. A. (2011). Engaging citizens: The high cost of citizen participation in high technology. *Public Understanding of Science, 20*(2), 221–240. doi: 10.1177/0963662509347137

Ladwig, P., Anderson, A. A., Brossard, D., Scheufele, D. A., & Shaw, B. (2010). Narrowing the nano discourse? *Materials Today, 13*(5), 52–54. doi: 10.1016/S1369-7021(10)70084-5

Lazarsfeld, P. F., Berelson, B., & Gaudet, H. (1944). *The people's choice: How the voter makes up his mind in a presidential campaign* (3rd ed.). New York: Columbia University Press.

Lewenstein, B. V. (2003). Models of public communication of science and technology. *Public Understanding of Science, 16*, 1–11.

Li, N., Anderson, A. A., Brossard, D., & Scheufele, D. A. (2014). Channeling science information seekers' attention? A content analysis of top-ranked vs. lower-ranked sites in Google. *Journal of Computer-Mediated Communication, 19*(3), 562–575. http://doi.org/10.1111/jcc4.12043

Luskin, R. C., Fishkin, J. S., & Jowell, R. (2002). Considered opinions: Deliberative polling in Britain. *British Journal of Political Science, 32*(3), 455–487. doi: 10.1017/S0007123402000194

Meltzer, K. (2014). Journalistic concern about uncivil political talk in digital news media: Responsibility, credibility, and academic influence. *The International Journal of Press/Politics*. doi: 10.1177/1940161214558748

Meraz, S. (2009). Is there an elite hold? Traditional media to social media agenda setting influence in blog networks. *Journal of Computer-Mediated Communication, 14*(3), 682–707. http://doi.org/10.1111/j.1083-6101.2009.01458.x

Meraz, S., & Papacharissi, Z. (2013). Networked gatekeeping and networked framing on #Egypt. *The International Journal of Press/Politics, 18*(2), 138–166. doi: 10.1177/1940161212474472

Metzger, M. J. (2007). Making sense of credibility on the Web: Models for evaluating online information and recommendations for future research. *Journal of the American Society for Information Science and Technology, 58*(13), 2078–2091. doi: 10.1002/asi.20672

Miller, S. (2001). Public understanding of science at the crossroads. *Public Understanding of Science, 10*(1), 115–120. doi: 10.1088/0963-6625/10/1/308

Mitchelstein, E., & Boczkowski, P. J. (2009). Between tradition and change: A review of recent research on online news production. *Journalism, 10*(5), 562–586. http://doi.org/10.1177/1464884909106533

Papacharissi, Z. (2002). The virtual sphere: The internet as a public sphere. *New Media & Society, 4*(1), 9–27. doi: 10.1177/14614440222226244

Papacharissi, Z. (2004). Democracy online: Civility, politeness, and the democratic potential of online political discussion groups. *New Media & Society*, *6*(2), 259–283. doi: 10.1177/1461444804041444

Pew Research Center (2013a). The role of news on Facebook: Common yet incidental. Retrieved from http://www.journalism.org/files/2013/10/facebook_news_10-24-2013.pdf

Pew Research Center (2013b). Twitter reaction to events often at odds with overall public opinion. Retrieved from http://www.pewresearch.org/2013/03/04/twitter-reaction-to-events-often-at-odds-with-overall-public-opinion/

Powell, M. C., & Colin, M. (2009). Participatory paradoxes: Facilitating citizen engagement in science and technology from the top-down? *Bulletin of Science, Technology & Society*, *29*(4), 325–342. doi: 10.1177/0270467609336308

Powell, M., Colin, M., Lee Kleinman, D., Delborne, J., & Anderson, A. (2011). Imagining ordinary citizens? Conceptualized and actual participants for deliberations on emerging technologies. *Science as Culture*, *20*(1), 37–70. doi: 10.1080/09505430903567741

Powell, M., Delborne, J., & Colin, M. (2011). Beyond engagement exercises: Exploring the US National Citizens' Technology Forum from the bottom-up. *Journal of Public Deliberation*, *7*(1), 4.

Purcell, K., Rainie, L., Mitchell, A., Rosenstiel, T., & Olmstead, K. (2010). Understanding the participatory news consumer. *Pew Internet and American Life Project*, *1*. Retrieved from http://www.pewinternet.org/~/media/Files/Reports/2010/Understanding%20the%20Participatory%20News%20Consumer.pdf

Rowe, G., & Frewer, L. J. (2000). Public participation methods: A framework for evaluation. *Science, Technology & Human Values*, *25*(1), 3–29. doi: 10.1177/016224390002500101

Scheufele, D. A. (2011). Modern citizenship or policy dead end? Evaluating the need for public participation in science policy making, and why public meetings may not be the answer. Joan Shorenstein Center on the Press Politics and Public Policy Discussion Paper Series. Retrieved from http://shorensteincenter.org/wp-content/uploads/2012/03/r34_scheufele.pdf

Scheufele, D. A., & Lewenstein, B. V. (2005). The public and nanotechnology: How citizens make sense of emerging technologies. *Journal of Nanoparticle Research*, *7*(6), 659–667. doi: 10.1007/s11051-005-7526-2

Science & Engineering Indicators. (2014). Science and technology: Public attitudes and understanding. Retrieved from http://www.nsf.gov/statistics/seind14/index.cfm/overview

Shoemaker, P. J. (1997). A new gatekeeping model. In D. Berkowitz (Ed.), *Social meanings of news: A text-reader* (pp. 57–71). Thousand Oaks, CA: Sage Publications.

Shoemaker, P. J., Eichholz, M., Kim, E., & Wrigley, B. (2001). Individual and routine forces in gatekeeping. *Journalism & Mass Communication Quarterly*, *78*(2), 233–246. doi: 10.1177/107769900107800202

Smith, A. (2013). Civic engagement in the digital age. *Pew Internet & American Life Project*. Retrieved from http://www.mobilemarketer.rcrwireless.pewinternet.com/~/media/Files/Reports/2013/PIP_CivicEngagementintheDigitalAge.pdf

Sturgis, P., & Allum, N. (2004). Science in society: Re-evaluating the deficit model of public attitudes. *Public Understanding of Science*, *13*(1), 55–74. http://doi.org/10.1177/0963662504042690

Su, L. Y.-F., Akin, H., Brossard, D., Scheufele, D. A., & Xenos, M. A. (2015). Science news consumption patterns and their implications for public understanding of science. *Journalism & Mass Communication Quarterly*. doi: 10.1177/1077699015586415

Suler, J. (2004). The online disinhibition effect. *Cyberpsychology & Behavior*, 7(3), 321–326. doi: 10.1089/1094931041291295

Sunstein, C. (2007). *Republic.com 2.0*. Princeton, NJ: Princeton University Press.

Tewksbury, D. (2005). The seeds of audience fragmentation: Specialization in the use of online news sites. *Journal of Broadcasting & Electronic Media*, 49(3), 332–348. doi:10.1207/s15506878jobem4903_5

Thorson, K., Vraga, E., & Ekdale, B. (2010). Credibility in context: How uncivil online commentary affects news credibility. *Mass Communication and Society*, 13(3). doi: 10.1080/15205430903225571

Trench, B. (2012). Vital and vulnerable: Science communication as a university subject. In B. Schiele, M. Claessens, & S. Shi (Eds.), *Science communication in the world—Practices, theories and trends* (pp. 241–257). Dordrecht: Springer.

Vraga, E. K., Anderson, A. A., Kotcher, J. E., & Maibach, E. W. (2015). Issue-specific engagement: How Facebook contributes to opinion leadership and efficacy on energy and climate issues. *Journal of Information Technology & Politics*, 12(2), 200–218. doi: 10.1080/19331681.2015.1034910

Watts, D. J., & Dodd, P. S. (2007). Influentials, networks, and public opinion formation. *Journal of Consumer Research*, 34(40), 441–458. doi: 10.1086/518527

Westerman, D., Spence, P. R., & Van Der Heide, B. (2014). Social media as information source: Recency of updates and credibility of information. *Journal of Computer-Mediated Communication*, 19(2), 171–183. doi: 10.1111/jcc4.12041

5
HOW WE TALK AND WHY IT MATTERS

Myiah Hutchens

Close your eyes and picture your last political discussion. Are you in front a computer screen or are you with a person or a group? Are you engaging in a heated debate or venting to a sympathetic ear about the latest decision to come out of Washington? Is it a challenge for you to remember when was the last time you had a discussion like this, or is this a regular occurrence for you? Did you leave the discussion with a new piece of information, or a changed point of view, or did it reinforce the beliefs you already had? All of these questions represent various conditions that political discussion scholars seek to better understand. From a strategic communication perspective, understanding how individuals are communicating, and the effects of that communication, can serve to enable practitioners to better understand their publics, and how to create more effective spaces for engagement between stakeholders.

The role of discussion in U.S. politics has been prominent in the political realm harkening back to the days of the coffee houses of Colonial America (Marcus, 1988), and discussion has been an important area of research for communication scholars. For instance, the two-step flow of communication posited that the influence of mass media reached the public through interpersonal communication with opinion leaders in the community (Katz & Lazarfeld, 1955). Although interest in interpersonal political communication has waxed and waned among communication scholars, the study of political discussion is an important area of research to understand the influence of communication on public opinion. Scholars have spent significant time studying political discussion because of the important role it plays in the democratic process. Discussing politics is generally seen to be essential to an ideally functioning citizenry. Talking about politics is associated with a variety of beneficial outcomes. The most common outcomes examined by communication scholars include increased levels of political knowledge (Eveland, 2004; Holbert, Benoit, Hansen, & Wen, 2002) and political engagement (Knoke, 1990; Verba, Scholzman, & Brady, 1995). Engaging in political conversations allows us to gain new information, and can lead to cognitive processes that encourage deeper elaboration about important issues facing society. Discussing politics also creates opportunities for individuals to learn about potential engagement opportunities that they may have not heard about otherwise.

While much is known about the benefits of discussion, we by no means have a complete picture of how discussion functions in a democracy. However, recent studies have made important contributions to the political discussion literature. First, scholars have begun to understand the underlying cognitive processes that occur during group deliberations, and the effects of deliberative events on attitudes about public policy (Hutchens, PytlikZillig, et al., 2014; PytlikZillig et al., 2013). Given that the foundation for most research on political discussion relies on the framework of deliberative democracy, better understanding what it is about deliberation that produces beneficial will be crucial for better understanding how everyday discussions can be useful. This line of research has revealed the importance of cognitive engagement during deliberation activities for producing greater enjoyment, knowledge, and satisfaction with the resulting policy suggestions (Hutchens et al., 2014; PytlikZillig et al., 2013).

The second area I will examine focuses on everyday discussion in online contexts, in particular aggressive discussion. Scholars have become interested in examining the use of aggressive communication tactics when discussing politics online (Papacharissi, 2004). Scholars have used the term political flaming to describe situations in which people use aggressive communication tactics when discussing politics in chat rooms, discussion boards, or in the comments sections of a news story. Scholars have made recent strides in documenting how frequently people use aggressive tactics (Coe, Kenski, & Rains, 2014) and figuring out the characteristics and conditions that lead people to use hostile communication tactics in online settings, otherwise known as political flaming (Hmielowski, Hutchens, & Cicchirillo, 2014; Hutchens, Cicchirillo, & Hmielowski, 2015). These studies also look at the impact that flaming has on important democratic outcome variables.

Finally, scholars have made strides in addressing the methodological issues associated with measuring exposure to disagreement in everyday discussion by teasing apart the various characteristics of discussion networks. The importance of disentangling discussion means that scholars can now make important distinctions between different types of discussion. Specifically, scholars have explained that it is important to understand the differences between frequency, dangerous (i.e., hearing opinion challenging views), safe (i.e., hearing opinion supportive information), and assessing the diversity of opinions in a person's social network (Eveland & Hively, 2009). Additionally, further breaking down the components of one commonly used measure of dangerous discussion is critical for understanding why conflicting findings have emerged (Hutchens, Eveland, & Morey, 2014).

In this chapter, I will provide a more in depth review of these three recent contributions to the discussion literature. I will do this by providing a general overview of the important empirical questions that drive this work and provide an overview of the findings from these recent studies. In addition, I will outline potential next steps for communication scholars to examine relative to these important issues and how strategic communication scholars can put his information to work.

Deliberation

That vast majority of our political discourse occurs in everyday, casual conversations (Mansbridge, 1999). However, while most individuals are much more likely to engage in these informal discussions, much of the groundwork for the research on everyday discussion comes from the deliberation literature. Participating in deliberative events is consistently seen as benefiting communities and those who participate in them. Exploring how individuals' process diverse views in deliberative settings is important for scholars to understand how deliberative processes have beneficial outcomes. Additionally, as more communities look to obtain citizen input in local issues, understanding people's experience in these formal deliberative events is also important in order to create the best deliberative experience possible, and a variety of companies have been created to facilitate these goals. America Speaks was an organization whose purpose was to facilitate citizen discussions, and functioned in multiple communities for nearly two decades. The Oregon Citizens' Initiative Review has a similar goal, in that they bring in community members to discuss various initiative and referendum measures prior to elections, which has been shown to have multiple positive effects (Knobloch, Gastil, Richards, & Feller, 2013). Employing the tactics of successful deliberations is a tool that could greatly help strategic communication scholars. Deliberations could be useful when trying to better understand organizations' primary stakeholders, or to help resolve conflicts that may exist between various stakeholder groups.

Deliberation is conceptualized as a tool which informs a public through discussion of all sides of an issue with the goal of reaching a decision (Gastil & Dillard, 1999; Goodin & Niemeyer, 2003; Mansbridge, 1999; Sanders, 1997). While some do not require that a decision be made in their conceptual definition of deliberation, the need to engage in thoughtful consideration of alternatives is consistently invoked (Delli Carpini, Cook, & Jacobs, 2004; Dutwin, 2003). Deliberations are generally structured events, which, according to theorists, is necessary in order to ensure three key aspects for successful deliberations can be present; non-tyranny, that the event be held in public, and participants are viewed as having equal status and participate equally

(Dutwin, 2003; Gastil & Dillard, 1999; Goodin & Niemeyer, 2003; Sanders, 1997). These characteristics are necessary to ensure that all points of view are heard, which theoretically leads to the best decision being made based on all available information. This sharing of multiple perspectives is considered crucial to an effective deliberation. It is the sharing of views, and their resulting positive findings, that serve as the backbone for the theoretical justifications when examining exposure to disagreement in more informal settings.

Research has suggested that engaging in a deliberation has positive outcomes. For decades, public participation in deliberations has been promoted by the National Research Council due to these beneficial effects (Delli Carpini et al., 2004; Gastil, 2008; Ryfe, 2005). Researchers find that individuals who participate in deliberations have an enhanced belief in the benefit of democratic values (Chambers, 2003; Fishkin, 1997; Gastil, 2000), more trust in government (Price & Cappella, 2002), and increased sophistication in their political and social reasoning (Gastil & Dillard, 1999; Muhlberger, 2006). Participating in engagement activities has been found to be enjoyable and educational for members of the public (Powell & Kleinman, 2008) and to stimulate further discussions with friends and family beyond the formalized engagement setting (Besley, Kramer, Yao, & Toumey, 2008). From a democratic perspective, research has found participation increases policy-relevant knowledge, opinion sophistication, and levels of satisfaction (Barabas, 2004; Gastil & Dillard, 1999); and has positive influences on policy preferences such as willingness to endorse an increase in taxes (Tomkins et al., 2015).

However, deliberating policy can be fraught with issues, especially when dealing with complex technical situations which may require specialized knowledge to fully grasp (Powell & Kleinman, 2008). Additionally, contradictory evidence suggests deliberative events do occasionally result in negative outcomes (Delli Carpini et al., 2004; Sanders, 1997; Sunstein, 2000), such as participant dissatisfaction (Karpowitz & Mansbridge, 2005; Smith & Wales, 2000) and group conflict and attitude polarization (Gastil, Bacci, & Dollinger, 2010; Sunstein, 2002). How to best create these deliberative experiences and avoid these negative effects is still an issue that needs more research. Specifically, scholars need to determine what aspects of the deliberative process actually lead to these beneficial effects and when and why they do so (PytlikZillig & Tomkins, 2011). For example, do deliberative participants learn most from the discussion or the pre-deliberation materials, or is their learning more a function of what individuals do when exposed to either activity? Is learning most likely when the discussion, materials or individual differences induce positive states such as active learning and open-mindedness (PytlikZillig et al., 2013), or is it more important to reduce negative states such as closed-mindedness and boredom? A promising place to start to understand what variables explain desirable outcomes—defined as learning from the process, and seeing the value in contributing to deliberative events—such as trying to increase critical thinking, and to understand how participants are cognitively engaging in the materials they are presented with in the deliberation.

Research in areas such as cognitive and educational psychology finds that one of the most important predictors of positive learning outcomes is how individuals engage with information. That is, the cognitive process involved when individuals engage with materials is often just as important, or more important, than the materials themselves. For example, Dunlosky and colleagues (2013) conducted an extensive review and evaluation of techniques used by learners in the classroom and judged that one of the most effective methods was "distributed practice" of the targeted learning outcomes. Other researchers have constructed measures of different types of study strategies, categorizing ways of studying new materials as involving surface-level versus deep cognitive processing, or as being strategic and conscientious. This research on learning finds that both deep cognitive processing and strategic/conscientious approaches to learning are effective for different types of outcomes.

To systematically examine the effects of various types of cognitive engagement, Hutchens and colleagues (Hutchens, PytlikZillig et al., 2014) used data from three longitudinal studies that examined the impact of engaging in a deliberative process focused on the issue of nanotechnology. Students enrolled at a large public institution over various time points in the semester participated in a deliberative event which included exposure to pre-deliberation materials and participating in a group deliberation. Afterwards they filled out surveys measuring their levels of knowledge and cognitive engagement. Across all three studies, students demonstrated higher levels of knowledge after participating in the deliberative activity. This finding suggests that there were some long-term effects of the deliberation event, which is consistent with prior research. They also found that conscientious engagement, active learning engagement, and creative engagement while participating in the deliberation had a positive relationship with subjective knowledge across all three studies. In essence, those who indicated they were paying closer attention, were actively engaging with the materials, and were thinking creatively about the issues were more likely to indicate that they learned more over the course of the deliberative event. Most of the negative forms of engagement, such as anger and closed-mindedness, were not associated with the measures of knowledge in any of the studies. One exception was feeling bored or uninterested during the deliberative activities, which was frequently associated with lower levels of knowledge. Overall, it appears that individuals do learn from deliberation materials and events. Experiencing positive cognitive engagement while participating also increases the extent to which they felt they have learned.

This study also examined a second important factor tied to deliberation. Specifically, they assessed whether or not being encouraged to critically think while reading the pre-deliberation material influenced individuals' level of engagement and subsequently how much they felt they learned throughout the experience. In other words, they assessed whether or not cognitive engagement mediated the effect of being instructed to think critically. Consistently they found participants who were prompted to think critically while participating in the deliberative event reported higher levels of conscientiousness, open-minded engagement, and active learning. This suggests that being asked to critically evaluate the deliberation materials results in a more positive engagement experience with the pre-deliberation materials. Given the findings indicating that positive engagement is associated with increases in knowledge, this finding indicates that the critical thinking condition has the potential to influence knowledge indirectly through increases in positive engagement, and a formal test of mediation indicated this was the case.

The results of these studies help scholars understand why deliberation can lead to positive outcomes when individuals are exposed to new or counter-attitudinal information. Reminding participants to be critical of information led to more positive experiences for the participants, which in turn led to greater knowledge. While these findings provide a solid foundation to understand how message processing occurs in deliberative groups, more can be done. In these studies, students were dealing with an unfamiliar and somewhat controversial topic. While students heard multiple perspectives during the deliberations, the students themselves typically held weak opinions about nanotechnology. How individuals would respond with a more polarized political issue that is often addressed in online settings still needs to be addressed. Additionally, while it is expected that individuals are exposed to disagreement and diverse views during the deliberation, it is still unknown how the specific make-up of the group influences the deliberation. For example, explicitly manipulating the balance of pro- and counter-attitudinal views within a deliberative group could result in different findings regarding the types of cognitive engagement that participants experience.

Disagreement Online: The Case of Political Flaming

While deliberations tend to be very civil events, another area of research that has gained interest among political communication scholars is the extent to which people use incivility when discussing politics online. New communication technologies have allowed people to communicate with each other without the same time and space constraints tied to more traditional forms of communication (e.g., face-to-face discussion). From a democratic perspective, the increasing popularity of blogs and online news sources requires scholars to look at the ability of the online public sphere to increase or inhibit political engagement. A potential concern regarding political discussion online is associated with high levels of incivility used when discussing politics. While scholars tout the benefits of exposure to a variety of viewpoints, how these views are expressed is generally not considered. Incivility is considered to be a more detrimental form of disagreement in that it doesn't add any substance to the discussion (Brooks & Geer, 2007). In essence, there is a difference between providing criticism and using insults and slurs when providing criticism. Concerns about incivility are not tied only to online politics. This work stems from previous studies showing high levels of incivility in people's day-to-day lives. Philips and Smith (2003) found high levels of what they call "everyday incivility," such as instances of road rage or overhearing inappropriate language. One concern held by these scholars is that these instances of everyday incivility may affect important political variables such as social capital (Putnam, 1996). Strategic communication scholars likely would like to reduce the amount of incivility that appears in online discussion forums and comment sections associated with their organizations. Understanding what features of the commenters, and the situations themselves are associated with increases in uncivil comments could help practitioners encourage more civil discussions online.

A popular context that is currently being addressed is the extent of incivility in politics. Scholars have determined that incivility exists in a variety of political contexts. Citizens can witness incivility when tuning into cable programming (Sobieraj & Berry, 2011) or when watching interactions among Congress members on CSPAN (Uslander, 1993). Incivility is so pronounced these days that is has become a common occurrence in online political discussion boards (Papacharissi, 2004; Upadhyay, 2010). Papacharissi (2004) found that nearly one-third of discussions in online contexts are uncivil. However, few studies have examined what variables best predict people engaging in uncivil online political discussions.

These aggressive online discussions can be tied to the often studied concept of "flaming." Computer-mediated communication (CMC) scholars have studied this phenomenon since at least the mid-1990s (Aiken & Waller, 2000; Kayany, 1998; Thompsen & Foulger, 1996). The general definition provided for flaming behaviors incorporates both the sending and interpretation of aggressive or hostile messages across various forms of online communication (e.g., email, instant messaging, chat groups). Research on flaming has studied how situational factors (e.g., anonymity and aggression) and individual-level factors (e.g., traits and communication) both contribute to flaming in non-political contexts. Anonymity is important because it is easy to achieve online. In CMC settings, anonymity is typically achieved through the use of avatars or screen names, as opposed to individuals' actual names. That is, people build online personas while hiding their true identity. The ability to use a manufactured persona is associated with a loss of self-awareness (Spears & Lea, 1992), which other scholars have tied it to increases in uninhibited behaviors and a perception of a lack of consequences for actions (Hardaker, 2010). For example, Alonzo and Aiken (2004) found that the anonymity of online communication increases disinhibition, which increases flaming motivations. Another commonly addressed situational contributor to flaming is the perception of aggression. That is, individuals can respond aggressively when they perceive a threat, regardless of if a threat was present or not (Dodge & Coie, 1987). In essence, people might flame because of a perceived threat or insult against themselves or their preferred group.

Individual level factors have also been shown to be important predictors of using hostile communication strategies in face-to-face contexts, which could provide an understanding of flaming behaviors. One individual difference variable that could explain flaming behaviors is verbal aggression. Verbal aggression has been shown to be a strong predictor of hostile communication strategies. Individuals high in verbal aggression are more likely to use character attacks, teasing, ridicule, or even profanity when trying to get their point across. Johnson and colleagues (2007) found trait verbal aggression predicted the use of verbal aggression tactics during arguments. People high in verbal aggression are also more likely to use aggressive tactics across a variety of different conversational contexts (Rocca & Vogl-Bauer, 1999). Another individual level factor that predicts the use of aggressive behaviors is perceived social norms. A number of studies in the aggression literature have focused on the importance of the perception of what is acceptable behavior when predicting aggressive behaviors and behavioral intentions (Gracia & Herrero, 2006; Henry et al., 2000). Much of this work emphasizes that people are socialized to regard certain aggressive behaviors as acceptable (Anderson & Huesmann, 2004). Moreover, these studies have shown that people who see aggressive behaviors as acceptable or normative tend to engage in aggressive behaviors or report intention to behave aggressively.

To determine if these variables predict flaming in explicitly political contexts, Hutchens and colleagues (Hmielowski et al., 2014; Hutchens et al., 2015) conducted research to examine political flaming intentions and to better understand the theoretical process that would lead to higher intentions to flame. Looking at both a student sample and a sample of bloggers they found some results that replicated across both samples, while other findings were constrained to just one sample. In regard to the situational factors, within the student sample, and contrary to prior research, anonymity was not a significant predictor of flaming intention. Anonymity, however, was associated with higher flaming intentions for the blogger sample. They also determined that participants reported higher levels of flaming intention when others directly challenged their political views when compared to simply seeing a political statement they disagreed with directed at someone else. In terms of individual difference variables, they determined that trait verbal aggression and viewing flaming as acceptable were significant predictors of intention to engage in flaming, across a variety of hypothetical scenarios, within both samples.

To better understand what conditions lead people to engage in aggressive online communication behaviors, Hmielowski, Hutchens, and Cicchirillo (2014) examined a moderated mediation model incorporating verbal aggression and the belief that flaming is acceptable behavior. Across both samples, they find that online political discussion socializes individuals to see flaming as an acceptable behavior. This increase in perceived acceptability in turn increases intention to flame. Furthermore, this increase in intention to flame is greater among those with high levels of verbal aggression. These results point to a few important takeaway points. It demonstrates that the prevalence of flaming in online contexts (Papacharissi, 2004; Upadhyay, 2010) may lead people to see aggressive behaviors as acceptable. That is, behaving aggressively in the face of disagreements is seen as normal. This effect is heightened when individuals already have higher levels of trait verbal aggression, which is consistent with prior research showing people with high levels of trait aggression show greater aggressive tendencies (e.g. Anderson, 1997).

These studies confirmed that many of the predictors of general flaming also are relevant when examining explicitly political situations. Additionally, it improved our understanding of how various individual-level variables work together to predict these negative responses. However, many questions still need to be answered in regard to how political flaming is triggered and how it can be avoided. The first step moving this line of research forward will be to conduct experiments to observe if what predicted flaming intentions in the surveys actually predict flaming behaviors in a laboratory setting. There are also elements of the website or discussion board, and how other members behave within these spaces, that need to be more explicitly researched. The first of these is the extent to which the tone of the website comment section, or the tone on a Facebook wall, influences the extent to which individuals will engage in flaming. Flaming could be seen as acceptable on websites that foster heated discussions, while this same tactic could be seen as unacceptable on other website. On websites that have a more consistently negative tone, participants may observe respondents being rewarded for their flaming responses. From a Social Learning Theory perspective, one reason why people may see flaming as acceptable is because they see others rewarded for flaming on sites that are geared more towards aggressive commentary. Carnagey and Anderson (2005) found that rewarding aggressive behaviors increases the likelihood of acting aggressively. It will also be important to understand whether acceptability of flaming varies by the type of comment. Flaming could be seen as acceptable when directed at "trolls"—individuals who are generally seen to be purposefully harming the discussion—but seen as unacceptable in response to a civil comment that challenges someone's beliefs.

Additional research should also examine how additional individual-level variables may serve as moderators between independent variables and political flaming. For example, knowledge and party identification could interact in predicting flaming intentions, with individuals higher in knowledge and with weaker party identification being less likely to engage in flaming behaviors compared to those with low levels of political knowledge and high party identification. Future studies could also explore interactions based on the context (e.g., strong party identification and direct attack vs. non-direct attack) and examine these relationships in an experimental setting.

Because people may be learning that it is common to use aggressive language when discussing politics online, it becomes important to postulate ways to increase civility in online discussions. This increase in civility could enable online discussion boards to be associated with the more beneficial outcomes associated with participating in deliberative events. One potential solution could be increased policing of the discussion forums, which could be done by those running the website or by the users themselves. However, this tactic could also have a counteractive effect, in that policing aggressive language may only increase users' animosity toward the website, particularly among partisans. Another tactic could be to have users flag inappropriate content. A potential pitfall with this strategy is this could result in users flagging any comment that challenges their existing opinions. This could create a situation in which flagging is no longer taken seriously by members of the online community, and would hamper the potential democratic benefit of a diverse online community.

Disentangling Discussion

The final area of political discussion research that will be addressed here is scholars' attempts to classify various forms of discussion. Any strategic communication practitioner engaged in evaluation research will be familiar with concerns surrounding having accurate measurement. At the broadest level, political discussion would subsume any conversation regarding governance whether it be policy, electoral, or community based. The majority of the discussion literature allows respondents to determine for themselves what "politics" entails. Much research is survey-based and asks them to indicate how often they discuss politics, or occasionally "important matters." As previously mentioned, the literature has consistently found positive relationship between these general measures of discussion and democratic outcomes. The literature on political discussion, however, has moved from an emphasis on focusing simply on the frequency of discussion to the characteristics of the conversation itself or the nature of the social networks in which the conversations take place.

The most frequently examined characteristic of discussion is the extent to which individuals are exposed to opposing viewpoints in their conversations. The rationale for the focus on disagreement is that exposure to differing views is critical for increasing levels of knowledge and participation. However, this line of research focused on opposing viewpoints has been fraught with inconsistent findings across studies. For instance, Mutz (2006) has found that exposure to disagreement is associated with lower levels of political participation. She posits that this relationship is due to increased levels of ambivalence that occur when individuals are exposed to counter-attitudinal views. As individuals become more ambivalent, they delay decisions such as who to vote for in upcoming elections

(Nir, 2005) or even become disengaged from the political process and decide not to vote (Mutz, 2006). A different branch of research (Brundidge, 2010; McLeod et al., 1999; Scheufele, Hardy, Broddard, Waismel-Manor, & Nisbet, 2006; Scheufele, Nisbet, Brossard, & Nisbet, 2004), however, consistently finds higher levels of participation in the presence of heterogeneous networks, which is a measure that incorporates multiple indicators of exposure to opposing views.

In an attempt to clarify these contradictory findings, Eveland and Hively (2009) undertook an in-depth analysis of the various conceptual and operational issues involved with measuring how often people talk to individuals who hold opposing views on important political issues. One of the problems they outline with this literature is the inconsistent use of terms across studies. A variety of terms have previously been used to describe the makeup of an individual's discussion network, all which generally assess the extent to which individuals in a network agree or disagree with the survey respondent. These terms include cross-cutting exposure (Mutz, 2002a, 2002b), ambivalent networks (Nir, 2005), heterogeneous networks (Marsden, 1987; McLeod et al., 1999; Moy & Gastil, 2006; Scheufele et al., 2006; Scheufele et al., 2004), dangerous networks (Eveland & Shah, 2003), diverse exposure (Huckfeldt & Sprague, 1995; Marsden, 1987), and disagreement (Huckfeldt & Mendez, 2008; McClurg, 2006; Pattie & Johnston, 2008; Price, Cappella, & Nir, 2002). The conceptual definitions associated with these various terms also have slight variations. However, the general emphasis here is on understanding the extent to which people hear opposing points of view.

Eveland and Hively (2009) determined that there are actually three distinct concepts that are intertwined in the various measures that assess exposure to opposing views. They broke down the single concept of heterogeneity into three components: exposure to disagreement (dangerous discussion), the very rarely measured exposure to agreement (safe discussion), and the proportion of safe and dangerous views in one's network (diversity). Additionally, they undertook a closer examination of the role of controlling for general frequency when examining safe, dangerous and diverse discussion's relationship with common political outcomes, namely knowledge and participation. They determined that safe discussion was positively associated with political participation, regardless of controls. Dangerous discussion, however, worked differently when controlling for general frequency. The results showed that, prior to controlling for frequency, the simple correlation between dangerous discussion and participation was positive. This correlation became non-significantly negative after controlling for frequency. Diversity, while matching the often used conceptual definition of being exposed to a variety of views, was found to not be a strong predictor of democratic outcomes, although a small but significant negative effect on participation was observed. Dangerous discussion and diverse discussion were associated with higher levels of knowledge, both before and after controlling for discussion frequency.

While this research appeared to indicate that differences could be attributed to differences in controlling for overall frequency of discussion (Eveland & Hively, 2009) or that varying the conceptualization of exposure to disagreement could account for the differences observed in outcomes (Eveland & Hively, 2009; Klofstad, Sohkey, & McClurg, 2013; Nir, 2011), questions remained. Scholars continued to find positive relationships between heterogeneous networks even when controlling for general frequency of discussion (Kim, Scheufele, & Han., 2011), which went against Eveland and Hively's (2009) findings. With this in mind, Hutchens, Eveland, and Morey (2014), took a more in-depth look at the operationalization utilized by scholars who use measures of heterogeneity when examining political outcomes. Although minor differences exist across studies, the traditional measure of "heterogeneity" incorporates a mix of demographic and political measures of difference (Brundidge, 2010; Kim et al., 2011; Kwak, Williams, Wang, & Lee, 2005; McLeod et al., 1999; Moy & Gastil, 2006; Quintelier, Stolle, & Harell, 2012; Rojas, 2008; Scheufele et al., 2006; Scheufele et al., 2004). This is in stark contrast to other measures used in the discussion literature. Most other measures of disagreement in the literature utilize a single item of political difference. For example, other studies examine how many discussion partners voted for the opposing candidate for president (Huckfeldt & Mendez, 2008), or how many days per week the respondent discussed politics with someone from a different political party (Eveland & Hively, 2009). Among those using heterogeneity, scholars commonly ask respondents to list how often they talk with individuals who have a variety of demographic characteristics (e.g., gender, ethnicity) in addition to individuals who have certain political characteristics. In addition to assessing discussion with individuals who vary on partisanship, respondents are asked to report frequency of political discussion with "individuals who have extreme views" on the left and the right. Empirically, anyone who is not in the most extreme position on the ideological scale is considered to be exposed to difference when talking to individuals with extreme views on both the left and the right. For those holding extreme views, only talk with those at the opposite end of the political spectrum counts as exposure to extreme views.

Hutchens, Eveland, and Morey (2014) disaggregated the commonly used heterogeneity measure to determine why studies were still showing this measure was positively related to political participation, which is a finding that was not replicated when measures of political difference were utilized. Their results suggested two potential reasons for the inconsistent findings across studies. The first explanation is tied to the incorporation of the "extreme views" measure. It appears that discussion with those who have extreme political views is an important, though rarely discussed, component of heterogeneity when considering predictors of knowledge and voting. It was the only individual component of the heterogeneity measure that was associated with increases in political participation. Moreover, when they compared a measure of heterogeneity that included the extreme views item with one that didn't, the measure that included extreme views was a significant predictor of participation whereas the measure that excluded extreme views was not. The second potential explanation for inconsistent findings is how missing data is treated. Allowing for missing data or not in the heterogeneity measure effectively either included or excluded independents, due to the construction of one of the political difference items that is included in the heterogeneity index. When independents were included, their heterogeneity score was artificially lowered, but a significant positive relationship between heterogeneity and participation was observed. When independents were excluded, no significant relationship was present.

While this research illuminates potential reasons for inconsistent findings across the political discussion literature, more research is needed. In particular, these findings suggest exciting new insights that will allow scholars to link the literature on polarization, partisan echo chambers, and exposure to political disagreement. Future research should study the nature of interpersonal expression of extreme views with an eye toward how those expressions are incorporated into memory structures by those who hold more moderate positions, or extreme opinions on the opposite end of the political spectrum. Moderates may be the least likely to hear opposing views. In addition, the ideological difference to which strong partisans are exposed is also quantitatively "more different" than could possibly be experienced by moderates. This suggests discussion scholars begin to consider exposure to counter-attitudinal views not just as dichotomy. Rather, scholars must consider "difference" on a continuum, from small amounts of difference (e.g. a liberal with an extreme liberal) to a great deal of difference (e.g. a liberal with a conservative). Understanding the actual content of the discussions that are taking place is also a common concern in the literature that has yet to be fully addressed, and may further our understanding of how individuals experience disagreement.

Summary

The role of political discussion between citizens is an important issue to examine when trying to understand democratic behaviors. Decades of research have demonstrated that simply discussing politics more often increases knowledge and levels of political engagement. Despite this long history of research, questions remain regarding the make-up of individuals' networks, how new communication technologies impact the relationships between these commonly addressed variables, and how practitioners can modify structured discussion to elicit the most desirable responses.

As this summary of the research shows, examining various ways to operationalize aspects of discussion reveals that there are layers of nuance that can be considered when examining who individuals discuss politics with. What might seem like small changes in measurement can produce contradictory findings. Therefore, scholars should pay closer attention to the operationalization of network measures. Indeed, decisions about measurement strategies should be thought through and explicitly addressed as those decisions can impact the democratic conclusions that are drawn.

Discussing politics online will only continue to grow in importance. Research showing that people see the use of these tactics as normal the more they discuss politics online is concerning. Thinking uncivil discussion is normal varies dramatically from the democratic ideal espoused when discussing differing perspectives. Aggressive behavior is more likely to occur in anonymous situations, situations where individuals feel they are being directly threatened, if the individual has higher levels of trait verbal aggression, and if the individual thinks aggressive behavior is acceptable. Knowing this, steps can be taken to try to reduce these aggressive behaviors in online political discussion spaces.

Research on best practices for structured discussions, in which a variety of viewpoints will be presented, suggests that encouraging individuals to think critically will increase their positive cognitive engagement with materials you present them with, and with the deliberation itself.

All of these conclusions that are being drawn in a political discussion context could also be applied to strategic communication practitioners. Understanding how we talk in various situations helps illuminate why we behave the way we do in situations, and can help us better determine how to elicit desirable behaviors in the future. While the research presented here generally focuses on improving democratic behaviors, these findings could be applied to multiple contexts. Encouraging critical thinking and reducing uncivil responses are salient aims in most public arenas, and would likely improve the relationships between organizations and their publics.

References

Aiken, M., & Waller, B. (2000). Flaming among first-time group support system users. *Information & Management*, *37*(2), 95–100. doi: 10.1016/S0378-7206(99)00036-1

Alonzo, M., & Aiken, M. (2004). Flaming in electronic communication. *Decision Support Systems*, *36*(3), 205–213. doi: 10.1016/S0167-9236(02)00190-2

Anderson, C. A. (1997). Effect of violent movies and trait hostility on hostile feelings and aggressive thoughts. *Aggressive Behavior*, *23*(3), 161–178. doi: 10.1002/(SICI)1098-2337(1997)23:33.0.CO;2-P

Anderson, C. A., & Huesmann, L. (2004). Human aggression: A social-cognitive view. In M. A. Hogg & J. Cooper (Eds.), *The Sage handbook of social psychology*. Thousand Oaks, CA: Sage.

Barabas, J. (2004). How deliberation affects policy opinions. *American Political Science Review*, *98*(04), 687–701. doi: 10.1017/S0003055404041425

Besley, J. C., Kramer, V. L., Yao, Q., & Toumey, C. (2008). Interpersonal discussion following citizen engagement about nanotechnology: What, if anything, do they say? *Science Communication*, *30*(2), 209–235. doi: 10.1177/1075547008324670

Brooks, D. J., & Geer, J. G. (2007). Beyond negativity: The effects of incivility on the electorate. *American Journal of Political Science*, *51*(1), 1–16. doi: 10.1111/j.1540-5907.2007.00233.x

Brundidge, J. (2010). Encountering "difference" in the contemporary public sphere: The contribution of the internet to the heterogeneity of political discussion networks. *Journal of Communication*, *60*(4), 680–700. doi: 10.1111/j.1460-2466.2010.01509.x

Carnagey, N. L., & Anderson, C. A. (2005). The effects of reward and punishment in violent video games on aggressive affect, cognition, and behavior. *Psychological Science*, *16*(11), 882–889. doi: 10.1111/j.1467-9280.2005.01632.x

Chambers, S. (2003). Deliberative democratic theory. *Annual Review of Political Science*, *6*(1), 307–326. doi: 10.1146/annurev.polisci.6.121901.085538

Coe, K., Kenski, K., & Rains, S. A. (2014). Online and uncivil? Patterns and determinants of incivility in newspaper website comments. *Journal of Communication*, *64*(4), 658–679. doi: 10.1111/jcom.12104

Delli Carpini, M. X., Cook, F. L., & Jacobs, L. R. (2004). Public deliberation, discursive participation, and citizen engagement: A review of the empirical literature. *Annual Review of Political Science*, *7*, 315–344. doi: 10.1146/annurev.polisci.7.121003.091630

Dodge, K. A., & Coie, J. D. (1987). Social-information-processing factors in reactive and proactive aggression in children's peer groups. *Journal of Personality and Social Psychology*, *53*(6), 1146–1158. doi: 10.1037/0022-3514.53.6.1146

Dunlosky, J., Rawson, K. A., Marsh, E. J., Nathan, M. J., & Willingham, D. T. (2013). Improving students' learning with effective learning techniques promising directions from cognitive and educational psychology. *Psychological Science in the Public Interest*, *14*(1), 4–58. doi: 10.1177/1529100612453266

Dutwin, D. (2003). The character of deliberation: Equality, argument, and the formation of public opinion. *International Journal of Public Opinion Research*, *15*(3), 239–264. doi: 10.1093/ijpor/15.3.239

Eveland, W. P. (2004). The effect of political discussion in producing informed citizens: The roles of information, motivation, and elaboration. *Political Communication*, *21*(2), 177–193. doi: 10.1080/10584600490443877

Eveland, W. P., & Hively, M. H. (2009). Political discussion frequency, network size, and "heterogeneity" of discussion as predictors of political knowledge and participation. *Journal of Communication*, *59*, 205–224. doi: 10.1111/j.1460-2466.2009.01412.x

Eveland, W. P., & Shah, D. V. (2003). The impact of individual and interpersonal factors on perceived news media bias. *Political Psychology*, *24*(1), 101–117. doi: 10.1.1.321.268

Fishkin, J. S. (1997). *The voice of the people: Public opinion and democracy*. New Haven CT: Yale University Press.

Gastil, J. (2000). *By popular demand*. Berkeley, CA: University of California Press.

Gastil, J. (2008). *Political communication and deliberation*. Thousand Oaks, CA: Sage.

Gastil, J., Bacci, C., & Dollinger, M. (2010). Is deliberation neutral? Patterns of attitude change during "The Deliberative Polls™." *Journal of Public Deliberation*, *6*(2). Retrieved from http://www.publicdeliberation.net/jpd/vol6/iss2/art3

Gastil, J., & Dillard, J. P. (1999). Increasing political sophistication through public deliberation. *Political Communication*, *16*(1), 3–23. doi: 10.1080/105846099198749

Goodin, R. E., & Niemeyer, S. J. (2003). When does deliberation begin? Internal reflection versus public discussion in deliberative democracy. *Political Studies*, *51*(4), 627–649. doi: 10.1111/j.0032-3217.2003.00450.x

Gracia, E., & Herrero, J. (2006). Acceptability of domestic violence against women in the European Union: A multilevel analysis. *Journal of Epidemiology and Community Health, 60*(2), 123–129. doi: 10.1136/jech.2005.036533

Hardaker, C. (2010). Trolling in asynchronous computer-mediated communication: From user discussions to academic definitions. *Journal of Politeness Research, 6*(2). doi: 10.1515/jplr.2010.011

Henry, D., Guerra, N., Huesmann, R., Tolan, P., VanAcker, R., & Eron, L. (2000). Normative influences on aggression in urban elementary school classrooms. *American Journal of Community Psychology, 28*(1), 59–81.

Hmielowski, J. D., Hutchens, M. J., & Cicchirillo, V. J. (2014). Living in an age of online incivility: Examining the conditional indirect effects of online discussion on political flaming. *Information, Society and Communication, 17*(10), 1196–1211. doi: 10.1080/1369118X.2014.899609

Holbert, R. L., Benoit, W. L., Hansen, G. J., & Wen, W.-C. (2002). The role of communication in the formation of an issue-based citizenry. *Communication Monographs, 69*, 296–310. doi: 10.1080/03637750216549

Huckfeldt, R., & Mendez, J. M. (2008). Moths, flames, and political engagement: Managing disagreement within communication networks. *The Journal of Politics, 70*(1), 83–96.

Huckfeldt, R., & Sprague, J. (1995). *Citizens, politics, and social communication: Information and influence in and election campaign.* New York: Cambridge University Press.

Hutchens, M. J., Cicchirillo, V. J., & Hmielowski, J. D. (2015). How could you think that?!?!: Understanding intentions to engage in political flaming. *New Media & Society, 17*(10), 1196–1211. doi: 10.1177/1461444814522947

Hutchens, M. J., Eveland, W. P., & Morey, A. C. (May, 2014). *Dissecting heterogeneity in political discussion networks: The critical role of discussion with people holding extreme views.* Presented to the Political Communication Division of the International Communication Association Annual Conference, Seattle, WA.

Hutchens, M. J., PytlikZillig, L. M., Muhlberger, P., Tomkins, A. J., Anderson, R. A., Walther, J. C., & Gonzalez., F. J. (May, 2014). *Message or process? Learning about nanotechnology through engaged deliberation.* Presented to the Information Systems Division of the International Communication Association Annual Conference, Seattle, WA.

Johnson, A. J., Becker, J. A. H., Wigley, S., Haigh, M. M., & Craig, E. A. (2007). Reported argumentativeness and verbal aggressiveness levels: The influence of type of argument. *Communication Studies, 58*(2), 189–205. doi: 10.1080/10510970701341154

Karpowitz, C. F., & Mansbridge, J. (2005). Disagreement and consensus: The importance of dynamic updating in public deliberation. In J. Gastil & P. Levine (Eds.), *The deliberative democracy handbook: Strategies for effective civic engagement.* San Francisco: Jossey-Bass.

Katz, E., & Lazarsfeld, P. F. (1955). *Personal influence: The part played by people in the flow of mass communication.* Glencoe, IL: The Free Press.

Kayany, J. M. (1998). Contexts of uninhibited online behavior: Flaming in social newsgroups on usenet. *Journal of the American Society for Information Science, 49*(12), 1135–1141. doi: 10.1002/(SICI)1097-4571(1998)49:12<1135::AID-ASI8>3.0.CO;2-W

Kim, E., Scheufele, D., & Han, J. Y. (2011). Structure or predisposition? Exploring the interaction effect of discussion orientation and discussion heterogeneity on political participation. *Mass Communication and Society, 14*(4), 502–526. doi: 10.1080/15205436.2010.513469

Knobloch, K. R., Gastil, J., Richards, R., & Feller, T. (2013). *Evaluation report on the 2012 Citizens' Initiative Reviews for the Oregon CIR Commission*. Available online at http://www.la1.psu.edu/cas/jgastil/CIR/ReportToCIRCommission2012.pdf

Knoke, D. (1990). *Political networks: The structural perspective* New York: Cambridge University Press.

Klofstad, C. A., Sokhey, A. E., & McClurg, S. D. (2013). Disagreeing about disagreement: How conflict in social networks affects political behavior. *American Journal of Political Science*, 57(1), 120–134. doi: 10.1111/j.1540-5907.2012.00620.x

Kwak, N., Williams, A. E., Wang, X., & Lee, H. (2005). Talking politics and engaging politics: An examination of the interactive relationships between structural features of political talk and discussion engagement. *Communication Research*, 32(1), 87–111. doi: 10.1177/0093650204271400

Mansbridge, J. (1999). Everyday talk in the deliberative system. In S. Macedo (Ed.), *Deliberative politics: Essays on democracy and disagreement* (pp. 211–239). New York: Oxford University Press.

Marcus, G. E. (1988). Democratic theories and the study of public opinion. *Polity*, 21(1), 25–44. doi: 10.2307/3234922

Marsden, P. V. (1987). Core discussion networks of Americans. *American Sociological Review*, 52(1), 122–131.

McClurg, S. D. (2006). The electoral relevance of political talk: Examining disagreement and expertise effects in social networks on political participation. *American Journal of Political Science*, 50(3), 737–754. doi: 10.1111/j.1540-5907.2006.00213.x

McLeod, J. M., Scheufele, D. A., Moy, P., Horowitz, E. M., Holbert, R. L., Zhang, W., Zubric, S., & Zubric, J. (1999). Understanding deliberation: The effects of discussion networks on participation in a public forum. *Communication Research*, 26(6), 743–774. doi: 10.1177/009365099026006005

Moy, P., & Gastil, J. (2006). Predicting deliberative conversation: The impact of discussion networks, media use, and political cognitions. *Political Communication*, 23(4), 443–460. doi: 10.1080/10584600600977003

Muhlberger, P. (2006). Should e-government design for citizen participation? Stealth democracy and deliberation. In *Proceedings of the 2006 International Conference on Digital Government Research* (pp. 53–61). San Diego, California: Digital Government Society of North America. doi: 10.1145/1146598.1146620

Mutz, D. (2002a). Cross-cutting social networks: Testing democratic theory in practice. *American Political Science Review*, 96(1), 111–126. doi: 10.1017/S0003055402004264

Mutz, D. C. (2002b). The consequences of cross-cutting networks for political participation. *American Journal of Political Science*, 46(4), 838. doi: 10.2307/3088437

Mutz, D. C. (2006). *Hearing the other side: Deliberative versus participatory democracy*. New York: Cambridge University Press.

Nir, L. (2005). Ambivalent social networks and their consequences for participation. *International Journal of Public Opinion Research*, 17(4), 422–442. doi: 10.1093/ijpor/edh069

Nir, L. (2011). Disagreement and opposition in social networks: Does disagreement discourage turnout? *Political Studies*, 59(3), 674–692. doi: 10.1111/j.1467-9248.2010.00873.x

Papacharissi, Z. (2004). Democracy online: Civility, politeness, and the democratic potential of online political discussion groups. *New Media & Society*, 6(2), 259–283. doi: 10.1177/1461444804041444

Pattie, C., & Johnston, R. (2008). It's good to talk: Talk, disagreement and tolerance. *British Journal of Political Science*, 38, 677–698. doi: 10.1017/S0007123408000331

Phillips, T., & Smith, P. (2003). Everyday incivility: Towards a benchmark. *The Sociological Review*, *51*(1), 85–108. doi: 10.1111/1467-954X.00409

Powell, M., & Kleinman, D. L. (2008). Building citizen capacities for participation in nanotechnology decision-making: the democratic virtues of the consensus Conference model. *Public Understanding of Science*, *17*(3), 329–348. doi: 10.1177/0963662506068000

Price, V., & Cappella, J. N. (2002). Online deliberation and its influence: The electronic dialogue project in campaign 2000. *IT & Society*, *1*, 303–329. doi: 10.1.1.9.5945

Price, V., Cappella, J. N., & Nir, L. (2002). Does disagreement contribute to more deliberative opinion? *Political Communication*, *19*, 95–112. doi: 10.1080/105846002317246506

Putnam, R. (1996, December 1). The strange disappearance of civic America. *The American Prospect*, *7*(24), 34–48.

PytlikZillig, L. M., Hutchens, M. J., Muhlberger, P., Wang, S., Harris, R., Neiman, J. L., & Tomkins, A. J. (2013). The varieties of individual engagement (VIE) scales: Confirmatory factor analysis across two samples and contexts. *Journal of Public Deliberation*, *9*(2). Retrieved from http://www.publicdeliberation.net/jpd/vol9/iss2/art8/

PytlikZillig, L. M., & Tomkins, A. J. (2011). Public engagement for informing science and technology policy: What do we know, what do we need to know, and how will we get there? *Review of Policy Research*, *28*(2), 197–217. doi:10.1111/j.1541-1338.2011.00489.x

Quintelier, E., Stolle, D., & Harell, A. (2012). Politics in peer groups: Exploring the causal relationship between network diversity and political participation. *Political Research Quarterly*, *65*(4), 868–881. doi: 10.1177/1065912911411099

Rocca, K. A., & Vogl-Bauer, S. (1999). Trait verbal aggression, sports fan identification, and perceptions of appropriate sports fan communication. *Communication Research Reports*, *16*(3), 239–248. doi: 10.1080/08824099909388723

Rojas, H. (2008). Strategy versus understanding—How orientations toward political conversation influence political engagement. *Communication Research*, *35*(4), 452–480. http://doi.org/10.1177/0093650208315977

Ryfe, D. M. (2005). Does deliberative democracy work? *Annual Review of Political Science*, *8*(1), 49–71. doi:10.1146/annurev.polisci.8.032904.154633

Sanders, L. M. (1997). Against deliberation. *Political Theory*, *25*(3), 347–376. doi: 10.1177/0090591797025003002

Scheufele, D. A., Hardy, B. W., Brossard, D., Waismel-Manor, I. S., & Nisbet, E. (2006). Democracy based on difference: Examining the links between structural heterogeneity, heterogeneity of discussion networks, and democratic citizenship. *Journal of Communication*, *56*(4), 728–753. doi: 10.1111/j.1460-2466.2006.00317.x

Scheufele, D. A., Nisbet, M. C., Brossard, D., & Nisbet, E. C. (2004). Social structure and citizenship: Examining the impacts of social setting, network heterogeneity, and informational variables on political participation. *Political Communication*, *21*(3), 315–338. doi: 10.1080/10584600490481389

Smith, G., & Wales, C. (2000). Citizens' juries and deliberative democracy. *Political Studies*, *48*(1), 51–65. doi: 10.1111/1467-9248.00250

Spears, R., & Lea, M. (1992). Social influence and the influence of the "social" in computer-mediated communication. In M. Lea (Ed.), *Contexts of computer-mediated communication* (pp. 30–65). London: Harvester-Wheatsheaf.

Sobieraj, S., & Berry, J. M. (2011). From incivility to outrage: Political discourse in blogs, talk radio, and cable news. *Political Communication*, *28*(1), 19. doi:10.1080/10584609.2010.542360

Sunstein, C. R. (2000). *Infotopia: How many minds produce knowledge.* New York: Oxford University Press.

Sunstein, C. R. (2002). The law of group polarization. *Journal of Political Philosophy, 10*(2), 175–195. doi: 10.1111/1467-9760.00148

Thompsen, P. A., & Foulger, D. A. (1996). Effects of pictographs and quoting on flaming in electronic mail. *Computers in Human Behavior, 12*(2), 225–243. doi: 10.1016/0747-5632(96)00004-0

Tomkins, A. J., Hoppe, R. D., Herian, M. N., PytlikZillig, L. M., Abdel-Monem, T., & Shank, N. C. (2012). Public input for city budgeting using e-input, face-to-face discussions, and random sample surveys: The willingness of an American community to increase taxes. *Electronic Journal of e-Government, 12*(2), 698–707.

Upadhyay, S. R. (2010). Identity and impoliteness in computer-mediated reader responses. *Journal of Politeness Research, 6,* 105–127. doi: 10.1515/JPLR.2010.006

Uslander, E. M. (1993). *The decline of comity in Congress.* Ann Arbor, MI: University of Michigan Press.

Verba, S., Scholzman, K. L., & Brady, H. E. (1995). *Voice and equality: Civic voluntarism in American politics* Cambridge, MA: Harvard University Press.

6
STRATEGIC COMMUNICATION AND U.S. NATIONAL SECURITY AFFAIRS

Critical-Cultural and Rhetorical Perspectives

Hamilton Bean

> This chapter is dedicated to the late H. L. "Bud" Goodall, Jr.

Policymakers, officials, and commentators have long been concerned with the influence of global public opinion on U.S. foreign policy and national security (Farwell, 2012). The last 100 years have witnessed the establishment, consolidation, division, reform, or abolishment of numerous overt and covert agencies designed to influence foreign audiences (Arndt, 2005). Traditionally, the U.S. Department of State has led overt foreign influence activities, while the CIA has led covert operations, both of which reached their zenith during the Cold War (Simpson, 1996). In the post-September 11, 2001-era, prominent examples of U.S. strategic communication activities have included the Bush Administration's "Shared Values" initiative in 2002 (Fullerton & Kendrick, 2006) and President Obama's Executive Order 13584, which established the Center for Strategic Counterterrorism Communications in 2011 to counter terrorist propaganda within interactive digital environments (Center for Strategic Counterterrorism Communications, 2013, para. 1). In order to align and synchronize foreign influence activities, in 2010 the White House issued the first *National Framework for Strategic Communication*, which defined strategic communication as:

> (a) the synchronization of our words and deeds and how they will be perceived by others, as well as (b) programs and activities deliberately aimed at communicating and engaging with intended audiences, including those implemented by public affairs, public diplomacy, and information operations professionals. (White House, 2010, p. 2)

In addition to the White House, U.S. Department of State, and the CIA, the Department of Defense (DoD) conducts strategic communication, which it defines as government "efforts to understand and engage key audiences to create, strengthen, or preserve conditions favorable for the advancement of United States Government interests, policies, and objectives through the use of coordinated programs, plans, themes, messages, and products synchronized with the actions of all instruments of national power" (Paul, 2011a, p. 19). Over the last decade, the U.S. military has played a much larger role in strategic communication activities given the government's interest in using communication as a weapon in the fight against terrorism (Nakamura & Weed, 2009). Despite U.S. efforts, worldwide terrorist attacks soared to a record high in 2012 (Burke, 2013) and the United States' image remains weak in the Middle East and North Africa and volatile elsewhere in the world (Stokes, 2013). Specifically, in 2007, the BBC reported that in 18 nations polled, only 29% of respondents said the United States was a positive influence in the world (BBC, 2007). By 2010, that number had jumped to 46% (BBC, 2010). But by 2013, public opinion of the United States had plummeted, placing it just ahead of Iran as the world's most unpopular country (Kierman, 2013). The U.S. Government Accountability Office (GAO) recently concluded that the DoD's strategic communication programs were inadequately tracked, their impact was unclear, and the military did not know if it was "targeting the right foreign audiences" (Vanden Brook, 2013, para. 1). The U.S. military's increased involvement in foreign influence activities thus raises critical questions concerning U.S. strategic communication's premises, new and evolving forms, unintended consequences, and tangible results.

The DoD appeared to try to halt internal use of the term "strategic communication" in 2012 due to the confusion it created among some officials given its conceptual similarity to public affairs (*USA Today*, 2012, para. 2). Public affairs focuses on media relations and involves engaging both foreign and domestic audiences "with the goal of furthering U.S. foreign policy and national security interests as well as broadening understanding of American values" (U.S. Department of State, 2014, para. 1). However, both overt and covert strategic communication efforts endure under different names, as well as within other government agencies (*USA Today*, 2012; White House, 2010, 2012). Exploring how U.S. strategic communication activities have shaped the decade's volatile shifts in global public opinion, the surge in terrorism, and the future of U.S. foreign policy and national security is a task that should entice communication scholars—especially scholars who affiliate with critical-cultural and rhetorical traditions. Critical-cultural and rhetorical scholarship historically has been confined to the role of critiquing U.S. foreign policy; but in recent years, such scholarship has begun to inform U.S. strategic communication practice (Corman, Trethewey, & Goodall, 2008). Thus, the purpose of this chapter is two-fold: (1) it advocates for the increased use of critical-cultural and rhetorical perspectives within the domain of applied strategic communication research; and (2) it promotes critical-cultural and rhetorical approaches vis-à-vis the development of U.S. strategic communication.

The chapter unfolds in five sections. The first section argues that themes related to security ought to become more central to the overall agenda of strategic communication research. The second section defines key concepts and tensions in order to map the terrain of U.S. strategic communication research and practice.[1] This section also describes what critical-cultural and rhetorical communication scholarship entails. The third section establishes the need for a new research agenda that emphasizes critical-cultural and rhetorical perspectives. The fourth section describes how my research advances this new agenda, and the concluding section points to research opportunities for scholars who work at the intersection of communication and security.

Security's Presence and Absence Within Strategic Communication Research

In 2007, the editors of the newly founded *International Journal for Strategic Communication* (*IJSC*) defined strategic communication as "the purposeful use of communication by an organization to fulfill its mission" (Hallahan, Holtzhausen, Van Ruler, Verčič, & Sriramesh, 2007, p. 3). Studying strategic communication involved examining "how the organization itself presents and promotes itself through the intentional activities of its leaders, employees, and communication practitioners" (p. 7). As a new journal, *IJSC* sought to define the field of strategic communication, assess the role of theory, and support multidisciplinary approaches and international voices. Hallahan et al. placed communication practices associated with national security under the moniker of "political communication," which included "communications in support of public diplomacy and military stabilization" (p. 6). This placement permitted the authors to briefly acknowledge strategic communication's militaristic antecedents, but they lamented, "Associating *strategic* as a war metaphor in connection with communication practice can . . . strengthen the existing negative perceptions of the field" (p. 12; emphasis original).

Still, despite the emphasis of Hallahan et al. (2007) on commercial (versus government) domains, the authors did acknowledge, "Research can be informed by looking beyond the bounds of traditional communications disciplines to include such diverse activities as public diplomacy, psychological operations by the military, and social marketing" (p. 27). Along these lines, Arizona State University's Consortium for Strategic Communication (CSC) was noted for its promotion of "advanced research, teaching, and public discussion of the role of communication in combating terrorism, promoting national security, and successfully engaging in public diplomacy worldwide" (p. 4). This note was particularly appropriate given that national security concerns have played an integral role in the development of strategic communication (Paul, 2011a; Simpson, 1996). As Dwayne Winseck (2008) explains:

> In the past, the US had hastily cobbled together the Committee on Public Information and the Office of War Information in the crises-ridden contexts of the First and Second World Wars, respectively. That changed forever in 1953 as permanent tools of persuasion and propaganda were created: the Voice of America (VOA), the United States Information Agency (USIA), Radio Free Europe and a slew of newspapers, books and magazines, journalists and intellectuals financed by the CIA in a bid to cultivate a global milieu of opinion favourably disposed to the US view of the world. (p. 421)

However, despite their acknowledgement of this history, Hallahan et al. (2007) defined the field of strategic communication research in terms of four "academic clusters" that potentially obscured the field's origins in relation to national security and related strategic communication: (1) corporate communication; (2) marketing, advertising, and public relations; (3) business communication; and (4) organizational communication. The term "public diplomacy" was not deemed worthy of its own academic cluster, perhaps because associated research has been published within leading public relations journals and volumes (Dutta-Bergman, 2006; Hayden, 2012; Mor, 2007; Signitzer & Wamser, 2006; Zhang, 2010).

Public diplomacy is defined as "government's efforts to conduct foreign policy and promote national interests through direct outreach and communication with the population of a foreign country," and it is characterized by messages broadcast via mass media, disseminated over the Internet, or through cultural and educational exchange (Nakamura & Weed, 2009, p. 2). An argument in favor of the creation of a distinct academic cluster for public diplomacy research comes from Bruce Gregory (2008), who cites a cohesive analytical framework and a body of relevant scholarship to support his claim that public diplomacy "differs from education, journalism, advertising, public relations, branding, and other ways in which people communicate in societies" and constitutes an emerging academic field in its own right (p. 276).

Therefore, it might be useful to recognize a fifth, distinct academic cluster of strategic communication research beyond those four clusters identified by Hallahan et al. (2007)—a cluster comprised of research that focuses primarily on public diplomacy, yet one that also does not omit the study of propaganda, given the role that propaganda has played in the evolution of public diplomacy. The U.S. military defines propaganda as any form of "adversary communication, especially of a biased or misleading nature, designed to influence the opinions, emotions, attitudes, or behavior of any group in order to benefit the sponsor, either directly or indirectly" (Aftergood, 2010, para. 4). Allying with Gregory's conceptualization of public diplomacy, the next section describes some of the key concepts and tensions associated with U.S. strategic communication research occurring within this proposed fifth academic cluster. It also explains what critical-cultural and rhetorical perspectives entail and how they fit within public diplomacy research.

Key Concepts and Tensions

It was only in 2001 that a Chairman of a Defense Science Board (DSB) task force, Vincent Vitto, first used the term "strategic communication" to refer to the sum total of the state's public affairs, public diplomacy, and propaganda activities (Paul, 2011b).[2] Definitional debates, operational differences, and contested genealogies aside, the terms "public affairs," "public diplomacy," "propaganda," and "strategic communication" bear a clear family resemblance (Arquilla & Borer, 2007; Cioppa, 2009; Creel, 1920; Cull, Culbert, & Welch, 2003; Dimitriu, 2012; Farwell, 2012; Forest, 2009; Kamalipour & Snow, 2004; Louw, 2003; Moloney, 2006; Munoz, 2012; Paul, 2011a; Snow & Taylor, 2006). As Ambassador Alberto Fernandez, Coordinator for the U.S. Department of State's Center for Strategic Counterterrorism Communications (CSCC), intimated, "What we try to do is not to affirm the positive about ourselves but to emphasize the negative about the adversary. It is about offense and not defense" (Fernandez, 2013, para. 23). Such sentiments are not new.

For example, Christopher Simpson (1996) has chronicled the post-World War II institutionalization of psychological warfare within the U.S. national security sector and its close connection to the founding fathers of the field of Mass Communication. Ambassador Fernandez's sentiments echo the long-held assumption that the skillful application of communication science can potentially mitigate conflict, as well as provide a cheap, flexible, and a "sometimes less brutal" alternative to war (p. 116). However, U.S. strategic communication's ties to the state, militarism, and the covert sphere generate unease among some scholars. As the RAND Corporation's Christopher Paul declared during a 2011 U.S. House of Representatives Armed Services subcommittee hearing, "In my view, strategic communication should be unashamedly about virtuous persuasion, but should be completely devoid of falsehood, partial truths and spin" (United States House Armed Services Subcommittee, 2011, p. 4). Paul thus sought to remove propaganda from the definition of strategic communication.

However, in their quest to influence audiences, both U.S. and foreign strategic communicators can and do draw upon a toolkit that includes half-truths, fallacies, and fabrications (Bockstette, 2010; Paul, 2011a; Snow, 2006). In a now infamous example, the government of Kuwait hired the Hill & Knowlton public relations firm to build global public support for a U.S.-led invasion of Iraq in 1991. Hill and Knowlton disseminated a news story claiming that Iraqi troops had brutally thrown Kuwaiti infants from their incubators and left them to die. Media outlets worldwide repeated the appalling—yet unsupported—story, which generated momentum for the U.S. intervention (Regan, 2002). More recently, the *Washington Post* reported in 2013 that the U.S. military is increasingly focused on "manipulating news and commentary on the Internet, especially social media, by posting material and images without necessarily claiming ownership" (Whitlock, 2013, para. 8). In 2014, the Associated Press revealed the details of a covert U.S. operation that involved the use of social media designed to undermine Cuba's communist government (Arce, Butler, & Gillum, 2014)—an effort duplicated with varying levels of transparency in "dozens" of other countries (Nixon, 2014, para. 3). The warrant for such activities can be traced to the demonstrated connection between media use and pro- or anti-American sentiment (Nisbet & Myers, 2011).

Consider the 2012 DoD-commissioned report "Science and Technology for Communication and Persuasion Abroad: Gap Analysis and Survey" (McCants, 2012), which offers a rare glimpse of the research underwriting U.S. strategic communication activities. While Cold War-era officials often relied on (government-funded) communication studies published in *Public Opinion Quarterly* (Simpson, 1996), today's strategic communicators draw upon research published in public relations and consumer research journals and volumes (Watts & Dodds, 2007; Wright & Hinson, 2009). These studies center upon developing "effective techniques for cultivating relationships and influencing people in the digital realm" (McCants, 2012, p. iv). Such research informs numerous government-funded projects (the details of which are usually concealed from public view) bearing names including: "Population Research and Analysis Planning Support to Military Information Support Operations;" "Real-Time Contextual Mapping and Visualization Dashboard for Muslim Social Movements;" "Influencing Violent Extremist Organizations Update;" "Early Warning, Analysis and Targeting for Hotspot Identification, Tracking and Intervention;" and "Global Assessment Program (GAP)."

As reported in *USA Today* in 2014, the latter GAP project has evolved into the U.S. Special Operations Command's Global Research Assessment Program, which seeks to "determine if [its] propaganda programs . . . are effective in convincing target audiences of U.S. policy aims" (Locker, 2014, para. 2). These projects, which accompany a phalanx of government, think-tank, corporate, and academic white papers, reports, policy memos, directives, field manuals, statements, and studies have advanced numerous approaches to strategic communication. Much of this material is generated from scholars associated with U.S. military and intelligence colleges and is produced outside of civilian universities (King, 2011), although this situation is changing.

The research informing U.S. strategic communication overwhelmingly relies on a "message influence model" that would be familiar to any student of communication (Corman et al., 2008). This model, developed in the 1950s, maintains that communication involves transmitting messages in order to influence people's attitudes, values, and beliefs. The model emphasizes the intentions of the message sender, which, in principle, can be successfully communicated to audiences by reducing or eliminating distortion, noise, and attenuation. The model presumes that people are instruments for meeting objectives, and that they can be successfully influenced, persuaded, or coerced by the "right" message.

The message influence model stands in contrast to recent public relations theorizing that emphasizes "dialogic" activities that foreground the *relationship* between speaker and audience and enact the principles of mutuality, propinquity (shared bonds), empathy, risk, and commitment (Kent & Taylor, 2002). Carl Botan and Maureen Taylor (2004) linked the development of dialogic communication to the broader transition within the field of public relations from functional, coercive approaches to "cocreational" ones. Cocreational approaches view publics as "cocreators of meaning" and "communication as what makes it possible to agree to shared meanings, interpretations, and goals" (p. 652). Cocreational approaches maintain that publics "are not instrumentalized but instead are partners in the meaning-making process" (p. 652).

Given the development of dialogic and cocreational approaches in other domains of communication research and practice, as well as the poor track record of U.S. strategic communication over the last decade in reducing terrorism and improving global public opinion of the United States (Vanden Brook, 2013), a key question becomes why U.S. strategic communication programs continue to rely on the message influence model. Three answers appear reasonable. First, officials confront the entrenchment of Cold War-era communication models and assumptions due to their perceived success in countering the threat posed by the Soviet Union (Simpson, 1996). U.S. agencies generally maintain risk-avoidant cultures that promote institutional inertia and the continued use of communication models developed for other times and contexts (Snow & Taylor, 2006). Second, private sector contractors stand to profit from officials' continued belief in the effectiveness of the message influence model. He who pays the piper calls the tune, and private sector contractors are rewarded for confirming officials' suppositions (Bean, 2011). Finally, as currently structured, U.S. strategic communication is fundamentally designed to influence, persuade, or coerce audiences—not allow for the dialogical transformation of the beliefs, interests, or actions of the speaker (Dutta-Bergman, 2006). This tension generates unique challenges in the context of U.S. national security affairs because it raises uncertainties about the legitimacy of speakers and speech acts, the role of cooperation and conflict in defining and solving security problems, and acceptable communication practices in relation to one's own values and beliefs (Comor & Bean, 2012). It follows that some scholars deride twenty-first-century U.S. strategic communication as a euphemism for propaganda in support of American imperialism (Hartnett & Goodale, 2008; Kumar, 2006, Snow, 2006). Skepticism of

U.S. government intentions often characterizes critical-cultural and rhetorical communication scholarship (Taylor & Harnett, 2000).

Critical-Cultural and Rhetorical Perspectives

Critical-cultural and rhetorical perspectives eschew the pursuit of a conceptualization of strategic communication that excludes its propagandistic tendencies, which include simplification, hostility, emotional manipulation, omission, and deception (Arthos, 2013). These perspectives also move beyond a simple message influence model, a model that only serves to blind message senders to the limits of intentionality (Heath & Feldwick, 2008). Instead, these perspectives challenge taken-for-granted assumptions about communication, as well as the roles of and relationships among U.S. government agencies, academic institutions, private sector enterprises, citizens, and foreign audiences.

"Critical" refers to studies where issues of power and politics are fundamental to the questions that scholars investigate. "Cultural" refers to how signs and symbols serve as both the means and medium for the generation of meaning. This is the site where power is achieved in the flow of speech and interaction, and where ideas become legitimate, justified, and binding (Barker, 2002). "Rhetorical" refers to studies that explore how shared values and ways of communicating construct, sustain, or transform the meanings of objects and concepts within communities of interest (Foss, 2004; Phillips & Hardy, 2002). Objects of study can include speech or writing, audio or video, art, or almost any type of media in cases where an object (or "artifact") is thought to contain narratives, metaphors, arguments, affects, or other units of rhetorical analysis (Foss, 2004). As Barbara Warnick (2002) explains, "[Rhetoric] focuses on making the invisible (what is transparent and unnoticed) visible" (p. 7). It does this by focusing on the interconnections among rhetors, audiences, situations, and messages. Critical-cultural and rhetorical research assists scholars in viewing uncertainty as a *productive* research outcome, as well as helps educate publics on issues of ethics, accountability, and the liberty/security tradeoff (Bean, 2013).

In the context of U.S. strategic communication, a critical-cultural perspective maintains that policy and practice can in no way be isolated from the dominant social, economic, and political order. Critical-cultural studies of U.S. strategic communication in this vein certainly are not new; "renegade" scholars have offered critiques for more than fifty years (Winseck, 2008, p. 420; Ellul, 1965; Herman & Chomsky, 1988; Smythe, 1981; Schiller, 1969). At one level, the tension between America's democratic ideals and its practical security objectives may be irresoluble (Ivie, 2005; Weinberg & Ben Dor, 2005). A new agenda, however, takes seriously the ideals of dialogue and co-creation in relation to institutional practice (Zaharna, 2010). By entering into dialogue and co-creational activities with multiple and diverse stakeholders, U.S. officials' potentially deepen their sense of empathy, responsibility, accountability, and discomfort with the status quo. Critical-cultural and rhetorical scholarship in this vein aims to make a difference by influencing stakeholders who can formulate, conduct, or shape U.S. strategic communication policy and practice (Seeger, 2009).

Agendas Old and New

Undergirded by the message influence model, the "old" agenda involves an approach to strategic communication that emphasizes core values of *efficiency* and *effectiveness* in support of status quo interests and policies. This approach's chief activities include *informing* and *persuading*, and achieving objectives requires *consensus, coordination,* and *consistency* (Paul, 2011a). At root, the old agenda is obsessed with *control*. This agenda is often accompanied by a rhetoric that extolls the virtues of dialogue among stakeholders while leaving the foundational premises of communication-as-domination intact. A representative example of this dualistic rhetoric comes from Paul (2011b), who stated:

> I have a vision of what successful strategic communication would look like. In this vision, we have clearly stated national objectives, which contain nested subordinate objectives, which contain nested intermediate or supporting objectives, nesting all the way down to the operational and tactical level. These clear statements make it easy to see which objectives can be realized through influence or persuasion, and which can be supported through such efforts . . . . In this vision communication is not just one-way broadcast, but is true two-way communication, engagement, or dialogue. In my vision this leads to policies shaped with our own interests as well as the interests and preferences of others in mind. (p. 14)

In principle, Paul's vision permits consideration of the interests and preferences of others. In translating principles into practices, however, Paul does not explain how the voices of others might *actually* be heard, assessed, and addressed in support of what he calls "true engagement" (p. 16). In fact, Paul undermines his own stated vision by allowing engagement to comingle with outright deception. He argued:

> If we must retain 'black' information capabilities (and I accept that there are compelling arguments for doing so), carve them off and sequester them from other sources of messages and signals. Do not have the same organizations and personnel conducting both truth-based and false messaging. Retain some kind of conduit or connection between those who deceive and manipulate and the rest of the communication community for deconfliction and coordination purposes, but keep such 'black' information capabilities small and away from the light. (2011b, p. 17)

Paul simultaneously bemoans and accepts the inevitability of deception within U.S. strategic communication practice—a situation that is not much different from the views expressed by Americans writ large. As Timothy Melley explains in *The Covert Sphere: Secrecy, Fiction, and the National Security State* (2012), citizens already presume the existence of (and repress knowledge of) the state's anti-democratic and unethical activities. From this perspective, "true engagement" is rhetorical; it is a concept designed to allow a speaker to symbolically embrace the ideals of dialogic communication in order to reduce that speaker's discomfort with the state's presumed use of propaganda and psychological warfare. Confirmation of the use of such techniques occasionally surface in the public domain, as when the press recently reported that the U.S. Army had ordered a team of soldiers specializing in psychological operations to manipulate U.S. senators into providing more troops and funding for war efforts (Hastings, 2011).[3]

A number of studies have illuminated the hypocritical propensities of twenty-first-century U.S. strategic communication (Dutta-Bergman, 2006; Hartnett & Goodale, 2008; Kumar, 2006; Snow & Taylor, 2006; Winseck, 2008). But instead of categorizing these studies as "new," I view these studies as representing the flipside of the "old" agenda. These studies generally oppose the secrecy and duplicity of U.S. strategic communication in ways that are reminiscent of earlier "renegade" scholarship. For example, Mohan Dutta-Bergman (2006) used the theory of communicative action to interrogate the long history of U.S. public diplomacy efforts in the Middle East. Dutta-Bergman found that "[a]fter more than five decades, the U.S. public diplomacy strategies reflect the same one-way flow of communication intended to convince publics in the Middle East of the virtues of the United States via information and entertainment programs" (p. 113). Dutta-Bergman concluded that, in the absence of meaningful, cultural dialogue and deliberation between U.S. and Middle Eastern message senders and receivers, public diplomacy efforts would continue to foster mutual mistrust and misunderstanding. However, Deepa Kumar (2006) observed that the development of such dialogue and deliberation was highly unlikely in an environment in which U.S. mainstream media generally were "complicit" with the objectives of the military–industrial complex (p. 64). As a result, Kumar called upon "dissenting voices in the academy" to produce "scholarship critical of the new imperialism" (p. 66).

Taking up Kumar's call, in "The Demise of Democratic Deliberation: The Defense Science Board, The Military–Industrial Complex, and The Production of Imperial Propaganda," Stephen John Hartnett and Greg Goodale (2008) argued:

> DSB's function has always been rhetorical. Indeed, because the DSB was founded to fulfill imperial functions in a way that appeared to honor the norms of democratic deliberation, even while burying them under

a barrage of Cold War subterfuge, the DSB stands among our nation's largely unseen but perpetually important forces shaping public arguments about U.S. foreign policy. (p. 12)

Hartnett and Goodale interpreted the recommendations contained in the DSB's *Strategic Communication* report as a call for a "revamped propaganda machine" (p. 22), and they too urged scholars to focus "attention on the DSB and the other military-industrial complex institutions charged with planning the empire" (p. 31). They argued that "democratic deliberation-destroying secrecy" jeopardized the nation's "best interests," and they advocated deliberation of the "decision-making process of the military-industrial complex" (p. 30). Likewise, in "The Revival of the Propaganda State: U.S. Propaganda at Home and Abroad since 9/11," Nancy Snow and Philip Taylor (2006) offered numerous examples of policies and programs that demonstrated how U.S. strategic communication relied upon an outdated Cold War-era philosophy that presumed that officials could successfully separate words from deeds in efforts to win "global hearts and minds" (p. 406; see also Snow, 2002, 2004, 2006). Connecting Hartnett, Goodale, Snow, and Taylor is the belief that improving America's image abroad requires strengthening democratic institutions and deliberation at home. "[T]he real challenge in the global struggle for hearts and minds" Snow and Taylor concluded, "is that in the process of selling democracy, you do not sell it out" (p. 406). Agreeing with Hartnett, Goodale, Snow, and Taylor, Winseck (2008) concluded that current trends "could erode the legitimacy of government, the media and democracy itself even further" (p. 437).

These studies usefully scrutinize some of the core assumptions and practices of twenty-first-century U.S. strategic communication. However, while these studies imply that institutional processes are antithetical to democratic deliberation, they do not clearly state what democratic deliberation ought to look like in the context of U.S. national security affairs. Since the earliest days of the republic, democratic deliberation has been a vague influence on national security policy development, and legislators have consistently given the president wide latitude to conduct foreign affairs (Zegart, 1999, 2011). It was only in the early twentieth century, with the simultaneous development of both public opinion polling and the field of public relations, that the belief that "there are things about which people can and should have opinions" gained currency (Olcott, 2013, p. 158). Despite the overall enlargement of democratic deliberation within the United States, a relatively small, interconnected group of technocratic elites has continued to dominate U.S. national security policy formation (Rothkopf, 2004). Therefore, most critiques of U.S. strategic communication have less to do with *preserving* a sense of democratic deliberation in the national security arena and more to do with *advocating* for one. Certainly, the assumption that opening up U.S. strategic communication policy to public scrutiny and deliberation would radically transform its underlying premises and objectives, or lead to better outcomes, requires more empirical support. Nevertheless, the development of dialogic and co-creational activities within U.S. national security affairs is an alluring proposition for researchers who share the commitments of critical-cultural and rhetorical scholarship.

A New Agenda

Using critical-cultural and rhetorical inquiry to reduce the metric distance between the ideals of democratic communication and the state's actual strategic communication practices is a goal of the "new" agenda of strategic communication research. H. L. Goodall, Jr. (2005) explained how misguided U.S. strategic communication efforts in the War on Terror served as the catalyst of this new agenda:

> We must begin now to combine the tools of academic critique with practical political action. And our political action should redirect our efforts away from resistance to full-partner participation in the communication and intercultural work that must be done if we are to be successful in reestablishing the image of America as a good thing, a positive force, in the world. (p. 21)

Scholarship produced by or in association with Arizona State University's CSC (Center for Strategic Communication), formed in 2005, exemplifies a move toward this new agenda (Bernardi, Cheong, Lundry, & Ruston, 2012; Corman, 2011; Corman et al., 2008; Halverson, Goodall, & Corman, 2011). Corman, Trethewey, and Goodall (2008) elaborated their perspective:

> As academics, we all firmly believe that critique is critical to understanding, and that theoretical advancements are built upon a solid foundation of criticism of existing ways of thinking. But we were also aware of the vast gap between academic critiques of the global war on terror and the practical considerations concerning communication practices of those charged with waging it. We hoped that our white papers would find an audience among the latter group and that from that prose introduction we would engage in some productive conversations aimed at changing the present course of applied communication in the global war of ideas. (p. viii)

For these scholars, moving beyond the legacy of the renegade scholars' vociferous critiques was necessary for productive institutional engagement and transformation. In *Weapons of Mass Persuasion: Strategic Communication in the Struggle Against Violent Extremism*, the authors noted that their work was "designed to reach broader public audiences, decision makers, and policy groups without giving up the cultural and critical foundations central to our scholarship" (p. ix).

"Critical foundations" are evident in a number of studies from CSC-affiliated researchers. For example, in "A 21st Century Model for Communication in the Global War of Ideas," Corman, Trethewey, and Goodall (2007) did not hesitate to call U.S. strategic communication "dysfunctional" and argued that it has "diminished [our] status among world opinion leaders and further[ed] the recruitment goals of violent extremists" (p. 2). But instead of asserting the need for tighter message control, the authors explored the productivity of acknowledging the fallibility of the United States' policies. "For instance," they stated, "rather than always promoting the virtues of democracy, the United States might try messages that discuss its problems and invite comparison of these faults to the problems of other forms of government" (p. 13). The authors urged officials to "deemphasize control and embrace complexity, replace repetition of messages with experimental variation, consider moves that will disrupt the existing system, and make contingency plans for failure" (p. 15).

In "The War of Ideas and the Battle of Narratives: A Comparison of Extremist Storytelling Structures," Furlow and Goodall (2011) acknowledged that extremism is found among groups in the Middle East, Asia, North Africa, Europe, *and* the United States. The authors argued that extremist narratives, whether at home or abroad, possess great similarities. Analysis of the structure of those narratives, they claimed, could help answer "questions about the relationship of words to violence" (p. 216). They found that extremists usually construct a core narrative that "posits a world in chaos and disorder that must be set right again by political action inspired and ordained by the divine" (p. 221). This narrative trajectory "begins with a desire to set right the world," and can only be resolved "by a hero who moves the action from the story line to the streets" (p. 221). Other examples of CSC scholarship move from analysis of extremist narratives to strategies to counteract their potency. For example, Goodall, Cheong, Fleischer, and Corman (2012) examined the "promise and pitfalls of humor and ridicule" as a tactic for combating extremism (p. 70). Focusing on language and/or images designed to "provoke laughter, disrupt ordinary arguments, and counter taken-for-granted truths," Goodall et al. found that deploying such "rhetorical charms" could undermine extremist ideology, but they also cautioned that such tactics could backfire among certain audiences (p. 70).

Not all CSC-affiliated scholarship emphasizes critical-cultural or rhetorical perspectives. For example, the Defense Advanced Research Projects Agency (DARPA)-sponsored "Toward Narrative Disruptors and Inductors: Mapping the Narrative Comprehension Network and its Persuasive Effects," employs multi-modal neuroimaging and evokes images of Cold War-era mind science. CSC-affiliated researchers also tend to not assert the need for increased democratic deliberation, dialogue, or cocreational activities to the same extent as their "renegade" colleagues. One of the main differences that distinguishes CSC-affiliated research from the harsher indictments of U.S. strategic communication cited herein is that the former acknowledges that some individuals and groups will not be interested in anything less than the destruction of the U.S. government and/or the death of U.S. citizens and allies: "For these others, only continued use of military solutions will bring a resolution of our differences. That is unfortunate, but it is also true" (Corman et al., 2008, p. x).

Despite the probable accuracy of this assessment, it is crucial that scholars continually reconsider how the category of "terrorist" is rhetorically constructed, maintained, or transformed (Puar, 2007). However, in sum, CSC-affiliated scholars' commitment to critical-cultural and rhetorical perspectives, institutional transformation, and audience-centered paradigms represents a move toward a new agenda of strategic communication research. Advancing this new agenda even further entails combining CSC's commitment to institutional engagement with a commitment to exploring the benefits of and possibilities for democratic deliberation, dialogue, and cocreational activities with U.S. national security affairs.

Intersections

Toward this end, my research program strives to exemplify how communication scholars might productively work at the intersection of communication, organization, and security. Within this overall framework, my approach to the study of strategic communication aligns with many of the examples of critical-cultural and rhetorical scholarship cited in this chapter. My own agenda, however, differs from CSC's because it involves a more inward-looking focus on institutional discourse, power, and change, as well as more a more explicit investigation of the possibilities for deliberative, dialogic, and cocreational activities within U.S. national security affairs.

For example, in an article for *International Communication Gazette*, Edward Comor and I critiqued what we termed "America's 'Engagement' Delusion" (Comor & Bean, 2012). The Obama administration initially embraced "engagement" as the dominant concept informing U.S. public diplomacy (White House, 2010). Yet, despite its emphasis on facilitating dialogue with and among Muslims overseas, we demonstrated that, in practice, engagement employed social media technologies to persuade skeptical audiences to empathize with U.S. policies. This engagement, we argued, actually perpetuated the communication-as-dominance underpinnings of U.S. strategic communication. We showed that this public diplomacy strategy was both contradictory and, ultimately, delusional.

While such a harsh assessment might seem at odds with a commitment to institutional transformation, we proposed an ethical public diplomacy that embraced genuine (rather than contrived) dialogue. Following Heath, Toth, and Waymer (2009), we claimed that an ethical communication strategy maintains that people have the right and prospective ability to obtain and judge messages and make decisions that affect them. This commitment requires that strategic communicators must be good listeners who sincerely want "to know, appreciate, and respect what others believe and think—and why they hold those positions" (Heath, 2009, p. 19). This commitment, however, also requires entering into dialogue and debate to enact the democratic process. It "presumes that any position voiced in public must be sufficiently compelling to withstand vigorous critiques by other [speakers] who believe their compelling ideas have merit" (p. 21). Thus, we argued that transforming America's persistently negative image in the Middle East should begin with an honest analysis of history and structural conditions, rather than a retooling of ineffective strategic communication messages.

Along these lines, at a 2014 conference on "International Educational Exchange and the Promotion of Peace, Development, and Intercultural Understanding" held in Ankara, Turkey, I argued that educational exchange evaluation at the U.S. Department of State's Bureau of Educational and Cultural Affairs aims to prove to funders that programs bolster America's positive image and reputation. While an implicit objective of educational exchange is for foreign participants to become more accommodating, understanding, or supportive of U.S. economic, political, social, or technological interests, values, and aims, rarely is it suggested that the values of others might inform how Americans view and conduct themselves in a globalized world. If educational exchange is evaluated using such limited snapshots that overwhelmingly showcase positive benefits, officials could be hindered in their ability to even recognize the ways that educational exchange might in some cases inadvertently contribute to negative international sentiment or political extremism.

Such analysis has influenced academic debates (Hayden, 2013), but like CSC researchers, I have hoped that U.S. officials would consider the implications of these critiques in relation to actual policy. It is significant that at the end of 2013, the word "engagement" was removed from one of the U.S. State Department's definitions of public diplomacy (John Brown's Notes and Essays, 2013, para. 1). Thus, critical-cultural and rhetorical perspectives can inform and influence U.S. strategic communication.

Conclusion

A goal of critical-cultural and rhetorical scholarship should be to square U.S. strategic communication policy with the ideals of democracy, dialogue, and co-creation. As this chapter has indicated, some scholars find U.S. strategic communication and democracy incompatible, while others see opportunities—however delicate—for reconciliation. Opportunities abound for scholars interested in developing critical-cultural and rhetorical studies of strategic communication. This chapter has suggested a few: A new agenda involves a more explicit move toward institutional engagement—an approach that is usually absent from the large body of work critical of U.S. imperialism. For CSC-affiliated scholars, future research priorities include investigating strategic communication in relation to domestic terrorism threats, state-state conflicts, health and public safety, and risk and crisis communication. Critical-cultural and rhetorical work, however, offers scholars considerable insights concerning the historical and structural premises, drivers, and consequences of strategic communication. Critique remains a—if not *the*—core task of critical-cultural and rhetorical scholarship. Nevertheless, more work is needed to understand the actual and potential role and shape of democratic deliberation, dialogue, and co-creation in relation to national security strategy and communication. Without compelling alternatives to the status quo, institutional change will remain difficult to achieve.

With transformation in mind, the influence of commercial imperatives in an increasingly privatized U.S. strategic communication sector also requires more scrutiny. The door between government and industry is a revolving one. It is no secret that some commercial enterprises employ personnel trained in psychological warfare—the militarization of community relations efforts by the U.S. natural gas industry being a recent high-profile example (Javers, 2011). Thus, even as dialogic and cocreational communication models gain more institutional advocates, scholars would do well to track the lingering influence of the message influence model. Dialogue should not be used as a mere buzzword to make message influence campaigns more appealing. Commitment to a critical impulse can and should encompass critique of both U.S. adversaries *and* misguided institutional practices. Institutional actors not only undertake strategic communication campaigns designed to influence foreign audiences, U.S. policymakers, officials, and citizens are audiences for institutional messages as well (Mitchell, 2000, 2006), and critical-cultural and rhetorical analysis of internal communication is needed.

Finally, this chapter has focused on U.S. national security; however, strategic communication is a global phenomenon, and similar to the trend in public diplomacy research (Hayden, 2012), international perspectives should be cultivated (McKie & Munshi, 2007). Developments in "prosumption," "transmediation," and resistance impact strategic communicators globally. Prosumption refers to the trend of media consumers simultaneously serving as media producers, while transmediation refers to the additive and iterative forms of media generated when audiences appropriate or resist messages to create new texts. As Pauline Hope Cheong and Chris Lundry (2012) note, these trends are rapidly undermining "the stratagems of the state to control their communication outreach and corresponding symbolic battlefield of ideas" (p. 489). Gordon Mitchell (2002) notes that such technological trends are giving rise to new forms of argumentation with "potential to shape events in ways that are only beginning to be understood" (p. 69). Given such conditions, the accelerated development of critical-cultural and rhetorical perspectives is an agenda worth pursuing—urgently.

Notes

1 Scholarship reviewed in this chapter was identified using databases including Communication and Mass Media Complete and Google Scholar and keyword combinations including "strategic communication," "security," and "propaganda." Those texts' citations were, in turn, scrutinized for additional, relevant materials.
2 The DSB is a committee of up to 45 civilian experts appointed to advise the DoD on various scientific and technical matters.
3 While current U.S. propaganda materials are occasionally exposed as such, institutional secrecy makes them difficult to verify. The National Security Archive at George Washington University maintains an extensive collection of historical U.S. propaganda documents.

References

Aftergood, S. (2010, January 19). DoD "clarifies" doctrine on psychological operations. *Secrecy News*. Retrieved from http://blogs.fas.org/secrecy/2010/01/psyop/

Arce, A., Butler, D., & Gillum, J. (2014, April 3). U.S. secretly created "Cuban Twitter" to stir unrest. *Washington Post*. Retrieved from http://www.washingtonpost.com/politics/us-secretly-created-cuban-twitter-to-stir-unrest/2014/04/03/8a2dc77c-bafa-11e3-80de-2ff8801f27af_story.html

Arndt, R. T. (2005). *The first resort of kings*. Dulles, VA: Potomac Books.

Arquilla, J., & Borer, D. A. (Eds.). (2007). *Information strategy and warfare: A guide to theory and practice*. New York: Routledge.

Arthos, J. (2013). The just use of propaganda (?): Ethical criteria for counter-hegemonic communication strategies. *Western Journal of Communication*, 77, 582–603. doi:10.1080/10570314.2013.785014

Barker, C. (2002). *Making sense of cultural studies: Central problems and critical debates*. Thousand Oaks, CA: Sage.

BBC. (2007, January 23). View of US's global role "worse." Retrieved from http://news.bbc.co.uk/2/hi/americas/6286755.stm

BBC. (2010, April 19). Global views of United States improve while other countries decline. Retrieved from http://www.bbc.co.uk/pressoffice/pressreleases/stories/2010/04_april/19/poll.shtml

Bean, H. (2011). *No more secrets: Open source information and the reshaping of U.S. intelligence*. Santa Monica, CA: Praeger.

Bean, H. (2013). Rhetorical and critical/cultural intelligence studies. *Intelligence and National Security*, 28, 495–519. doi:10.1080/02684527.2012.699284

Bernardi, D. L., Cheong, P. H., Lundry, C., & Ruston, S. W. (2012). *Narrative landmines: Rumors, Islamist extremism, and the struggle for strategic influence*. New Brunswick, NJ: Rutgers University Press.

Bockstette, C. (2010). *Jihadist terrorist use of strategic communication management techniques*. Darby, PA: Diane Publishing Co.

Botan, C. H., & Taylor, M. (2004). Public relations: State of the field. *Journal of Communication*, 54, 645–661. doi:10.1111/j.1460-2466.2004.tb02649.x

Burke, D. (2013, October 28). Terrorist attacks and deaths hit record high, report shows. *CNN Belief Blog*. Retrieved from http://religion.blogs.cnn.com/2013/10/28/terrorist-attacks-and-deaths-hit-record-high-report-shows/

Center for Strategic Counterterrorism Communications. (2013). Center for Strategic Counterterrorism Communications. Retrieved from http://www.state.gov/r/cscc/

Cheong, P. H., & Lundry, C. (2012). Prosumption, transmediation and resistance: Terrorism and man-hunting in Southeast Asia. *American Behavioral Scientist, 56*, 488–510. doi: 10.1177/0002764211429365

Cioppa, T. M. (2009). Operation Iraqi Freedom strategic communication analysis and assessment. *Media, War & Conflict, 2*, 25–45. doi: 10.1177/1750635208101353

Comor, E., & Bean, H. (2012). America's "engagement" delusion: Critiquing a public diplomacy consensus. *International Communication Gazette, 74*, 203–220. doi: 10.1177/1748048511432603

Corman, S. R. (2011). Understanding the role of narrative in extremist strategic communication. In L. Fenstermacher & S. Canna (Eds.), *Countering violent extremism: Scientific methods and strategies* (pp. 36–43). Dayton, OH: Air Force Research Laboratory.

Corman, S. R., Trethewey, A., & Goodall Jr., H. L. (2007). A 21st century model for communication in the global war of ideas. Retrieved from http://csc.asu.edu/wp-content/uploads/pdf/114.pdf

Corman, S. R., Trethewey, A., & Goodall Jr., H. L. (Eds.). (2008). *Weapons of mass persuasion: Strategic communication to combat violent extremism*. New York: Peter Lang.

Creel, G. (1920). *How we advertised America: The first telling of the amazing story of the Committee on Public Information that carried the gospel of Americanism to every corner of the globe*. New York: Harper & Brothers.

Cull, N., Culbert, D., & Welch, D. (2003). *Propaganda and mass persuasion: A historical encyclopedia, 1500 to the present*. Santa Barbara, CA: ABC–CLIO.

Dimitriu, G. R. (2012). Winning the story war: Strategic communication and the conflict in Afghanistan. *Public Relations Review, 38*, 195–207. Retrieved from http://dx.doi.org/10.1016/j.pubrev.2011.11.011

Dutta-Bergman, M. J. (2006). U.S. public diplomacy in the Middle East: A critical-cultural approach. *Journal of Communication Inquiry, 30*, 102–124. doi: 10.1177/0196859905285286

Ellul, J. (1965). *Propaganda: The formation of men's attitudes*. New York: Knopf.

Farwell, J. P. (2012). *Persuasion and power: The art of strategic communication*. Washington, DC: Georgetown University Press.

Fernandez, A. (2013, December 10). Remarks, Alberto Fernandez, Coordinator for the Center for Strategic Counterterrorism Communications. Terrorist, regime, and western media: The war of ideas in the disinformation age. Conference at the Newseum. Washington DC. Retrieved from http://www.state.gov/r/cscc/releases/218606.htm

Forest, J. J. (2009). *Influence warfare: How terrorists and governments fight to shape perceptions in a war of ideas*. Santa Barbara, CA: Praeger.

Foss, S. K. (2004). *Rhetorical criticism: Exploration and practice* (3rd ed.). Long Grove, IL: Waveland Press.

Fullerton, J. A., & Kendrick, A. (2006). *Advertising's war on terrorism: The story of the U.S. State Department's shared values initiative*. Spokane, WA: Marquette Books.

Furlow, R. B., & Goodall, Jr., H. L. (2011). The war of ideas and the battle of narratives: A comparison of extremist storytelling structures. *Cultural Studies—Critical Methodologies, 11*, 215–223. doi: 10.1177/1532708611409530

Gregory, B. (2008). Public diplomacy: Sunrise of an academic field. *The ANNALS of the American Academy of Political and Social Science, 616*, 274–290. doi: 10.1177/0002716207311723

Goodall, Jr., H. L. (2005). Qualitative inquiry and the war on terror, or: How I learned to give up my liberal biases and accept personal responsibility for the consequences of official U.S. government messages policies and narratives. Paper presented at the

First International Congress of Qualitative Inquiry. University of Illinois, Urbana-Champaign, IL, May 5–7. Retrieved from http://www.iiqi.org/C4QI/httpdocs/qi2005/papers/goodal.pdf

Goodall, Jr., H. L., Cheong, P. H., Fleischer, K., & Corman, S. R. (2012). Rhetorical charms: The promise and pitfalls of humor and ridicule as strategies to counter extremist narratives. *Perspectives on Terrorism*, *6*, 70–79. Retrieved from http://www.terrorismanalysts.com/pt/index.php/pot/article/view/goodall-et-al-rhetorical/html

Hallahan, K., Holtzhausen, D., Van Ruler, B., Verčič, D., & Sriramesh, K. (2007). Defining strategic communication. *International Journal of Strategic Communication*, *1*, 3–35. doi: 10.1080/15531180701285244

Halverson, J. R., Goodall, H. L., Jr., & Corman, S. R. (2011). *Master narratives of Islamist extremism*. Basingstoke, UK: Palgrave Macmillan.

Hartnett, S. J., & Goodale, G. (2008). The demise of democratic deliberation: The Defense Science Board, the military–industrial complex, and the production of imperial propaganda. In D. Timmerman & T. McDorman (Eds.), *Rhetoric and democracy: Pedagogical and political practices* (pp. 181–224). East Lansing: Michigan State University Press.

Hastings, M. (2011, February 23). Another runaway general: Army deploys psy-ops on U.S. senators. *Rolling Stone*. Retrieved from http://www.rollingstone.com/politics/news/another-runaway-general-army-deploys-psy-ops-on-u-s-senators-20110223

Hayden, C. (2012). *The rhetoric of soft power: Public diplomacy in global contexts*. Lanham, MD: Lexington Books.

Hayden, C. (2013). Logics of narrative and networks in U.S. public diplomacy: Communication power and U.S. strategic engagement. *Journal of International Communication*, *19*, 196–218. doi: 10.1080/13216597.2013.775070

Heath, R. L. (2009). The rhetorical tradition: Wrangle in the marketplace. In R. L. Heath, E. L. Toth, & D. Waymer (Eds.), *Rhetorical and critical-cultural approaches to public relations II* (pp. 17–47). New York: Routledge.

Heath, R. L., & Feldwick, P. (2008). Fifty years using the wrong model of advertising. *International Journal of Market Research*, *50*, 29–59. Retrieved from https://www.mrs.org.uk/ijmr_article/article/87203

Heath, R. L., Toth E. L., & Waymer, D. (Eds.). (2009). *Rhetorical and critical-cultural approaches to public relations II*. New York: Routledge.

Herman, E., & Chomsky, N. (1988). *The manufacture of consent*. New York: Pantheon.

Ivie, R. L. (2005). *Democracy and America's war on terror*. Tuscaloosa, AL: University of Alabama Press.

Javers, E. (2011, November 8). Oil executive: Military-style "psy ops" experience applied. *CNBC*. Retrieved from http://www.cnbc.com/id/45208498

John Browns Note's and Essays. (2013, December 21). "Engaging" seems to have disappeared from one of the State Department's definitions of public diplomacy. Retrieved from http://johnbrownnotesandessays.blogspot.com/2013/12/engaging-seems-to-have-disappeared-from.html

Kamalipour, Y. R., & Snow, N. (2004). *War, media, and propaganda: A global perspective*. Oxford: Rowman & Littlefield.

Kent, M. L., & Taylor, M. (2002). Toward a dialogic theory of public relations. *Public Relations Review*, *28*, 21–37. doi: 10.1016/S0363-8111(02)00108-X

Kierman, R. (2013, June 24). BBC poll: World's opinion of U.S. lowest since Bush presidency. *CNSNews.com*. Retrieved from http://cnsnews.com/news/article/bbc-poll-world-s-opinion-us-lowest-bush-presidency#sthash.Lvphh0Gr.dpuf

King, S. B. (2011). Military social influence in the global information environment: A civilian primer. *Analyses of Social Issues and Public Policy*, *11*, 1–26. doi: 10.1111/j.1530-2415.2010.01214.x

Kumar, D. (2006). Media, war, and propaganda: Strategies of information management during the 2003 Iraq war. *Communication and Critical/Cultural Studies*, *3*, 48–69. doi: 10.1080/14791420500505650

Locker, R. (2014, April 30). Special Operations wants help to see if propaganda works. *USA Today*. Retrieved from http://www.usatoday.com/story/nation/2014/01/16/socom-global-research-assessment-program/4523289/

Louw, E. P. (2003). The "war against terrorism": A public relations challenge for the Pentagon. *Gazette: The International Journal for Communication Studies*, *65*, 211–230. doi: 10.1177/0016549203065003001

McCants, W. (2012). Science and technology for communication and persuasion abroad: Gap analysis and survey. Retrieved from http://www.cna.org/research/2012/science-technology-communication-persuasion-abroad

McKie, D., & Munshi, D. (2007). *Reconfiguring public relations: Ecology, equity, and enterprise*. London: Routledge.

Melley, T. (2012). *The covert sphere: Secrecy, fiction, and the national security state*. Ithaca, NY: Cornell University Press.

Mitchell, G. R. (2000). *Strategic deception: Rhetoric, science, and politics in missile defense advocacy*. East Lansing, MI: Michigan State University Press.

Mitchell, G. R. (2002). Public argument-driven security studies. *Argumentation & Advocacy*, *39*, 57–71.

Mitchell, G. R. (2006). Team B intelligence coups. *Quarterly Journal of Speech*, *92*, 144–173. doi: 10.1080/00335630600817993

Moloney, K. (2006). *Rethinking public relations* (2nd ed.). New York: Routledge.

Mor, B. D. (2007). The rhetoric of public diplomacy and propaganda wars: A view from self-presentation theory. *European Journal of Political Research*, *46*(5), 661–683. doi: 10.1111/j.1475-6765.2007.00707.x

Munoz, A. (2012). U.S. military information operations in Afghanistan: Effectiveness of psychological operations 2001–2010. RAND. Retrieved from http://www.rand.org/pubs/monographs/MG1060.html

Nakamura, K. H., & Weed, M. C. (2009, December 18). U.S. public diplomacy: Background and current issues. *Congressional Research Service*. Retrieved from http://www.fas.org/sgp/crs/row/R40989.pdf

Nisbet, E. C., & Myers, T. (2011). Anti-American attitudes as a media effect? Arab media, political identity, and public opinion in the Middle East. *Communication Research*, *38*, 684–709 doi: 10.1177/0093650211405648

Nixon, R. (2014, April 25). U.S. says it built digital programs abroad with an eye to politics. *New York Times*. Retrieved from http://www.nytimes.com/2014/04/26/world/us-ran-social-media-programs-in-afghanistan-and-pakistan.html?_r=0

Olcott, A. (2013). What "white" propaganda can learn from "gray." In G. Dalziel (Ed.), *Rumor and communication in Asia in the internet age* (pp. 156–166). Abingdon, UK: Routledge.

Paul, C. (2011a). *Strategic communication: Origins, concepts, and current debates*. Santa Monica, CA: ABC-CLIO.

Paul, C. (2011b). Getting better at strategic communication. Testimony presented before the House Armed Services Committee, Subcommittee on Emerging Threats and Capabilities on July 12, 2011. Retrieved from http://armedservices.house.gov/index.cfm/files/serve?File_id=bc69c7a3-5641-4614-a647-ffc4e2d39357

Phillips, N., & Hardy, C. (2002). *Discourse analysis: Investigating processes of social construction*. Thousand Oaks, CA: Sage.

Puar, J. K. (2007). *Terrorist assemblages: Homonationalism in queer times*. Durham, NC: Duke University Press.

Regan, T. (2002, September 6). When contemplating war, beware of babies in incubators. *The Christian Science Monitor*. Retrieved from http://www.csmonitor.com/2002/0906/p25s02-cogn.html

Rothkopf, D. (2004). *Running the world: The inside story of the National Security Council and the architects of American power*. New York: Public Affairs.

Schiller, H. (1969). *Mass communications and American empire*. New York: A.M. Kelley.

Seeger, M. (2009). Does communication research make a difference: Reconsidering the impact of our work. *Communication Monographs, 76*, 12–19.

Signitzer, B., & Wamser, C. (2006). Public diplomacy: A specific governmental public relations function. In C. H. Botan & V. Hazleton (Eds.), *Public relations theory II* (pp. 435–464). New York: Routledge.

Simpson, C. (1996). *Science of coercion: Communication research and psychological warfare, 1945–1960*. Oxford: Oxford University Press.

Smythe, D. (1981). *Dependency road: Communications, capitalism, consciousness, and Canada*. Norwood, NJ: Ablex.

Snow, N. (2002). *Propaganda, Inc.* (2nd ed.). New York: Seven Stories Press.

Snow, N. (2004). *Information war*. New York: Seven Stories Press.

Snow, N. (2006). *The arrogance of American power*. Lanham, MD: Rowman & Littlefield.

Snow, N., & Taylor, P. M. (2006). The revival of the propaganda state: U.S. propaganda at home and abroad since 9/11. *International Communication Gazette, 68*, 389–407. doi: 10.1177/1748048506068718

Stokes, B. (2013, July 26). America's international image slipping. *CNN*. Retrieved from http://globalpublicsquare.blogs.cnn.com/2013/07/26/americas-international-image-slipping/

Taylor, B. C., & Harnett, S. J. (2000). "National security, and all that it implies . . .": Communication and (post-) cold war culture. *Quarterly Journal of Speech, 86*, 465–491. doi: 10.1080/00335630009384311

United States House Armed Services Sub-Committee on Evolving Threats and Capabilities. (2011). Ten years on: The evolution of strategic communication and information operations since 9/11. Retrieved from http://www.gpo.gov/fdsys/pkg/CHRG-112hhrg67796/pdf/CHRG-112hhrg67796.pdf

U.S. Department of State (2014). Bureau of Public Affairs. Retrieved from http://www.state.gov/r/pa/

USA Today (2012, December 3). Pentagon drops "strategic communication." Retrieved from http://www.usatoday.com/story/news/nation/2012/12/03/pentagon-trims-strategic-communication/1743485/

Vanden Brook, T. (2013, May 23). Report raps military propaganda efforts as ineffective. *USA Today*. Retrieved from http://www.usatoday.com/story/news/nation/2013/05/23/military-propaganda-operations-poorly-coordinated-often-ineffective/2354235/

Warnick, B. (2002). *Critical literacy in a digital era: Technology, rhetoric, and the public interest*. Mahwah, NJ: Lawrence Erlbaum.

Watts, D. J., & Dodds, P. S. (2007). Influentials, networks, and public opinion formation. *Journal of Consumer Research, 34*(4), 441–458.

Weinberg, L., & Ben Dor, G. (2005). Democracy and security: Introduction. *Democracy and Security, 1*, 1–3. doi: 10.1080/17419160500248548

White House. (2010). *National framework for strategic communication*. Retrieved from www.fas.org/man/eprint/pubdip.pdf

White House. (2012). *National framework for strategic communication*. Retrieved from http://mountainrunner.us/files/2012/03/President-response-to-NDAA-1055-of-2009.pdf

Whitlock, C. (2013, July 7). Somali American caught up in a shadowy Pentagon counter-propaganda campaign. *Washington Post*. Retrieved from http://www.washingtonpost.com/world/national-security/somali-american-caught-up-in-a-shadowy-pentagon-counterpropaganda-campaign/2013/07/07/b3aca190-d2c5-11e2-bc43-c404c3269c73_story.html

Winseck, D. (2008). Information operations "blowback": Communication, propaganda and surveillance in the global war on terrorism. *International Communication Gazette, 70*, 419–441. doi: 10.1177/1748048508096141

Wright, D. K., & Hinson, M. D. (2009). An updated look at the impact of social media on public relations practice. *Public Relations Journal, 3*(2), 1–27.

Zaharna, R. S. (2010). *Battles to bridges: US strategic communication and public diplomacy after 9/11*. New York: Palgrave Macmillan.

Zegart, A. B. (1999). *Flawed by design: The evolution of the CIA, JCS, and NSC*. Stanford, CA: Stanford University Press.

Zegart, A. B. (2011). *Eyes on spies: Congress and the United States intelligence community*. Stanford, CA: Hoover Institution Press.

Zhang, J. (2010). Exploring rhetoric of public diplomacy in the mixed-motive situation: Using the case of President Obama's "nuclear-free world" speech in Prague. *Place Branding and Public Diplomacy, 6*(4), 287–299. doi: 10.1057/pb.2010.31

7

MARKETER-CONSUMER LANGUAGE COOPERATION IN STRATEGIC COMMUNICATION

Ann Kronrod

Bill Barnes, one of the creators of www.unshelved.com, once said "It's not that we don't like ads, we just don't like ads when they are out of place." This memorable quote begs the question, "When are ads out of place and when are ads in place?" This chapter suggests that when marketers fail to be cooperative and do not provide ads that fit into consumers' expectations, these ads are "out of place" and consequently consumers react in a non-cooperative fashion against the ads, resulting in disliking, reactance and overall ineffectiveness of the ad. In this chapter, I describe how language is used pragmatically in strategic communication to achieve certain goals and how these language choices impact receivers of strategic communication. I will cite research that highlights language phenomena in marketing and advertising, and explain how the assumption of cooperation in natural conversation is translated into the field of strategic communication.

Conversational Cooperation—A Primer in the Philosophy of Language

What Is Linguistic Cooperation?

Looking to Grice's (1975) Cooperative Principle in Conversation, which serves as the conceptual foundation of this chapter, conversation can be seen as a means to achieve one's goal. In other words, when we have a goal that can be promoted by conversing with someone, we engage in a conversation in order to fulfill that goal (Austin, 1962). For example, when the goal is to learn the time, I may stop a passer-by and ask "What time is it, please?" Importantly, the way I phrase my request should be such that the passer-by would want to tell me the time, or at least engage in a conversation with me. Therefore I would make all efforts to be, what Grice (1975) calls "cooperative" in my language. The passer-by would also be "cooperative" within this conversation, if this conversation has potential to help her achieve her goal (e.g. she is in a hurry and the quickest way to keep on her way is to tell me the time). Thus, when conversation parties believe the conversation is a means to achieve a mutual goal (Grice, 1975, 1989) or separate goals (Austin 1962; Kasher, 1976, 1982), they will communicate with each other cooperatively in order for the conversation to succeed.

What does it mean, therefore, to be cooperative in a conversation? How is cooperation realized in the language behaviors of the conversational parties? Generally speaking, when communicating, a cooperative speaker would make all efforts to be understood and a cooperative hearer would make all efforts to understand the speaker (Grice 1975; Kasher 1982; Lumsden 2008). For the speaker, this effort is realized through making assumptions and inferences about the hearer, including previous knowledge, mutual knowledge, relationship hierarchy, contextual cues, theory of mind, etc. (Dumontheil, Küster, Apperly, & Blakemore, 2010; Lin, Keysar, & Epley, 2010; Searle 1969; Sperber & Wilson, 1986; Stemmer, 1994; Swinney, 1979). The hearer, in an effort to better understand the speaker, also makes assumptions and inferences about the speaker's intended meaning, relying on contextual cues, previous knowledge, etc. Moreover, both the speaker and the hearer hold a basic assumption about each other—the assumption that each conversation party is being cooperative in the conversation and will behave in a linguistically cooperative way, that is to make all efforts to understand and be understood. The assumption of cooperation is key to communication success, and has implications for the ensuing conversation.

The Linguistic Cooperation Assumption in Interpersonal Conversation

As mentioned, according to the Cooperation Principle (Grice, 1975; Levinson, 2000), normally in communication the speaker and the hearer assume that their party in conversation is being cooperative (otherwise why would they be engaged in conversation in the first place?). One of the ways to be cooperative is to adhere to certain accepted norms (Grice, 1975)—thus conversation parties expect each other to adhere to those norms. For example, when asking for the time, it is a norm to do it politely. If I address the passer-by with a phrase like "Tell me the time!" she would not only be surprised that I did not adhere to the politeness norm, but—being a cooperative conversation partner—she would look for a possible reason for this violation of the norms. In other words, she would try to find an intended meaning behind my impoliteness. Thus, *the search for an intended meaning is an integral part of conversational cooperation*. Speakers employ the cooperation assumption when choosing the language to employ in conversation. For example, when using irony (as in "you look so fresh this morning!") the speaker assumes that the hearer will figure out the intended meaning ("you look exhausted") based on contextual inferences, mutual knowledge, etc.

An example of speakers adhering to conversational (and cultural) norms is Caldwell-Harris, Kronrod, and Yang's (2013) work on the differences between Chinese and American cultures in the use of the phrase "I love you" (我爱你—"Wo ai ni" in Chinese). The authors find that generally young Americans say "I love you" significantly more often than young Chinese. Moreover, when asked about different ways of addressing others, American respondents reported more frequent use of "I love you" with parents, grandparents and siblings than with friends, whereas Chinese respondents reported significantly lower use of "I love you" with their family members, compared with friends. The authors suggest that the reason for this difference in language use is cultural-normative: being a low-context culture, American culture requires greater verbalization of feelings (Gudykunst et al., 1996; Hall, 1976; Lindholm, 1988, p. 232), whereas conversation in Chinese culture, being a high context culture (Gudykunst et al., 1996; Hall, 1976), is characterized by emotional verbal reticence (Fukuyama & Greenfield, 1983, p. 429; Kleinman, 1980), especially with authority figures (Fukuyama & Greenfield, 1983). Therefore young Chinese reported refraining from saying "I love you" to parents and grandparents, who are part of the Chinese traditional family hierarchy, but being more comfortable saying "I love you" to friends, who are not part of the traditional Chinese circle. Young Americans, adhering to the American communicational norm "If you don't say it, it isn't happening," reported generally saying "I love you" more frequently, but especially to closer family members such as parents and grandparents. Thus, communicational norms may govern cooperative speakers to use or refrain from using language in various social situations.[1]

At times, speakers do not employ the most direct phrasing of their intended meaning, and can veil their meaning in indirect language, which compels the listener to put forth additional effort to figure out the intended meaning. Literature suggests that considerations of a conversational effect that goes beyond the plain meaning may be one of the reasons for employing indirect language (e.g. Sperber & Wilson, 1986). For example, when saying to my friend, "You look fresh this morning!" but meaning "you look exhausted," I not only express my notice of my friend's physical state, but also contribute my *attitude* towards her exhaustion. What's more, by using indirect language I signal to my friend that our relationships are close enough for me to use indirect language and to trust my fellow to understand the intended meaning behind my ironic comment. Research suggests that a vast majority of conversations include the use and interpretation of indirect language (Lumsden, 2008). The assumption that the conversation parties will cooperate is the main reason for such prevalence of indirect language in conversations. Thus, the assumption for conversational cooperation is an inherent part of language use in interpersonal communication. Consider the following example:

A: "*Where is Jane?*"

B: "*She said her hair looks awful and that she needs new shoes.*"

On the face of it, B is not being cooperative because she is not answering A's question. But in fact, B is being very cooperative. She just makes a few extra-assumptions about what A knows and uses those assumptions to cooperatively contribute to the conversation. Here is a brief description of what happens in A's mind after hearing B's reply:

B said "she." Since I was talking about Jane, and B had no reason to change the subject, B probably means Jane when she says "she."

B did not say where Jane was, but contributed some information about what Jane had said, which can help me figure out where she is.

Based on what B said, Jane may be either at the hairstyle salon, or at the shoe store.

Why didn't B directly say that Jane is there? Well, probably because B is not sure about that and wanted me to know that she wasn't sure.

This long processing description is actually automatic and happens within milliseconds in our brain as part of our language comprehension system. The bottom line of this process, though, is that B not only answered A's question, but also signaled by her indirect answer that she is not quite sure where Jane is, and that she can only conclude about Jane's whereabouts from what Jane had said. Thus, B is being exceptionally cooperative in this conversation, even though her answer is seemingly irrelevant to A's question.

Now, consider another example: an ad for *The Economist* magazine, reads: "*Great minds like a think.*" The phrase is unusual, because it is both grammatically flawed and a variation on the saying "Great minds think alike." The phrase is therefore violating conversational norms. Is this an example of non-cooperative communication? In fact, this phrase is super-cooperative, because it not only suggests that clever people like to think, but also that the readers of *The Economist* are clever people, and that the magazine *appreciates it*. The magazine chose a clever way to show this: understanding and appreciating this word play requires some extra thought, which is exactly what clever people presumably like to do. So the phrase, by its very essence, suggests that it is meant for people who like reading this kind of phrase, and who would understand it. This is an example of the cooperation assumption realized in strategic communication.

I will next elaborate on the similarities and differences in the cooperation assumption between interpersonal and strategic communication.

Conversational Cooperation Assumption in Strategic Communication

Basic Differences Between Strategic and Natural Communication

Many strategic communication instances are based on the goal to persuade (Cialdini, 2004; Cook, 2001). Research on interpersonal communication suggests adherence to conversational norms leads to more persuasive communications (Brown and Levinson, 1987; Burgoon and Aho, 1982; Gibbs, 1985; Grice, 1975). For example, Xu and Wyer (2010) find that message effectiveness suffers when the language of a product description does not fit the media in which it appears (popular vs. professional magazine). This implies that strategic communication may have different conversational assumptions, compared with interpersonal communication. Kronrod and Danziger (2013) suggest a number of differences in the communicational expectations between interpersonal and strategic communication. First, interpersonal communication is typically perceived to be objective (Sen & Lerman, 2007), as well as, natural and spontaneous (Moore, 2012; Schellekens, Verlegh, & Smidts, 2010; Sen & Lerman, 2007). Conversely, strategic communication is perceived as a biased, professionally pre-planned mass communication (Sweldens, Van Osselaer, & Janiszewski, 2010). Therefore the conversational norms for persuasive communication may include expectations of the audience for higher use of rhetoric linguistic tactics. This may in some way resemble our expectations of art to include tactics that intensify the emotional and perceptual effect on receivers (Hahn, 2009; Murken-Altrogge, 1978; Spitzer, 1978). For example, it is a norm that strategic communication is exaggerated and emotionally intensified (Campbell & Kirmani, 2000; Rotfeld & Rotzoll, 1980; Simonson & Holbrook, 1993; Toncar & Fetscherin, 2012; Xu & Wyer, 2010). However, the mere existence of different norms for strategic versus interpersonal communication does not necessarily undermine the assumption for conversational cooperation in either of the contexts. In the following section I will describe and exemplify the idea that consumers and marketers hold a *conversation* between them, which is governed by expectations for *conversational cooperation*.

Is Conversational Cooperation Assumed in Strategic Communication?

Literature on persuasion knowledge (e.g. Ahluwalia & Burnkrant, 2004; Campbell & Kirmani, 2000; Friestad & Wright, 1994; McAlister & Cornwell, 2009) suggests that consumers hold assumptions about marketing communicators' motives in most instances of marketer-consumer communication. For example, consumers use what they assume about the intended meaning behind marketers' communication in order to form attitudes towards products (Friestad & Wright, 1994). I suggest that assumptions such as persuasion knowledge are representations of conversational cooperation: although marketers and consumers have different goals (marketers hold the purpose of persuading, whereas consumers have the goal of making the right consumption decisions), for both parties the moment of the conversation between them is a means to achieve their goals. To that end, a consumer may perceive a marketer's communication about a product to be largely irrelevant to his consumption decisions about this product, and prefer to base himself on communication from his friends, on online reviews or other information. But even in this case, both parties (consumer and marketer) would be cooperative in this "conversation," making assumptions and inferences in order to use this conversation to best serve their ends. This would be defined as communicational cooperation, and this cooperation manifests itself in the language marketers use, and in the way consumers interpret this communication. In the following section I will report literature which examined the pragmatics of strategic communication, and show how it exemplifies conversational cooperation.

Manifestation of Conversational Cooperation in Strategic Communication

As explained above, consumers' linguistic cooperation in marketing conversations yields linguistic expectations (that is, expectations for certain language to be used and certain language not to be used). Marketers, being cooperative speakers, are governed by their assumptions regarding consumers' linguistic expectations, and by their own goals (as in the case of strategic use of polysemy,[2] see Puntoni, Schroeder, & Ritson, 2010). For example, when trying to persuade consumers to behave in a more responsible manner towards the environment, marketers tend to use highly assertive language, as in "Stop the catastrophe!" by Greenpeace. Assertive language uses imperious and forceful expressions, such as "You must!" or plain commands like "Recycle!" Non-assertive language uses mild, gentle and polite expressions like "Please recycle" or "Thank you for not smoking." Kronrod, Grinstein, and Wathieu (2012a) demonstrate that when consumers deem an environmental issue important (e.g. water conservation, recycling, air and water pollution) they both expect and react better to environmental communication that uses assertive language, than non-assertive language. One of the reasons for this is that when people feel an issue is important and urgent, more assertive language is in line with the feeling of urgency and importance of the matter. Non-assertive language, in this case, would signal under-evaluation of the importance of the issue and therefore makes an impression of non-cooperative talk. To show how it works in actual consumer environments, the authors connected with a non-profit organization in Israel that fought for pure water and water conservation. Kronrod and colleagues posted a sponsored link on the Google search engine, encouraging people to sign a petition to keep the Mediterranean Sea clean. The sponsored links were phrased either assertively ("You must save the Mediterranean Sea! Sign the petition here!") or non-assertively ("You could save the Mediterranean Sea. You may sign the petition here"). The researchers identified people who typed in the search box words that are related to the Mediterranean Sea or water pollution as a high issue-importance group. Conversely, people who typed in miscellaneous words, such as *news, knitting instructions,* were considered a low issue-importance group. Both groups of people got an assertive or a non-assertive sponsored link in their search results. We counted the number of clicks on our sponsored links and found that those people who typed words related to the Mediterranean Sea in the search box on Google, were more likely to click on our assertive sponsored links. Conversely, people who searched for general issues were less prone to click on our assertive links and were more likely to click on our non-assertive links. Thus, this work implies that when marketers and consumers are linguistically cooperative (i.e., when marketers' language fits with consumers' linguistic expectations), strategic communication will be more successful in persuading consumers to be more pro-environmental.

Another case showing that persuasiveness of assertive language is higher when it suits consumers' linguistic expectations is reported by Kronrod, Grinstein, and Wathieu (2012b). In that work, focused on language concerning hedonic and utilitarian consumption, the authors show that hedonic consumption brings consumers in a positive mood, which in turn elevates expectations for more direct and assertive language (Forgas, 1999; Gibbs, 1985). Therefore marketers are more successful at communicating about hedonic consumption when they employ assertive language (e.g. Sprite's "Obey your thirst"). Moreover, Kronrod et al. (2012b) find that when consumers encounter assertive language, (being cooperative conversation partners) they infer that the communication is probably related to hedonic consumption, rather than utilitarian consumption. In an experiment, participants judged whether a fictitious product is more hedonic or more utilitarian after seeing an assertive or a non-assertive advertisement for the product. The authors discovered that when a product was assertively presented, like in "You must try QUILE!" participants tended to think it was more hedonic than when it was advertised in a less assertive tone, like in "Why don't you have a QUILE?" In sum, one way linguistic cooperation manifests itself is in fitting the language of strategic communication to linguistic expectations of the audience.

In a work focusing on field experiments (Grinstein & Kronrod, 2016), I expand my definition of assertive language and suggest that assertive tone is an intensifier of whatever is being conveyed. Specifically, I explore the appropriateness of assertive tone in marketing communication encouraging desired behaviors, such as hand hygiene, financial planning or pro-social behavior. I find that when such behaviors are encouraged by praising consumers for their actions (e.g. "You have been doing a lot"), assertiveness makes this communication even more effective in mobilizing people for action. Conversely, when behavior is promoted by scolding (e.g. "You have not done enough"), assertiveness may inhibit the effectiveness of this communication. The reason I suggest for this effect is that assertiveness is not merely a positive or a negative tone of communication, but rather an intensifier of the meaning being conveyed. Therefore scolding, which can be classified as a positive form of communication, benefits from assertiveness, whereas scolding does not, because it is largely a negative form of communication which may evoke guilt and avoidance. In this work, I implement the use of assertiveness in a variety of field experiments, which include encouraging people to sign a petition concerned with water pollution, encouraging visitors of public restrooms to wash their hands with soap, and disseminating an educative video about retirement planning among university employees. This work demonstrates the communicative role of assertiveness as an intensifier, which is beyond merely fitting communicational expectations.

Cooperation in Word of Mouth (WOM) and User Generated Content (UGC)

Linguistic cooperation is also evident in consumer-to-consumer Word of Mouth. For example, Schellekens, Verlegh, and Smidts (2010, 2012) find that consumers use more abstract terms when they describe experiences that are in line with the valence of their product attitudes, or with their expectations of the experience with the product. Further, when a consumer has the goal to convince another consumer of the high quality of a product (versus no persuasion goal), she would use more abstract descriptions of *positive* experiences with the objects, but more concrete language to describe negative experiences. On the receiver side, abstract language in positive word of mouth leads to the inference that the sender has a more favorable product attitude and elevated purchase intention for the product. Similarly, using concrete language led receivers to believe the author's attitude towards the product was negative, and consequently reduced purchase intention for the product. Putting these results in the framework of conversational cooperation, it appears that both the transmitters and the receivers of WOM make inferences about each other's linguistic expectations in order to achieve their goals: since abstractness is an outcome of and also implies positivity (e.g. Beukeboom & Semin, 2006), consumers receiving WOM infer positive attitudes from abstract language use. At the same time, transmitters of WOM intuitively use abstractness, especially when they have a strategic goal to persuade their listeners in the positive quality of the product.

In other work, which examines UGC, Kronrod and Danziger (2013) report that consumers tend to use figurative language (i.e., metaphor, hyperbole and word play) in reviews of hedonic consumption (things you do for fun), rather than utilitarian consumption (things you do because you need to). For example, a consumer wrote "Wii will rock you!" but another consumer wrote about a vacuum cleaner, "A great small-sized vacuum!" These results hold for positive and negative reviews. The explanation to this phenomenon relies on literature suggesting that hedonic consumption elicits more emotional attitudes, whereas utilitarian consumption elicits more rational attitudes (e.g., Adaval, 2001; Kivetz & Simonson, 2002 Wertenbroch & Dhar, 2000). Further, research on language and emotion indicates that when people are more emotionally aroused, they tend to use more figurative language (Fainsilber & Ortony, 1987; Fussel, 1992, 2002; Fussel & Moss, 1998). Combining these two bodies of research, Kronrod and Danziger (2013) suggest that consumers would use more figurative language when describing hedonic consumption, because of the emotional arousal this context induces. But even more importantly for our issue, the authors also show that, although consumers may get equally emotional about utilitarian consumption (e.g., a vacuum cleaner that stopped working after only three weeks of use), they will refrain from using figurative language when describing utilitarian experiences, no matter how emotional they are about this experience. The authors demonstrate that this difference is caused by the different communicational norms consumers hold regarding hedonic and utilitarian consumption. In other words, consumers would not use figurative language to describe utilitarian experiences because they are being cooperative speakers and therefore adhere to conversational norms about utilitarian consumption, which discourage the use of figurative language. To illustrate how language can influence perceptions of products through linguistic expectations, the authors ran a semi-field study, where they described a student store on campus using either literal language ("The store has a large inventory of products and they are very nicely ordered on the shelves and dispensers") or figurative language ("The store has a wide inventory, like in a king's palace, and the products are ordered on the shelves like soldiers in a military inspection"). Participants were asked to read one of these descriptions of the store and then to select a product out of a list that featured both hedonic products (music CD) and utilitarian products (course work CD). Interestingly, participants who read the figurative description chose dramatically more hedonic products than participants who read the literal description.

Yet another example of cooperation in UGC which is reflected in adjusting language to expectations is found in Kronrod, Grinstein, and Shuval (2016), who show that in a task where participants had to convince an imaginary person (John) to lead healthier lifestyle, they used less assertive language if they were scolding John for being not healthy enough, but more assertive language if they were praising John for leading healthy life already. For example, scolding participants would say: "John, if you continue eating unhealthy food you may incur health problems, so how about a few more veggies per day?" but praising participants would say: "John, you are doing great! Keep it up – get a bunch of veggies per day!" Kronrod, Grinstein, and Wathieu (2015) demonstrate that in communication encouraging people to act for their own good (e.g., invest in their retirement, maintain healthy lifestyle), communicators' (advice givers') language choices are governed by their assessment of the receiver's need for advice (based on their objective condition), while ignoring the receiver's wish for advice. However, advice receivers' reaction to this communication is governed by their wish for advice, regardless of their objective need for advice. This gap in motivations creates language cooperation discrepancy which can be evidenced in the relatively low success of pro-social campaigns.

Contextual and Situational Effects on Conversational Cooperation

Conversational cooperation and resulting linguistic expectations may vary depending on context and other situational variables. For example, Kronrod and Huber (2015) demonstrate that the effect of advertising repetition may switch from causing annoyance at a certain point in time, to elevating preference for the advertised brand at another point in time. The authors suggest this change takes place because initial annoyance with the overly repeated ad decays much quicker than the relatively high memory for the ad and the brand. The difference in the rate of decay between memory and annoyance gives an advantage to frequently promoted brands over less frequently promoted brands over time. Thus, the same brand that was frequently advertised and therefore annoying at a certain point in time, becomes the more preferred one after time passes, because annoyance as an effect of repetition is reduced but memory remains almost at the same level. Importantly, this result can happen only when the product category does become relevant after time. For example, diapers may be irrelevant to young adults until they have a baby. At this point, diapers become highly relevant. Now, the relevance of a product category influences conversational cooperation regarding this product. Namely, when a product is irrelevant to consumers, repetition of information about the product is deemed conversationally non-cooperative, and therefore may elicit annoyance. However, when the product is relevant, consumers would be cooperative in conversations about it, and therefore repetition would elicit familiarity and higher preferences for the product (Belch, 1981; Campbell & Keller, 2003; Janiszewski & Meyvis, 2001).

To illustrate how relevance can convert annoyance into preference, Kronrod and Huber (2015) conducted a field study on campus. In September, when Halloween was in the far future and therefore irrelevant, they posted ads for Halloween products by fictitious brand names (CreepyCrap and Boo Inc.) on billboards in two residence halls. In one hall, they posted CreepyCrap ads for ten days, and Boo Inc. ads for only four days. In the other hall, they posted the CreepyCrap ads for only four days and the Boo Inc. ads for the full ten days. After ten days all ads were removed and residents of the halls were asked which one is more annoying. Not surprisingly, the residents were more annoyed by the ad that was there for ten days. The researchers came back to the halls only three days before Halloween, with two boxes of Halloween decoration products. One box featured the CreepyCrap brand, and the other featured the Boo Inc. brand. Passers-by were offered to choose a free give away from one of the boxes. This time, three days before Halloween, the more frequently advertised brand in each hall—the same one that was more annoying two months ago—was now chosen more often. In this experiment the authors showed how situation-dependent relevance can change perceptions of cooperativeness of marketing communication, and how this can invert annoyance into product preference.

Xie and Kronrod (2012) also relate to situational effects on cooperation and linguistic expectations, though in a different way. The authors demonstrate that consumers' knowledgeableness can change their skepticism about green advertising and the inferences they make from the numerical precision employed in the ad. In their experiments, Xie and Kronrod (2012) found that people who are not particularly skeptical about advertising in general, tend to be influenced by numerical precision in ads and to think that the company represented in the ad is more competent and reliable. For example, when participants read an ad that employed precise numbers: "Introducing the green car: 12% reduction in carbon emission," they thought the car manufacturer was more proficient and credible, compared with when the ad read: "Introducing the green car: 10% reduction in carbon emission." This is because employing more precise numbers implies higher competence of the communicator, and elevates trust towards the source of communication—the firm (Xie & Kronrod, 2012; Zhang & Schwarz, 2012). However, people who are more skeptical towards advertising in general, are not impressed by numerical precision. All this was true when the advertisement talked about carbon emissions—a feature of a car that most people know. But when the authors presented participants with ads claiming: "Introducing the green car: 12% thermal efficiency," even people who were generally skeptical about advertising, were influenced by numerical precision and thought the car manufacturer was more competent and reliable. To sum, Xie and Kronrod (2012) find that low knowledge may cause even highly skeptical consumers to be influenced by numerical precision. Transmitters of strategic communication would benefit from being cooperative in their conversation with consumers and by considering linguistic expectations of consumers in different situations and contexts.[3]

Conclusion

Summary

In this chapter, I described one of the most prominent processes in conversation, Linguistic Cooperation. Through examples from different research works, I explained how linguistic cooperation manifests itself in strategic communication. Strategic Communication is traditionally seen as a one-way process, whereby marketers convey messages to consumers, adjusting the message to consumer needs, wants, culture etc. A vision of Strategic Communication through the linguistic-pragmatic lens suggests a Strategic *Conversation* account. This account is useful for understanding processes in the depth of strategic communication, because it explains the foundations underlying choices, and perceptions, of language and helps predict their outcomes. One of the processes in society that allows such novel perspective on strategic communication is that communication is no longer initiated solely by marketers: consumers today take active part in the conversation about products, communicating with each other and with marketers. I will relate to these changes in more depth in the following section.

The Future of Linguistic Inquiry of Strategic Communication

It is possible that cooperation assumptions about marketing communication today are more similar to interpersonal communication, rather than strategic communication, because consumers rely more and more on Word of Mouth and prefer to trust non-professional communication about consumption experiences (Ghose & Ipeirotis, 2009; Li & Hitt, 2008; Moe & Schweidel, 2012). Nevertheless, I suggest in this chapter that when consumers choose to share consumption experiences online, they do that not merely for the sake of emotional outlet or social interaction, but in fact, consumers also have persuasive goals, such as convincing others to consider or to *not* consider purchasing or using a certain product (Daugherty, Li, & Biocca, 2008; Forman, Ghose, & Wiesenfeld, 2008). In fact, we are all strategic communicators: we rarely say things without thinking about the effect our words would have on our audience. Therefore, the research of consumers as persuaders, albeit naïve persuaders, offers us an interesting new set of assumptions, assumptions which are different from those regarding either interpersonal communication or strategic communication. This is a novel type of consumer-generated strategic communication, where people contribute product reviews, blog content, Facebook updates, Tweets and other social media interactions, in a process of "lay persuasive" communication. In lay persuasive communication, the assumptions of cooperation in conversation take into account both the interpersonal character of the communication, and the goals of the communicator to convince the audience of the truthfulness of their tale, and ultimately in the righteousness of their point of view. Thus, research on the language of consumer-generated strategic communication could focus on trust, source verification and authentication, as well as audience's continuous testing of the source's cooperation in conversation.

As online communication today exceeds offline communication in volume and capacity (Ansari, Essegaier, & Kohli, 2000; Ghose & Ipeirotis, 2009; Moe & Schweidel, 2012), as well as the extent to which consumers rely on it (Daugherty et al, 2008; Flanagin & Metzger, 2013), future methods of exploring the language of social networks and consumer communication will employ computational linguistics and Big Data analysis tools (e.g., Hancock et al., 2007; Mayzlin, Dover, & Chevalier, 2012; McAfee & Brynjolfsson, 2012; Netzer, Feldman, Goldenberg, & Fresko, 2012; Ramanathan & Sarulatha, 2013; Zhang & Segall, 2010). The main barrier for progress in computational analysis of the pragmatics of online communication today is that computational tools are relatively limited in their ability to detect linguistic cooperation and inferences of intended meaning. To bridge this shortcoming, Kronrod and Tirunillai (2016) combine computer science and language behavior theory to create an automatic detector of fake reviews and deceptive user-generated content. Specifically, the researchers identify a tendency to be more abstract, to use more common language and expressions, and to avoid using the past tense as potential indicators of fake posts on Yelp. A computer code is employed to detect these linguistic aspects of online content. Thus, an optimistic view suggests that the need to assess pragmatic-linguistic behavior of consumers online will generate research and efforts to create tools for computational pragmatic analysis of online consumer-generated strategic communication.

Notes

1 Chinese respondents in Caldwell-Harris, Kronrod, and Yang (2013) reported slightly higher likelihood to substitute "I love you" with a phrase in another language. This behavior corresponds with the finding by Puntoni, de Langhe, and van Osselaer (2009), that advertising in one's native language is perceived as more emotional than advertising in a second language. This finding may also explain the replacement of taboo language with expressions in a foreign language.
2 Polysemy is the case when one word has several meanings. For example, the word "bank" has at least three meanings: a financial institution, the land alongside or sloping down to a river or lake, and a verb meaning to heap something into a mass or mound.
3 In a health communication context, Kronrod, Grinstein, and Wathieu (2015) demonstrate that a gap in linguistic expectations between communicators and receivers of health messages may cause reactance to, and inhibit compliance with, health messages in both interpersonal and public communication contexts.

References

Ansari, A., Essegaier, S., & Kohli, R. (2000). Internet recommendation systems. *Journal of Marketing Research, 37*, 363–376.
Adaval, R. (2001). Sometimes it just feels right: The differential weighting of affect consistent and affect-inconsistent product information. *Journal of Consumer Research, 28*(1), 1–17.

Ahluwalia, R., & Burnkrant, R. E. (2004). Answering questions about questions: A persuasion knowledge perspective for understanding the effects of rhetorical questions. *Journal of Consumer Research, 31*(1), 26–42.

Austin, J. L. (1962). *How to do things with words: The William James lectures delivered at Harvard University in 1955.* Oxford: Oxford University Press.

Belch, G. E. (1981). An examination of comparative and noncomparative television commercials: The effects of claim variation and repetition on cognitive response and message acceptance. *Journal of Marketing Research,* 333–349.

Beukeboom, C. J., & Semin, G. R. (2006). How mood turns on language. *Journal of Experimental Social Psychology, 42*(5), 553–566.

Brown, P. (1987). *Politeness: Some universals in language usage* (Vol. 4). Cambridge: Cambridge University Press.

Brown, P., & Levinson, S. C. (1987). *Politeness: Some universals in language usage* (Vol. 4). Cambridge: Cambridge University Press.

Burgoon, J. K., & Aho, L. (1982). Three field experiments on the effects of violations of conversational distance. *Communications Monographs, 49*(2), 71–88.

Caldwell-Harris, C., Kronrod, A., & Yang, J. (2013). Do more, say less: Saying "I love you" in Chinese and American cultures. *Intercultural Pragmatics, 10*(1), 41–69.

Campbell, M. C., & Keller, K. L. (2003). Brand familiarity and advertising repetition effects. *Journal of Consumer Research, 30*(2), 292–304.

Campbell, M. C., & Kirmani, A. (2000). Consumers' use of persuasion knowledge: The effects of accessibility and cognitive capacity on perceptions of an influence agent. *Journal of Consumer Research, 27*(1), 69–83.

Cialdini, R. (2004, January 1). The science of persuasion. *Scientific American Mind.* Retrieved from http://www.scientificamerican.com/article/the-science-of-persuasion/

Cook, G. (2001). *The discourse of advertising.* New York: Psychology Press.

Daugherty, T., Li, H., & Biocca, F. (2008). Consumer learning and the effects of virtual experience relative to indirect and direct product experience. *Psychology & Marketing, 25*(7), 568–586.

Dumontheil, I., Küster, O., Apperly, I. A., & Blakemore, S. J. (2010). Taking perspective into account in a communicative task. *Neuroimage, 52*(4), 1574–1583.

Fainsilber, L., & Ortony, A. (1987). Metaphorical uses of language in the expression of emotions. *Metaphor and Symbol, 2*(4), 239–250.

Flanagin, A. J., & Metzger, M. J. (2013). Trusting expert- versus user-generated ratings online: The role of information volume, valence, and consumer characteristics. *Computers in Human Behavior 29*(4), 1626–1634.

Forgas, J. P. (1999). Feeling and speaking: Mood effects on verbal communication strategies. *Personality and Social Psychology Bulletin, 25*(7), 850–863.

Friestad, M., & Wright, P. (1994). The persuasion knowledge model: How people cope with persuasion attempts. *Journal of Consumer Research, 21*(1), 1–31.

Forman, C., Ghose, A., & Wiesenfeld, B. (2008). Examining the relationship between reviews and sales: The role of reviewer identity disclosure in electronic markets. *Information Systems Research, 19*(3), 291–313.

Fukuyama, M. A., & Greenfield, T. K. (1983). Dimensions of assertiveness in an Asian-American student population. *Journal of Counseling Psychology, 30*(3), 429–432.

Fussell, S. R. (1992). *The use of metaphor in written descriptions of emotional states.* Unpublished manuscript, Carnegie Mellon University.

Fussell, S. R. (2002). The verbal communication of emotion: Introduction and overview. In S. R. Fussell (Ed.), *The verbal communication of emotion: Interdisciplinary perspectives* (pp. 1–16). Mahwah, NJ: Lawrence Erlbaum Associates.

Fussell, S., & Moss, M. (1998). Figurative language in emotional communication. In S. R. Fussell & R. J. Kreuz (Eds.), *Social and cognitive approaches to interpersonal communication* (pp. 113–143). Mahwah, NJ: Lawrence Erlbaum Associates.

Ghose, A., & Ipeirotis, P. (2009). The EconoMining project at NYU: Studying the economic value of user–generated content on the internet. *Journal of Revenue & Pricing Management, 8*(2), 241–246.

Gibbs Jr., R. W. (1985). Situational conventions and requests. In J. P. Forgas (Ed.), *Language and social situations* (pp. 97–110). New York: Springer.

Grice, H. P. (1975) Logic and conversation. In P. Cole & J. Morgan (Eds.), *Syntax and semantics 3: Speech acts* (pp. 41–58). New York, Academic Press.

Grice, H. P. (1989). *Studies in the way of words.* Cambridge, MA: Harvard University Press.

Grinstein, A., & Kronrod, A. (2016). Sparing the rod, spoiling the child? How praising, scolding, and assertive tone can encourage desired behaviors. *Proceedings of Association for Consumer Research International Conference, New Orleans, October 1–4 2016.*

Gudykunst, W. B., Matsumoto, Y., Ting-Toomey, Nishida, T., Kim, K., & Heyman, S. (1996). The influence of cultural individualism-collectivism, self construals, and individual values on communication styles across cultures. *Human Communication Research, 22*(4), 510–543.

Hahn, H. H. (2009). *Le Courrier français*, Géraudel cough drops, and advertising as art. In H. H. Hahn, *Scenes of Parisian modernity: Culture and consumption in the nineteenth century* (pp. 205–218). New York: Palgrave Macmillan.

Hall, E. T. (1976). *Beyond culture.* Garden City, NY: Anchor Press.

Hancock, J. T., Curry, L. E., Goorha, S., & Woodworth, M. (2007). On lying and being lied to: A linguistic analysis of deception in computer-mediated communication. *Discourse Processes, 45*(1), 1–23.

Janiszewski, C., & Meyvis, T. (2001). Effects of brand logo complexity, repetition, and spacing on processing fluency and judgment. *Journal of Consumer Research, 28*(1), 18–32.

Kasher, A. (1976). Conversational maxims and rationality. In A. Kasher (Ed.). *Language in focus: Foundations, methods and systems* (pp. 197–216), Dordrecht: Reidel.

Kasher, A. (1982). Gricean inference reconsidered. *Philosophica (Gent), 29,* 25–44.

Kivetz, R., & Simonson, I. (2002). Earning the right to indulge: Effort as a determinant of customer preferences toward frequency program rewards. *Journal of Marketing Research, 39*(2), 155–170.

Kleinman, A. (1980). *Patients and healers in the context of culture: An exploration of the borderland between anthropology, medicine, and psychiatry.* Berkeley: University of California Press.

Kronrod, A., & Danziger, S. (2013). "Wii will rock you!" The use and effect of figurative language in consumer reviews of hedonic and utilitarian consumption. *Journal of Consumer Research, 40*(4), 726–739.

Kronrod, A., Grinstein, A., & Shuval, K. (2016). Using praising, scolding and assertiveness to promote health: The role of guilt and optimism. Manuscript under review.

Kronrod, A., Grinstein, A., & Wathieu, L. (2012a). Enjoy! Hedonic consumption and compliance with assertive messages. *Journal of Consumer Research, 39*(1), 51–61.

Kronrod, A., Grinstein, A., & Wathieu, L. (2012b). Go green! Should environmental messages be so assertive? *Journal of Marketing*, 76(1), 95–102.

Kronrod, A., Grinstein, A., & Wathieu, L. (2015). Giving by the bucket, taking by the grain: The gap between health communicators and consumers. *Proceedings of the Society for Consumer Psychology International Conference, Phoenix, February 27–29, 2015*.

Kronrod, A., & Huber, J. (2015). The moderating role of time in the effects of ad repetition. *Proceedings of the American Academy of Advertising International Conference, Chicago, March 26–29 2015*.

Kronrod A., & Tirunillai S. (2016). Liars! Combining experimental and text analysis methods to detect insincerity in product reviews. Working Paper.

Levinson, S. C. (2000). *Presumptive meanings: The theory of generalized conversational implicature*. Cambridge, MA: MIT Press.

Li, X., & Hitt, L. M. (2008). Self-selection and information role of online product reviews. *Information Systems Research*, 19(4), 456–474.

Lin, S., Keysar, B., & Epley, N. (2010). Reflexively mindblind: Using theory of mind to interpret behavior requires effortful attention. *Journal of Experimental Social Psychology*, 46(3), 551–556.

Lindholm, C. (1988). The social structure of emotional constraint: The court of Louis XIV and the Pukhtun of Northern Pakistan. *Ethos*, 16(3), 227–246.

Lumsden, D. (2008). Kinds of conversational cooperation. *Journal of Pragmatics*, 40(11), 1896–1908.

Mayzlin, D., Dover, Y., & Chevalier, J. A. (2012). *Promotional reviews: An empirical investigation of online review manipulation* (No. w18340). National Bureau of Economic Research.

McAfee, A., & Brynjolfsson, E. (2012). Big data: The management revolution. *Harvard Business Review*, 90(10), 60–68.

McAlister, A. R., & Cornwell, T. B. (2009). Preschool children's persuasion knowledge: The contribution of theory of mind. *Journal of Public Policy & Marketing*, 28(2), 175–185.

Moe, W. W., & Schweidel, D. A. (2012). Online product opinions: Incidence, evaluation, and evolution. *Marketing Science*, 31(3), 372–386.

Moore, S. G. (2012). Some things are better left unsaid: How word of mouth influences the storyteller. *Journal of Consumer Research*, 38(6), 1140–1154.

Murken-Altrogge, C. (1978). Art as advertising—advertising as art. *Du-Europaische Kunstzeitschrift*, 446, 20.

Netzer, O., Feldman, R., Goldenberg, J., & Fresko, M. (2012). Mine your own business: Market-structure surveillance through text mining. *Marketing Science*, 31(3), 521–543.

Puntoni, S., De Langhe, B., & Van Osselaer, S. M. (2009). Bilingualism and the emotional intensity of advertising language. *Journal of Consumer Research*, 35(6), 1012–1025.

Puntoni, S., Schroeder, J. E., & Ritson, M. (2010). Meaning matters: Polysemy in advertising. *Journal of Advertising*, 39(2), 51–64.

Ramanathan, S., & Sarulatha, N. (2013). Big data: A marketers perspective of emerging marketing approach. *International Journal of Management Research and Reviews*, 3(5), 2872–2880.

Rotfeld, H. J., & Rotzoll, K. B. (1980). Is advertising puffery believed? *Journal of Advertising*, 9(3), 16–45.

Schellekens, G. A., Verlegh, P. W., & Smidts, A. (2010). Language abstraction in word of mouth. *Journal of Consumer Research*, 37(2), 207–223.

Schellekens, G. A., Verlegh, P. W., & Smidts, A. (2012). Linguistic biases and persuasion in communication about objects. *Journal of Language and Social Psychology*. doi: 0261927X12466083

Searle, J. R. (1969). *Speech acts: An essay in the philosophy of language* (Vol. 626). Cambridge: Cambridge University Press.

Sen, S., & Lerman, D. (2007). Why are you telling me this? An examination into negative consumer reviews on the web. *Journal of Interactive Marketing*, *21*(4), 76–94.

Simonson, A., & Holbrook, M. B. (1993). Permissible puffery versus actionable warranty in advertising and salestalk: An empirical investigation. *Journal of Public Policy & Marketing*, *12*(2), 216–233.

Sperber, D., & Wilson, D. (1986). *Relevance: Communication and cognition* (Vol. 142). Cambridge, MA: Harvard University Press.

Spitzer, L. (1978). Method of interpreting literature American advertising as popular art. *Poetique*, *34*, 152–171.

Stemmer, B. (1994). A pragmatic approach to neurolinguistics: Requests (re)considered. *Brain and Language*, *46*, 565–591.

Swinney, D. A. (1979). Lexical access during sentence comprehension: (Re)consideration of context effects. *Journal of Verbal Learning and Verbal Behavior*, *18*(6), 645–659.

Sweldens, S., Van Osselaer, S. M., & Janiszewski, C. (2010). Evaluative conditioning procedures and the resilience of conditioned brand attitudes. *Journal of Consumer Research*, *37*(3), 473–489.

Toncar, M., & Fetscherin, M. (2012). A study of visual puffery in fragrance advertising: Is the message sent stronger than the actual scent? *European Journal of Marketing*, *46*(1/2), 52–72.

Wertenbroch, K., & Dhar, R. (2000). Consumer choice between hedonic and utilitarian goods. *Journal of Marketing Research*, *37*(1), 60–71.

Xie, G. X., & Kronrod, A. (2012). Is the devil in the details? The signaling effect of numerical precision in environmental advertising claims. *Journal of Advertising*, *41*(4), 103–117.

Xu, A. J., & Wyer, R. S. (2010). Puffery in advertisements: The effects of media context, communication norms, and consumer knowledge. *Journal of Consumer Research*, *37*(2), 329–343.

Zhang, Y. C., & Schwarz, N. (2012). How and why 1 year differs from 365 days: A conversational logic analysis of inferences from the granularity of quantitative expressions. *Journal of Consumer Research*, *39*(2), 248–259.

Zhang, Q., & Segall, R. S. (2010). Review of data, text and web mining software. *Kybernetes*, *39*(4), 625–655.

8

HOW MARKETING COMMUNICATIONS INFLUENCE THE FORMATION OF FOOD HABITS PRIOR TO ADULTHOOD

Anna McAlister

Parents often express their feelings of frustration and confusion about how food and beverage marketers are so successful at shaping the dietary choices of young people. Given the alarming rates of obesity and diet-related diseases among today's youth, I am eager to answer questions about how purveyors of energy-dense, nutrient-poor foods[1] are successful at persuading children and teens to consume their offerings. Moreover, I am also interested in how competing communications (e.g., from parents, teachers, doctors, public service announcements) can be effective in countering this influence. In this chapter, I present findings from my own studies, as well as those reported by other researchers, to deliver to the reader a summary of the most recent insights on this topic. Given the old adage that "knowledge is power," the overarching goal of this chapter is to equip researchers, policy makers, and other child advocates with insights into how marketing communications work to influence young people. Once equipped with this understanding, they can begin to feel empowered to make more informed choices about how and when children should be exposed to food and beverage marketing, or when such exposure should be restricted.

The examination of children's responses to food and beverage marketing is highly relevant in a climate where concerns about childhood obesity abound. The obesity rate among preschool children has tripled over the past 30 years, and has quadrupled among children aged 6 to 11 years (Institute of Medicine, 2006). This epidemic is alarming because obese children are at greater risk for type 2 diabetes, heart disease, asthma, and psychological stress (Robert Wood Johnson Foundation, 2014). Perhaps most disturbing is the claim that, if the obesity epidemic is not reversed, the current generation of children will die at a younger age than their parents (Robert Wood Johnson Foundation, 2014).

Hence, research in the area of child-directed food marketing is very timely. It has real-world application to debates around current policy issues such as "fat taxes," restrictions on Happy Meal toys, and methods of displaying unit price information in retail settings.

To address the question of how young people's food choices are influenced by marketing communications (and what parents and other child advocates can do about it), this chapter is arranged into three distinct sections. It starts out with a general introduction to child development. This section is highly relevant since it is important to first understand the manner in which children are able to process persuasive messages before one can fully appreciate why children respond as they do to food and beverage marketing. Using this knowledge of child development as a foundation, the chapter then moves on to discuss children's susceptibility to persuasion. The focus here is on how children's openness to suggestion renders them quite receptive to promotion of healthy foods and beverages. The third section of this chapter gets to the crux of the issue by shedding light on current food and beverage marketing practices and discussing specific examples of how this knowledge of industry practices can be turned around to help those who wish to promote healthy food and beverage choices among young people. By the end of the chapter, readers will have a better understanding of how food and beverage marketing messages influence young people's food habits prior to adulthood. Readers will also be familiar with mechanisms that can be employed by various groups (e.g., retailers, parents, school lunchroom staff) to promote healthy food and beverage choices among children of all ages.

Traditional Versus Modern Theories of Child Development

Much of the existing literature on child-directed marketing was conducted in the late 1970s and early 1980s and was fueled by the FTC's proposal to ban television advertising aimed at young children. In 1978, the FTC encouraged public debate about the worthiness of various possible bans including an outright ban on all child-directed television or less strict alternatives, most of which focused on health-related concerns (e.g., banning advertising of foods high in sugar or requiring that all ads for sugared foods be counterbalanced equally by nutritional or health disclosures) (Beales, 2004). However, none of these bans was adopted and the Notice of Proposed Rulemaking[2] was ultimately shut down in 1981 (Beales, 2004).

From 1981 onwards, research on the topic of child-directed marketing plodded along, but with few new discoveries. Researchers continued to focus primarily on commercial television as the medium of choice for young children (Blosser & Roberts, 1985; Christenson, 1982; Levin, Petros, & Petrella, 1982; Macklin, 1985) and Piaget's theory of cognitive development[3] was the theoretical framework of choice for the vast majority of articles (see John, 1999).

Research in this area remained stagnant until the 2005 Fall issue of the *Journal of Public Policy and Marketing* shook things up. This special issue on marketing and advertising to children set the scene for renewed rigor in the field.

In that special issue, Friestad and Wright (2005) criticized the marketing literature for not keeping with the times. They argued that the majority of research could only be used to explain how children coped with television advertising in the 1970s and 1980s. These authors specifically called for new research to examine how children process marketing messages in the modern media environment where marketing is now more intrusive and pervasive. Further, Friestad and Wright proposed that modern studies of child-directed marketing should focus more so on the underlying psychological mechanisms that govern children's information processing, and criticized studies for taking a short-term view if they narrowly focused on children's behaviors as they related to one specific policy debate.

Consistent with Friestad and Wright (2005), Moses and Baldwin's (2005) article in the same special issue asserted the need for modern research to move away from the heavy reliance on Piaget's theory of child development. Moses and Baldwin pointed out that developmental psychologists started challenging the validity of Piagetian theory as early as the 1970s and 1980s, and that researchers in marketing had failed to keep pace with their interdisciplinary research. Throughout the article, Moses and Baldwin introduced readers to modern insights from developmental psychology. Specifically, for researchers who are unfamiliar with the modern psychology literature, Moses and Baldwin introduced "theory of mind" (a particular form of social development) and executive functioning (a particular form of cognitive development), and suggested these forms of development as important variables to be studied when examining children's responses to marketing messages.

Theory of Mind and Executive Functioning

In contrast to Piaget's (1970) theory of cognitive development, which groups together children of different ages and explains children's behavior in age stages (e.g., 3- to 7-year-olds are grouped together and 7- to 11-year-olds are lumped together), executive functioning researchers are concerned with *individual differences* in areas of cognitive functions including inhibitory control, categorization skills, impulse control, attention flexibility, planning behavior, and working memory (Hughes, 1998; McAlister & Cornwell, 2010; Zelazo, Carter, Reznik, & Frye, 1997). Similarly, theory of mind researchers consider *individual differences* in children's development of socio-cognitive competence (e.g., McAlister & Peterson, 2006, 2007; Peterson, 2000; Slaughter, Dennis, & Pritchard, 2002).

Theory of mind refers to the ability to mentally represent others' mental states, including their beliefs (true or false), knowledge, memory, and imagination

(McAlister & Peterson, 2007, 2013). A child's development of theory of mind brings with it the ability to make predictions about another's likely future behaviors, given what is known about the other's mental states and emotions. For example, if Lili knows that Aidan thinks dogs are dangerous, then Lili can predict that Aidan would most likely cross the street to avoid walking on the same sidewalk as someone who is running with their dog. Theory of mind development takes place largely during the preschool years, although it is also acknowledged that infancy is the starting point for this development and that mastery occurs beyond middle childhood (Moses & Baldwin, 2005).

Similar to theory of mind, executive functions begin to develop during infancy but with rapid development taking place during the preschool years (Moses & Baldwin, 2005). However, the development of executive functions is also more prolonged than that of theory of mind, with development continuing to "be refined and consolidated throughout adolescence and into early adulthood" (Moses & Baldwin, p. 195). Executive functions are central to behaviors that are not habitual. Habitual behaviors occur in all sorts of settings, including marketing contexts. Examples of habitual behaviors include riding a bike or routinely buying Coke at a vending machine. Once a person has performed one of these behaviors several times, then the behavior is said to be habitual because it requires very little planning or mental flexibility. On the other hand, novel behaviors require monitoring and control of thought and action. Novel behaviors occur in a variety of contexts, including marketing contexts. Examples of novel behaviors include driving a car for the first time, or selecting a meal from the menu at a restaurant you have never visited before. Both of these examples require a lot of thought and attention because they are new and therefore not well rehearsed. Hence, individual differences in executive functions are likely to explain the various ways in which children process and respond to novel experiences. This is true in all settings, including commercial settings.

The following sections provide examples of the ways in which theory of mind and executive functioning have been used in recent studies to explain different aspects of the consumer socialization process. I do not provide a review of the earlier studies that used Piagetian theory, since those studies have been argued to be outdated and of questionable validity (Friestad & Wright, 2005; Moses & Baldwin, 2005). For a thorough review of the literature from 1974 through 1999, the reader is referred to John's (1999) review paper. In short, the common thread among the vast majority of studies from that era was that the findings were tied closely to Piagetian theory and typically concluded that 3- to 7-year-olds felt positively about advertising, 7- to 11-year-olds felt negatively about ads, and that 11 to 16 years of age is the period for developing skepticism and critical thinking skills. Little, if any, attention was paid to individual differences within these age stages, and preschool children were largely excluded from sample frames.

Theory of Mind as It Relates to Consumer Socialization

As noted above, a young child with a developed theory of mind is equipped to understand the mental states of others. Just as Lili can predict that Aidan will likely cross the street to avoid encountering a dog (because she understand Aidan's beliefs about dogs), Lili can also predict that advertisers might not always tell the whole truth about their products (because she understands their persuasive intent and desire to sell products). Though the Piagetian studies concluded that children needed to be aged seven or older to detect persuasion and to know that ads are not always truthful (John, 1999), Moses and Baldwin's (2005) familiarity with the theory of mind literature led them to predict that children should be able to recognize the selling intent of commercials by around age three.

To test Moses and Baldwin's (2005) proposition, McAlister and Cornwell (2010) conducted a pioneering study in the area of child-directed marketing. This study was the first to examine individual differences in theory of mind and executive functioning as correlates of consumer socialization outcomes among preschool children. With a sample of 3- to 5-year-olds, they measured individual differences in theory of mind using well-established tests such as Baron-Cohen, Leslie, and Frith's (1985) "Sally-Ann" task and the misleading container task (Gopnik & Astington, 1988).

Both the Sally-Ann task and the misleading container task require the participant to think about the thoughts of others and to understand that another's beliefs can differ from one's own. In other words, these tasks require mental perspective taking. In the misleading container task, for example, the child sees a closed Bandaids box and is asked what s/he thinks is inside. Children typically respond by saying "Bandaids." The experimenter then opens the box to reveal that its true contents are crayons. After closing the box again, the experimenter asks the child what s/he thinks a friend would say, if the friend had never looked inside the box before. The correct answer is that the friend should guess there are Bandaids inside the box. As simple as this task is, children who have not yet developed the capacity for mental perspective taking will respond (incorrectly) by saying that their friend will guess that crayons are inside the box. The Sally-Ann task is similar in requiring children to think about the thoughts of others. Scores on these two tasks were combined to form an overall measure of theory of mind development. Consistent with prior studies of preschool children's theory of mind development (e.g., McAlister & Peterson, 2006, 2007; Peterson, 2000; Slaughter, Dennis, & Pritchard, 2002), McAlister and Cornwell (2010) observed no floor or ceiling effects in children's theory of mind scores. Preschool children showed great variance in their understanding of others' mental states.

McAlister and Cornwell (2010) were interested in using theory of mind development to explain variance in two dependent measures of consumer socialization, namely, brand representation ability and brand symbolism. Brand representation ability was defined as "the extent to which a child is capable of holding a schematic mental representation of a brand . . . including the brand's products, logo, trade characters, colors, typical sales venues, and so forth" (p. 209) and brand symbolism understanding refers to "an understanding of the meaning attributed to a brand name . . . [including] an appreciation of the ways in which a brand name symbolizes user qualities (e.g., popularity, user image) as well as information about the products or services encompassed by the brand (e.g., perceptions of brand use)" (p. 204). These outcome variables were assessed using purpose-built measures (i.e., measures that were designed specifically for the researchers' needs and had not previously been used in existing studies). Scores on each of these variables were then regressed onto predictor variables including theory of mind and, in both cases, theory of mind was found to be a significant predictor even after controlling for the effects of age and language development.

The researchers concluded that children whose theory of mind development is more advanced are better equipped to form mental representations of brands (McAlister & Cornwell, 2010). They also pointed out that theory of mind development is really the development of an ability to form mental representations of other people's mental states and so children whose theory of mind ability is advanced may show better scores on the brand representation task simply because they are better able to form mental representations in general. With regard to understanding brands as symbols, it was concluded that the ability to reason about the mental states of others might facilitate greater awareness of the ways in which brands are used as symbols in a social world. These findings are at odds with the Piagetian notion of preschoolers being egocentric and unable to think about others' mental states until age seven, however, this inconsistency can most likely be explained by the fact that McAlister and Cornwell's studies used age-appropriate tasks that allowed very young participants to show their understanding without the heavy language demands that were inherent in earlier studies.

Theory of mind has also been examined as a correlate of other consumer socialization outcomes among preschool children. For example, McAlister and Cornwell (2009) examined 3- to 5-year-olds' theory of mind development as a predictor of their persuasion knowledge. Persuasion knowledge is the ability to detect that advertisers "try to make you buy things" (Robertson & Rossiter, 1974, p. 13). In their study, McAlister and Cornwell measured persuasion knowledge in much the same way as Donohue, Henke, and Donohue had in 1980. Children were exposed to commercials and were then asked what the advertisers wanted them to do. In both studies, children were shown picture response options and were allowed to point to their answers. This non-verbal measurement tool reduced demands on children whose language skills were still developing.

Donohue and colleagues (1980) had originally reported that the majority of children in their preschool sample (some as young as 2 years old) could correctly identify the selling intent of a TV commercial. However, these results had been largely overlooked in the past because Macklin's (1985) attempt to replicate them failed (see John, 1999). When McAlister and Cornwell (2009) investigated preschoolers' persuasion knowledge, they asked why there might be inconsistent results between Donohue et al.'s and Macklin's findings. They suggested that if the inconsistent results were not due to methodological errors, it must be something about the child participants that explained the differences. The researchers noted that, even with the non-verbal picture response options, children needed some degree of receptive language skill to follow the task directions (McAlister & Cornwell, 2009). Hence, in addition to considering age, they controlled for individual differences in language ability when persuasion knowledge scores were regressed onto theory of mind scores. Not only was theory of mind significant in the prediction of persuasion knowledge, it accounted for 59% of variance. In the same paper, McAlister and Cornwell reported similar results in a second study, which was a replication conducted with a slightly more challenging test of persuasion knowledge. Overall, they concluded that children as young as three can detect persuasive intent in advertising, but that this ability emerges as theory of mind capacities are developed.

McAlister and her colleagues have also examined theory of mind in a slightly more applied context when they examined children's motivations to obtain collectible toys. In this study, the researchers designed a task where children obtained some toys from a collectible toy set (McAlister, Cornwell, & Cornain, 2011). The child participants then completed some assessments and, after that, were offered a choice of thank you gift for participating. Of the thank you gift options available, only one packet of toys contained the toy that was needed to complete the child's collectible set, but that packet came with a condition of sharing with a confederate child. McAlister and colleagues hypothesized that children would be more likely to share in order to obtain the desired collectible toy if they had more advanced theory of mind development. Indeed, this was what they found. After controlling for age and language effects, the children who were more likely to pay the "cost" of sharing were those who had higher scores on the theory of mind test battery. The researchers concluded that this sharing was unlikely to be altruistic and more likely reflects the fact that children whose theory of mind is more advanced are more aware of the social status associated with successful collecting (i.e., completing sets).

Taken together, findings from McAlister and colleagues' studies of brand representation and brand symbolism understanding (McAlister & Cornwell, 2010), persuasion knowledge (McAlister & Cornwell, 2009), and toy collecting (McAlister et al., 2011) lend strong support to Moses and Baldwin's (2005) proposition that theory of mind development is key to children's emerging understanding of the commercial marketplace. To date, no other published studies have examined the role of theory of mind in the process of children's consumer socialization, however, additional research is encouraged to test the boundaries of the effect. For example, one might argue that theory of mind may have little influence over decision making when it comes to privately consumed goods. Choosing a toothbrush, for example, comes with less social risk than choosing items that will be consumed or used publicly, such as toys (that may be shared during play with other children) or food (that will be eaten in front of other children at lunchtime). Since privately consumed goods have very little influence on one's social status, theory of mind may be less relevant in terms of children's thought processes around these items as social symbols.

Executive Functioning as It Relates to Consumer Socialization

As mentioned, executive functions encompass inhibitory control, impulse control, categorization skills, attention flexibility, planning behavior, and working memory (Hughes, 1998; McAlister & Cornwell, 2010; Zelazo et al., 1997), and are central to all forms of behavior that are not habitual (Luria, 1973; Moses & Baldwin, 2005). Children whose executive functions have begun to mature should be capable of switching their focus from one aspect of a persuasive communication message to another, in order to process the message in a holistic manner. The early studies in child-directed marketing argued that children below 7 or 8 years of age would be incapable of such attention flexibility (see John, 1999), however, findings from developmental psychology have shown, for decades, that the preschool years are a time for rapid development of attention flexibility as well as the various other executive functions (Carlson, Moses, & Hix, 1998; Luria, 1973; McAlister & Peterson, 2013).

In one of their studies of children's collectible toy sets, McAlister, Cornwell, and Cornain (2011) found that executive functioning played a significant role in preschool children's likelihood of engaging in goal-oriented collecting behavior. This finding is really not surprising, given that executive functions include planning behavior and impulse control. However, it was interesting to observe that children as young as three were inclined to ignore "distractor" toys and choose to obtain the final toy needed to complete a collectible set, even though they had not been given any instructions to collect all items of the set. This was true despite the fact that all of the toys used as stimuli had been pretested to ensure the "distractor" toys were no less appealing. When the researcher casually asked children why they chose as they did, the vast majority who selected the collectible toy said they did so in order to complete their set. Hence, the results show that children as young as three are capable of setting a goal and sticking to it.

Individual differences in executive functioning were also implicated in preschool children's performance on the mental brand representation task from McAlister and Cornwell's (2010) study, mentioned earlier. In addition to the significant influence of theory of mind, executive functioning also explained unique variance in children's ability to mentally represent various brands. The brand representation task required children to separate instances of competing brands from one another as well as from distractor items. For example, in one trial, children were asked to sort picture cards of Coca-Cola items (packaged beverages, cups, signage, etc.) from Pepsi items (packaged beverages, cups, signage, etc.) and "distractor" items (e.g., piggy bank, swim goggles). Since this task requires categorization skills and working memory (and perhaps control of any impulsive urge to place both soda brands together), it is not surprising that children with more advanced executive functioning skills performed better. On the flipside, it should be noted that some children—those with less advanced executive functions—performed poorly at the task. As simple as the task sounds (really one could do well simply by grouping together items sporting the same logo), children whose executive functioning was less well developed were challenged.

Theory of Mind and Executive Functioning Summary

Consistent with the conclusions regarding the role of theory of mind in the consumer socialization of young children, it appears that executive functioning is another area of development that acts as a catalyst to children's abilities to process information in commercial contexts. Whereas the early studies of child-directed marketing would lead readers to believe that children under the age of eight are passive recipients of commercial messages, McAlister and colleagues' findings regarding multiple socialization outcomes (i.e., children's formation of mental representations of brands, their understanding of the ways in which brands serve as social symbols, their ability to detect persuasion in advertising, and their processing of information about collectible sets of toys) come together to paint a picture of preschool children as being relatively sophisticated information processors whose abilities have been grossly underestimated in the past.

As their theory of mind and executive functions develop, these young people show emerging abilities to process marketplace information. I am by no means suggesting that preschoolers are so savvy as to not be regarded as a vulnerable group. In fact, quite the opposite is probably true. As Moses and Baldwin (2005) suggest, greater experience is likely a requirement for efficient information processing in any environment. Hence, in addition to needing theory of mind and executive functioning skills to process marketplace information, experience with the marketplace will improve children's abilities to cope with it over time. Moreover, since executive functions are important to children's self-protection and self-regulation (i.e., impulse control and resistance to interference would be key to developing healthy skepticism and avoiding unnecessary purchases)—and since these functions have a more protracted development than theory of mind (Moses & Baldwin, 2005)—it seems likely that children will experience a period of being especially vulnerable to marketing.

Between the age when children begin to understand the commercial marketplace (roughly around the preschool years when theory of mind and executive functions begin to blossom) and the age of mastery of socio-cognitive developments (possibly as late as the middle school years or into young adulthood), children are likely to "get" a lot of commercial messages and activities but will be ill-equipped to respond in a responsible manner. In other words, it appears that the period between preschool and middle school (or perhaps even later) will be an especially vulnerable time for children as they understand that advertisers want them to buy products but are not yet experienced enough in the marketplace to know which products are good for them or to have developed skepticism or resistance to persuasion. Given the current obesity epidemic, it seems especially prudent to monitor the types of food and beverage ads to which children and teens are exposed during this period of vulnerability, and to discuss policy interventions that might help to reduce the persuasive influence of ads that promote consumption of energy-dense, nutrient-poor foods.

Children's Susceptibility to Persuasion

In addition to the various ways in which children may be preyed upon by advertisers whose interests lie primarily in profiteering, there are, of course, those whose attempts to persuade children really have the kids' best interests at heart. Let us think for a moment about advertisers whose intentions are to persuade children to eat healthy foods, or parents who hope to encourage healthy behaviors at home. Research has shown that the commercial messages targeted to children are primarily used to encourage consumption of foods high in sugar, sodium, and fat (Mink, Evans, Moore, Calderon, & Deger., 2010; Powell, Szczypka, Chaloupka, & Braunschweig, 2007) and that budgets for promoting fresh fruits and vegetables or minimally processed foods pale in comparison to those of the major purveyors of processed foods (Moss, 2013). Those statistics, coupled with the alarming rate of childhood obesity in the United States (Centers for Disease Control and Prevention, 2013), have spurred research into the ways in which children's susceptibility to persuasion might be leveraged so as to encourage healthy eating.

The following sections highlight some of the recent developments in research focusing on the use of persuasive communications to promote healthy eating. One can think of these findings as serving the needs of children and those who care for them. By gaining insights into how communications can be structured to manipulate children to consume healthy food, researchers are helping to level the playing field for parents, teachers and other caregivers who often feel they have an uphill battle to fight against the extensive (and very successful) marketing of energy-dense, nutrient-poor foods.

Of course, it is prudent to mention that there are some folks who believe that *all* attempts to target persuasive messages to kids are inherently bad if the messages promote sales of products. One such group is the Campaign for Commercial-Free Childhood (CCFC). The CCFC is a non-profit group that "advocates for local, state, and federal policies that limit corporate marketers' access to children. [They] regularly submit petitions to the FTC and FCC and file comments aimed at enforcing and strengthening current regulations" (CCFC, 2014). As such, the CCFC protests directly against *all* child-directed marketing messages—even those promoting healthy food choices—and argues that any such messages are inherently exploitative.

The problem with the CCFC's argument for an outright ban on advertising to kids is two-fold. First, children who are raised in an entirely commercial-free environment will be ill equipped to cope when they are bombarded with commercial messages as adults (Can you imagine their first week at college?). As Moses and Baldwin (2005) clearly stated, a young person's ability to cope with advertising relies on having had some experience with advertising. Second, when corporations are forced to adhere to strict policies or are encouraged to engage in self-regulation, they typically improve their advertising in traditional media only. For example, companies may advertise their healthy food options on TV, but the less healthful alternatives will continue to be promoted online where regulation is much more difficult to enforce (Calvert, 2008). Hence, instead of advocating for an outright ban on child-directed marketing (which would be virtually impossible to impose), the remainder of this chapter is dedicated to discussion of the ways in which marketers, school lunchroom staff, parents, and other caregivers can use persuasive communication techniques to promote good food choices.

Promoting Good Food Choices

Promoting Healthy Eating

There is ample evidence to show how marketers can have a negative impact on children's diets (see Moss, 2013). For example, in the early 1980s, the Food and Drug Administration reported on the dangers of high sugar levels in Americans' diets. In response to criticisms surrounding sugared foods, "Kellogg and General Mills formed a group called the Flavor Benefits Committee . . . to conduct research that would help quiet the nay-sayers, putting sugar and other food additives in a more favorable light by emphasizing their nutritional benefits" (Moss, 2013, p. 18). This is just one of numerous examples from Moss's book, where he discusses the ways in which food and beverage companies look to formulate products to maximize taste appeal and get consumers "hooked," with little regard for improving the nutrition profiles of products, or any regard for the overall health of the consumer. There is, however, a potential silver lining to understanding the ways in which marketers of highly processed foods influence children's food choices. Specifically, parents who understand how marketing works are armed with knowledge that can help them to choose when their children are impacted and to circumvent undesirable influences if they so wish. Three examples of translating research findings into actionable changes are discussed briefly below.

Food Branding Influences Taste Perceptions

Robinson and colleagues (2007) have shown that children prefer foods that are clearly branded. In their experiment, these researchers served preschool children five different foods in pairs. The foods included three items from McDonald's (hamburger, fries, chicken nuggets) and two from a grocery store (1% milk, carrots). On each trial, children received the same food item within a pair (e.g., two hamburgers on one trial, two serves of fries on another trial). Hence the foods within a trial were identical, except for a packaging manipulation. Within each trial, one food was presented in McDonald's packaging and the other (identical) food was presented in plain white packaging. The 3- to 5-year-olds in this study showed a significant preference for the food with McDonald's packaging, stating that the branded food tasted better. This finding shows that the visual cue of the brand logo on a wrapper can overpower sensory stimulation of the taste palate to fool children into perceiving branded foods as tasting better.

Though the implications seem depressing for encouraging consumption of home-cooked meals, parents can take small steps to circumvent the influence of branding in children's perceptions of food. For example, a parent who decides to remove the presence of brand logos at their dinner table can do so in a variety of ways. Even on a night when a family gets take-out for dinner, the simple step of placing the food items on plates will mean the branded packaging is not present at the dinner table (or couch or wherever consumption takes place). Likewise, everyday items like the orange juice served at breakfast, or the soda served at lunch can be poured into cups in the kitchen so that no branded packaging is present when the drink is actually consumed. This second suggestion serves the dual purpose of controlling portion size, as it is often recommended to dish out what you plan to consume and to leave the package in the kitchen to avoid mindlessly reaching for a refill (e.g., Alliance for a Healthier Generation, 2013). By avoiding the presence of branded packaging during dining experiences, parents can exert control over the associations their children develop with the foods and drinks they consume.

Additionally, some parents may choose to leave brands visible when serving "healthy" offerings (e.g., they may want their child to learn to love Kashi cereal), while hiding branded packaging only when less ideal foods are served at home (e.g., serving Doritos in a bowl and leaving the packet in the pantry). The point is that, when parents understand the role that branding plays in shaping children's perceptions of food, then parents are empowered to pick and choose the brands to which their children are frequently exposed.

Collectible Toys Influence Food Choices

As mentioned earlier, McAlister et al. (2011) reported research findings that show how preschool children (especially those with developed executive functions and theory of mind) are motivated to engage in collecting behavior. In subsequent research, McAlister and Cornwell (2012) also showed that preschool children's motivation toward completing a set of collectible toys is sufficient to sway their perceptions of food appeal. This research consisted of two studies. The first study compared children's ratings of two different meals. The "healthful" meal consisted of plain milk, vegetables, and soup, while the "fast food" meal comprised pizza, fries, and a soda. Children viewed these meals when they were paired with a collectible toy premium, or a non-collectible toy premium, or when each meal was presented alone with no toy. In that first study, the researchers found that the collectible toy premium bore a significant influence in terms of encouraging children to give higher ratings to both the healthful and the fast food meals. In fact, the healthful meal on its own (i.e., with no toy included) received a lousy rating (2.25/5) compared to the fast food meal which, when presented without a toy, received a significantly higher rating (3.78/5). However, when the meals were each paired with a collectible toy, the difference disappeared—both meals received ratings around 4.5/5.

The findings from that first study suggest that collectible toy premiums could be paired with healthful meals to increase children's interest in consuming such meals (McAlister & Cornwell, 2012). However, the researchers needed to conduct a follow-up study to determine if the healthful meal would ever really be chosen over the typical fast food meal. Study 2 was similar to Study 1 in terms of using images of healthful and fast food meals that were either paired with a collectible toy or presented with no toy premium. However, Study 2 involved a choice task instead of a ratings task. Here, children were shown different meal options in pairs and asked which meal they would really choose. In this second study, the researchers found that the only condition under which children would really choose a healthful meal over the alluring "fast food" meal was if the healthful meal came with a collectible toy and the fast food meal came with no toy.

Findings from these studies hold strong implications for public policy. They suggest that an outright ban on the use of collectible toys in food marketing may do little to foster children's interest in healthy meals (McAlister & Cornwell, 2012). The data suggest that the move some policy makers adopted in 2010 is not sufficient to improve the dietary choices of young Americans. In 2010, several states imposed rulings that forbade fast food restaurants from pairing collectible toys with meals that did not meet strict nutritional guidelines (see Bernstein, 2010). Some restaurants responded by ceasing the use of collectible toys altogether. While this seems like a step in the right direction for not encouraging consumption of energy-dense foods, McAlister and Cornwell's (2012) data suggest that collectible toys are such a powerful tools that they should be considered as marketing tools, but only for use in promoting healthy meals. Sadly, these data paint a picture suggesting that children are likely to need the nudge from the collectible toy premium in order to want to choose a healthy meal over an unhealthy alternative. Of course, the study findings need to be replicated before being used as the basis for firm policy decisions.

Drink Choices Influence Food Consumption

Just as toy premiums can influence food choice, so too can the beverages that are present during food consumption. In a recent study, Cornwell and McAlister (2011) examined young people's perceptions of foods that "go together." The researchers conducted one study with college students and another with preschool children. In their survey of college students, they asked participants to rate their level of agreement (or disagreement) with statements that certain food and drink items "go together." College students felt very strongly about which foods soda "goes with" and had relatively neutral feelings about water, suggesting that water may be a reasonable complement to most foods. Soda, though, was seen as highly appropriate to pair with French fries or with pizza, and inappropriate as a partner to raw or cooked vegetables. Then in an experiment with preschoolers the researchers concluded that sweetened beverages do not pair well with raw vegetables. In the experiment, children were offered water or Hawaiian Punch and were then allowed to eat an unlimited amount of vegetables during the testing session. Kids ate more vegetables on the water trial, and vegetable consumption was significantly lower when children had consumed Hawaiian Punch (Cornwell & McAlister, 2011).

What can parents do with these findings? How can the findings help college students? The take home message is that it would be unwise to consume sweetened beverages like soda or Hawaiian Punch if you hope to facilitate healthy eating. Cornwell and McAlister's (2011) suggestions for intervention include parents serving only water with meals at home, and keeping sweetened beverages out of sight or not in the home at all. College students would likewise be advised to sip water with a meal so as to not dissuade their taste palates from raw or cooked vegetables. The researchers also suggested possible changes for restaurants to adopt on a voluntary basis to help their patrons. These could include offering water as the default drink with combo meals and limiting access to all-you-can-drink soda fountains (Cornwell & McAlister, 2011). Again, replication of these findings is needed prior to making any such policy decisions based on them.

Promoting Healthy Foods in Schools

Food Naming Interventions

Food naming interventions have recently been included in studies of behavioral economics. Behavioral economics is defined as the combination of "behavioral models of psychology with the decision models of economics to help highlight how biases in perception, memory, or thought processes may influence purchasing decisions" (Just & Wansink, 2009, p. 1). There is a wealth of literature on the use of behavioral economics to encourage children to make healthier choices at school. For example, Wansink, Just, Payne, and Klinger (2012) report that elementary school children consume significantly more vegetables when the dishes are labeled with attractive names (e.g., Power Punch Broccoli, Silly Dilly Green Beans), as opposed to being unnamed.

What is interesting about Wansink and colleagues' (2012) finding is that the attractive naming of the food had no significant impact on the amount of vegetable a child chose to put on their plate. Instead, the naming intervention influenced the amount of vegetable a child actually consumed. Though the researchers did not ask their child participants to rate the taste of the food items, the findings seem to suggest that the kids thought the vegetables tasted better when they were attractively named. This, of course, fits nicely with Robinson and colleagues' (2007) findings regarding the influence of branded packaging on children's perceptions of food.

Wansink et al.'s (2012) intervention in the lunchroom is promising because it illustrates how a simple intervention can encourage healthy eating without any need whatsoever to talk directly to kids about what foods they "should" eat. Moreover, the researchers demonstrated the feasibility of the intervention in a follow-up study, which showed that it was easily scalable at virtually no cost (see Wansink et al., 2012). To prove how simple the intervention was to implement, the follow-up study employed a high school student as a research assistant. In the intervention phase, the high school student selected fun names for vegetables offered in elementary school lunchrooms. He placed printed cards next to the food items in the lunch line. Vegetable sales from the intervention period were compared to sales from an earlier baseline period. The authors concluded, "Many of the interventions for school lunchrooms are not scalable because they are either too complicated, too labor-intensive, or too costly. The success of one student who implemented this at a negligible cost is a testament to its scalability across other schools" (Wansink et al., 2012, p. 332).

Menu Interventions

Given the success that Wansink and colleagues have had with their school lunchroom interventions (see www.smarterlunchrooms.org for a summary of multiple studies), it is interesting to question whether these minimalistic interventions (often referred to as "nudges") work precisely because they are minimal in nature. That is, one could question whether kids are less resistant to persuasive communications that they cannot detect. Unlike traditional advertising messages where young children can typically detect persuasive intent, the types of behavioral nudges used in modern school lunchroom interventions are so subtle that they may be resistant to children's skepticism because they are below the threshold of perception.

To test this hypothesis, Cash and McAlister (2016) investigated children's responses to a minimalistic lunchroom intervention. They interviewed children from a South Carolina middle school approximately six months after a subtle menu intervention had taken place in the school lunchroom. During the intervention, the regular menu had been altered to include images for different theme weeks (e.g., football theme, dinosaur theme, detective theme). On each of these weeks, healthier menu choices were highlighted in a subtle manner. For example, in the dinosaur week, the menu listed "triceratops's picks" as though the dinosaur had some favorite menu items. There was no information to suggest that the triceratops's picks were healthier food items, nor had children been instructed to choose these items. Cash and McAlister were interested in determining whether children remembered the intervention and, if so, whether they knew why it had occurred. The researchers found that the vast majority of children recalled the menu interventions, but that only about 50–60% were clued into the purpose (i.e., to promote healthy foods).

Though the data from this school menu study have yet to be fully analyzed, they are showing an interesting pattern. So far it appears that students can easily recall changes to their food environment, but that subtle nudges to encourage healthy eating are not fully processed as persuasive communications. Cash and McAlister (2016) have observed a trend in the data suggesting that those with higher executive functioning scores and more advanced language skills are better able to detect the persuasive intent of the intervention. If these trends are found to be significant, they would suggest that the most advanced children (in terms of language development and cognitive functions) may require the most tailored interventions to ensure they do not become overly skeptical and resistant to persuasive communications that are designed to enhance their health and wellbeing.

Communicating About Value in Retail Settings

Many consumers use price to guide their decision-making in retail settings (Devine & Marion, 1979; Zeithaml, 1982). Unit pricing—the practice of pricing goods on the basis of cost per unit of measure—is particularly helpful in assisting shoppers to save money (Sefcik, 2013). An example of unit pricing would be if the retail price of a 12oz can of soda is 99¢ and this is expressed as a unit price of 8.25¢ per oz. Research suggests that the presence of a unit price alongside the retail price of a product can help consumers to reduce their grocery bill by 1–3% (Russo, 1977).

Naturally, it is an admirable goal for retailers to want to help consumers navigate stores with ease and to save money. However, short-term savings on the grocery bill may result in long-term health costs if it turns out that the provision of unit price information dissuades consumers from purchasing food items of high nutritional value.

To question the likelihood of this issue arising, Cash, McAlister, and Lou (2014) conducted a lab experiment. These researchers anticipated that the presence of a unit price display might influence consumers' choices, particularly by reinforcing a perception that energy-dense foods provide better value. The study involved college student participants who viewed images of foods that were displayed in pairs using an online software tool. The display of these food pairs involved manipulation of three independent variables: price level (low vs. high), price display (retail price only vs. retail price accompanied by unit price vs. unit price only), and food type (fresh produce, packaged sweet snacks, or packaged salty snacks). As participants viewed the food displays (which looked like photos of real retail food displays), the researchers asked which food item they would select (from each food pair) if they were hungry and only had enough money to buy one item.

The primary hypotheses tested in this study were that the presence of a unit price display would be associated with a higher rate of individuals choosing (1) energy-dense foods, (2) less healthy foods (as measured by NuVal® scores), and (3) processed food items. The data supported the first hypothesis. The presence of a unit price display was associated with a higher rate of participants choosing more energy-dense foods. However, this was not the case for the selection of processed foods vs. fresh produce or choice of healthier food options as indicated by NuVal® ratings (Cash et al., 2014).

Cash and colleagues' (2014) findings suggest that the provision of unit pricing does serve to reinforce the value of energy-dense food options. However, it appears that this does not necessarily lead to less healthy food choices overall. Taken together, the findings suggest that there are some potential dangers around providing unit price displays and suggest the need to remind shoppers that value for money is a broad concept that should take into account not only how much product you get for your dollar but also what costs (e.g., future health costs) and benefits accompany one's food choices. Cash and colleagues also found that the choice of more energy-dense items was significantly related to respondents' ranking of price as an important attribute in making food purchase decisions. In other words, those who are most price-sensitive are likely to choose energy-dense foods because they see the value for money when unit price information is displayed. This suggests that price-sensitive consumers might be an especially vulnerable group who need to be reminded of the cost savings (e.g., healthcare savings) associated with more healthful food choices.

Recommendations and Future Directions

To date, this research stream has been focused on employing modern theories from developmental psychology to the study of young people's consumer behavior. Through this research, much has been learned about how marketers target children and how children process and respond to marketing messages. Future studies will move beyond learning about the effects of existing industry practices to examine new ways of communicating with children. The next steps in this research agenda will assess strategies designed to efficiently achieve the goal of improving dietary choices of children in the US. To this end, I will take what has been learned about current industry practices and use this knowledge to design and implement in-situ interventions in school lunchrooms and community settings (e.g., convenience stores and bodegas where children spend a significant portion of their pocket money on energy-dense, nutrient-poor snack foods).

Of particular interest is outreach work that will involve "real world" settings where children's food choices can be influenced. Cash, McAlister, and Economos's (2014–2015) first step in that direction is examining the influence of "kids only" coupons that will be distributed in corner stores and online via social media. These coupons are designed to discount "better for you" foods and to capitalize on children's tendencies to engage in activities that they perceive to be intended for them. Just as kids tend to grab at foods that are brightly colored or presented in "kid-friendly" packaging, Cash and colleagues anticipate being able to capture children's and teens' attention using coupons that are for youths only. The research team anticipates being able to apply what has been learned about children's responses to persuasive communications to design a real world intervention to improve the food choices of young children in the target area. The plan for 2015–2016 will then be to scale up the intervention to encompass several states within the US.

Other topics that are ripe for future research include parent and child responses to minimal interventions in the home. As mentioned, Wansink and colleagues have conducted numerous studies and continue to work towards a comprehensive understanding of how children's diets can be manipulated through "nudges" in the school lunchroom (see www.smarterlunchrooms.org). Very few studies have examined similar minimalistic changes in homes. One might envision such research being conducted as case studies or using ethnographic methods (e.g., observing in-situ changes in a number of homes and documenting parent and child responses—both behavioral and emotional). Moreover, the types of nudges being examined by Wansink's group in school lunchrooms could be examined in preschools and kindergartens.

Researchers have already reported that eating habits and taste preferences are established early in life and, after that time, are difficult to manipulate (Cornwell & McAlister, 2011). Moreover, some have suggested that the desirable effects achieved in one context may be "undone" by undesirable compensatory behaviors in other contexts (Cash & McAlister, 2011). For example, a successful school lunchroom intervention might encourage a child to eat a healthy lunch but then that same child might feel justified in selecting a candy bar and soda as an afternoon snack because they "were good" at lunchtime. For this reason, it is suggested that research into ways of counteracting the negative influences of child-directed food marketing focus on positive interventions in multiple contexts so that such compensatory behavior is reduced.

Notes

1 Energy-dense, nutrient-poor foods are those that are high in calories but low in nutritional value. Many fast food offerings and sodas fall into this category. This term is used by nutritionists to avoid the more vague term of "unhealthy food."
2 A notice of proposed rulemaking is a notice in the Federal Register that announces the intent of a government agency to add, edit, or remove a rule. Generally, when posting such a notice, an agency will also announce an opportunity for public comment.
3 See John (1999) for a detailed explanation of this theory. Piaget's theory of cognitive development groups children into age groups to explain development at different stages (e.g., birth–2 years, 3–7 years, 7–11 years, 11–16 years).

References

Alliance for a Healthier Generation (2013). Portion size vs. serving size. Retrieved from https://www.healthiergeneration.org/news__events/2013/07/10/801/portion_size_vs_serving_size

Baron-Cohen, S., Leslie, A. M., & Frith, U. (1985). Does the autistic child have a "theory of mind"? *Cognition, 21*, 37–46.

Beales, J. H. (2004). Advertising to kids and the FTC: A regulatory retrospective that advises the present. Retrieved from http://www.ftc.gov/public-statements/2004/03/advertising-kids-and-ftc-regulatory-retrospective-advises-present

Bernstein, S. (2010). It's a sad day for happy meals in Santa Clara County. Retrieved from http://articles.latimes.com/2010/apr/28/business/la-fi-happy-meals-20100428

Blosser, B. J., & Roberts, D. F. (1985). Age differences in children's perceptions of message intent: Responses to TV news, commercials, educational spots, and public service announcements. *Communication Research, 12*(October), 455–484.

Calvert, S. L. (2008). Children as consumers: Advertising and marketing. *The Future of Children, 18*(1), 205–234.

Carlson, S. M., Moses, L. J., & Hix, H. R. (1998). The role of inhibitory processes in young children's difficulties with deception and false belief. *Child Development, 69*(3), 672–691.

Cash, S. B., & McAlister, A. R. (2011). *Influence of developmental differences on children's response to information on foods.* Report to the United States Department of Agriculture, Economics Research Service, agreement number 59-5000-0-0075, pp. 43

Cash, S. B., & McAlister, A. R. (2016). *Salience and understanding of school lunch interventions involving pre-commitment to purchase decisions.* Manuscript in preparation.

Cash, S. B., McAlister, A. R., & Economos, C. (2014–2015). CHOMPS. Retrieved from http://www.nutrition.tufts.edu/chomps.

Cash, S. B., McAlister, A. R., & Lou, C. (2014, June). *Unit price displays are associated with higher rates of energy-dense food consumption.* Paper presented at Marketing and Public Policy Conference, Boston, MA.

CCFC (2014). Campaign for a commercial-free childhood. Retrieved from http://www.commercialfreechildhood.org/about-ccfc

Centers for Disease Control and Prevention (2013). Childhood obesity facts. Retrieved from http://www.cdc.gov/healthyyouth/obesity/facts.htm

Christenson, P. G. (1982). Children's perceptions of TV commercials and products: The effects of PSAs. *Communication Research, 9*(October), 491–524.

Cornwell, T. B. & McAlister, A. R. (2011). Alternative thinking about starting points of obesity: Development of child taste preferences. *Appetite, 56*(2), 428–439.

Devine, D. G., & Marion, B. W. (1979). The influence of consumer price information on retail pricing and consumer behavior. *American Journal of Agricultural Economics, 61*(2), 228–237.

Donohue, T. R., Henke, L. L., & Donohue, W. A. (1980). Do kids know what TV commercials intend? *Journal of Advertising Research, 20*(October), 51–57.

Friestad, M., & Wright, P. (2005). The next generation: Research for twenty-first-century public policy on children and advertising. *Journal of Public Policy & Marketing, 24*(2), 183–185.

Gopnik, A., & Astington, J. W. (1988). Children's understanding of representational change and its relation to the understanding of false belief and the appearance-reality distinction. *Child Development, 59*, 26–37.

Hughes, C. (1998). Executive function in preschoolers: Links with theory of mind and verbal ability. *British Journal of Developmental Psychology, 16*(2), 233–253.

Institute of Medicine (2006). *Progress in preventing childhood obesity: How do we measure up?* Washington, DC: National Academies Press.

John, D. R. (1999). Consumer socialization of children: A retrospective look at twenty-five years of research. *Journal of Consumer Research, 26*(December), 183–213.

Just, D. R., & Wansink, B. (2009). Smarter lunchrooms: Using behavioral economics to improve meal selection. *Choices, 24*(3), 1–7.

Levin, S. R., Petros, T. V., & Petrella, F. W. (1982). Preschoolers' awareness of television advertising. *Child Development, 53*(August), 933–937.

Luria, A. R. (1973). *The working brain: An introduction to neuropsychology.* New York: Basic Books.

Macklin, M. C. (1985). Do young children understand the selling intent of commercials? *Journal of Consumer Affairs, 19*(Winter), 293–304.

McAlister, A. R., & Cornwell, T. B. (2009). Preschool children's persuasion knowledge: The contribution of theory of mind. *Journal of Public Policy and Marketing, 28*(2), 175–185.

McAlister, A. R., & Cornwell, T. B. (2010). Children's brand symbolism understanding: Links to theory of mind and executive functioning. *Psychology and Marketing, 27*(3), 203–228.

McAlister, A. R., & Cornwell, T. B. (2012). Collectible toys as marketing tools: Understanding preschool children's responses to foods paired with premiums. *Journal of Public Policy and Marketing, 31*(2), 195–205. doi: 10.1509/jppm.10.067

McAlister, A. R., Cornwell, T. B., & Cornain, E. K. (2011). Collectible toys and decisions to share: I'll gift you one to expand my set. *British Journal of Developmental Psychology, 29*, 1–17.

McAlister, A., & Peterson, C. C. (2006). Mental playmates: Siblings, executive functioning and theory of mind. *British Journal of Developmental Psychology, 24*(4), 733–751.

McAlister, A. R., & Peterson, C. C. (2007). A longitudinal study of child siblings and theory of mind development. *Cognitive Development, 22*, 258–270.

McAlister, A. R., & Peterson, C. C. (2013). Siblings, theory of mind and executive functioning in children aged 3 to 6 years: New longitudinal evidence. *Child Development, 84*(4), 1442–1458.

Mink, M., Evans, A., Moore, C. G., Calderon, K. S., & Deger, S. (2010). Nutritional imbalance endorsed by televised food advertisements. *Journal of the American Dietetic Association, 110*(6), 904–910.

Moses, L. J., & Baldwin, D. A. (2005). What can the study of cognitive development reveal about children's ability to appreciate and cope with advertising? *Journal of Public Policy and Marketing, 24*(2), 186–201.

Moss, M. (2013). *Salt, sugar, fat: How the food giants hooked us*. New York: Random House.
Peterson, C. C. (2000). Kindred spirits: Influences of siblings' perspectives on theory of mind. *Cognitive Development, 15*, 435–455.
Piaget, J. (1970). Piaget's theory. In P. H. Mussen (Ed.), *Carmichael's manual of child psychology* (pp. 703–732). New York: Wiley.
Powell, L. M., Szczypka, G., Chaloupka, F. J., & Braunschweig, C. L. (2007). Nutritional content of television food advertisements seen by children and adolescents in the United States. *Pediatrics, 120*(3), 576–583.
Robert Wood Johnson Foundation (2014). Childhood obesity. Retrieved from: http://www.rwjf.org/en/topics/rwjf-topic-areas/health-policy/childhood-obesity.html
Robertson, T. S., & Rossiter, J. R. (1974). Children and commercial persuasion: An attribution theory analysis. *Journal of Consumer Research, 1*(June), 13–20.
Robinson, T. N., Borzekowski, D. L. G., Matheson, D. M., & Kraemer, H. C. (2007). Effects of fast food branding on young children's taste preferences. *Archive of Pediatrics and Adolescent Medicine, 161*(8), 792–797.
Russo, J. E. (1977). The value of unit price information. *Journal of Marketing Research, 14*(2), 193–201.
Sefcik, D. (2013, May). *UP*. Special session paper presented at Marketing and Public Policy Conference, Washington, DC.
Slaughter, V., Dennis, M. J., & Pritchard, M. (2002). Theory of mind and peer acceptance in preschool children. *British Journal of Developmental Psychology, 20*, 545–564.
Wansink, B., Just, D. R., Payne, C. R., & Klinger, M. Z. (2012). Attractive names sustain increased vegetable intake in schools. *Preventive Medicine, 55*(4), 330–332.
Zeithaml, V. A. (1982). Consumer response to in-store price information environments. *Journal of Consumer Research, 8*(4), 357–369.
Zelazo, P. D., Carter, A., Reznick, J. S., & Frye, D. (1997). Early development of executive function: A problem-solving framework. *Review of General Psychology, 1*(2), 1–29.

9

SOCIAL MEDIA AND CRISIS COMMUNICATION

Explicating the Social-Mediated Crisis Communication Model

Lucinda Austin and Yan Jin

High-profile organizational crises such as British Petroleum's (BP's) Deepwater Horizon oil spill in 2010 have shown the importance of social media in spreading (mis)information about crises. For example, BP shared updates and encouraged open dialogue through creation of dedicated Web and Facebook pages, and Twitter, Flickr, and YouTube sites, allowing publics to post uncensored messages about BP's response. Other publics responded by sharing information on their personal and organizational pages and created their own sites to share information about BP, such as a parody Twitter account with false information and a website dedicated for complaints. BP was simultaneously praised for its social media response and criticized for its public relations efforts. While the BP oil spill is a prominent example, other recent examples also illustrate the potential for social media to spread information that may lead to or further organizational crises, including:

- viral videos and photos of employee offenses, such as food tampering at restaurants including Dominos (2009), Burger King (2012, 2013), KFC (2013), Taco Bell (2012, 2013), Wendy's (2013), and others;
- viral YouTube videos of poor customer service, such as a FedEx delivery person throwing a fragile package over a fence instead of delivering to the door (2013); and
- Twitter campaigns gone wrong, such as McDonald's Twitter hashtag designed to share positive stories (#McDStories) that resulted in a backlash of negative stories about visits to McDonald's (2012).

Cases such as these further highlight the importance of monitoring social media and understanding effective crisis communication practices.

Crisis communicators facing high-stakes threats have an increasing need for evidence-based guidelines for crisis information to ensure the safety and welfare of publics and organizations and aid in crisis recovery. Scarce theory-grounded research explores how publics receive, seek, and share crisis information via social media. This chapter addresses the ways in which social media influence the practice of crisis communication, as a strategic communication area, and discusses the Social-Mediated Crisis Communication (SMCC) model, which serves as a framework for crisis and issues management in a rapidly evolving media landscape.

The SMCC model is the first theoretical model developed to address this need for empirical model development and testing specific to understanding crisis communication in the landscape of social media (Jin & Liu, 2010; Austin, Liu, & Jin, 2012). The SMCC model research has received wide attention: SMCC scholarship has been published and presented in a variety of outlets and received national and international attention, including top downloaded articles in the *Journal of Applied Communication, Journal of Public Relations Research, Public Relations Review,* and *Communication Research*. This research has also been funded by the Arthur W. Page Center for Integrity in Public Communication at Pennsylvania State University, and featured by NCA's *Communication Currents* magazine, by the Institute for Public Relations' Social Science of Social Media Research Center, in *New Media and Public Relations* (2nd edition), and in a forthcoming book on social media and crisis communication co-edited by authors of this chapter.

This chapter situates the SMCC model in the larger body of literature on social media and crisis communication, covers current and emerging issues in social media and crisis communication, provides an overview of dominant research streams and areas for special consideration (including characteristics of crises, organizations, audiences, and communication), and presents some important future directions for research in this area.

Social Media and Crisis Communication

Before expanding upon the research addressing social media and crisis communication, we first present common definitions for these two concepts. According to Fraustino, Liu, and Jin (2012), social media are "interactive digital tools that feature content users may generate, manipulate, or influence" (p. 7). From the perspective of public relations, Wright and Hinson (2009) operationalized social media broadly as various digital tools and applications that facilitate interactive communication and content exchange among and between publics and organizations.

An organizational crisis, according to Coombs (2012), is "an unpredictable event that threatens important expectancies of stakeholders related to health, safety, environmental and economic issues, and can seriously impact an organization's performance and generate negative outcomes" (p. 3). With this definition in mind, crisis communication, therefore, seeks to craft and manage responses that protect an organization's reputation in the wake of a crisis (Heath & Coombs, 2006). The rise of social media has changed the landscape of crisis communication in at least two important ways. First, social media can be the source or origin of an organizational crisis, such as a mishandled or poorly-designed social media campaign or message that damages the organization's reputation. Second, social media platforms have become major vehicles for damaging rumor transmission, negative opinion sharing, and aggregation of negative emotions regarding an organization.

Current and Emerging Issues

During crises, publics—groups of people who share common interests at a particular time and "share interpretations of events and actions in their environments" (Botan & Taylor, 2004, p. 655)—turn to social media for a wide variety of information and support, including emotional support (Macias, Hilyard, & Freimuth, 2009; Stephens & Malone, 2009). Social media play a role in both the amplification and attenuation of crises, as the choice of channel can strongly impact publics' perceptions of organizational reputation in certain circumstances. For example, one study found that when publics received information from an organization in crisis via Twitter they were less likely to attribute crisis responsibility to the organization (Schultz, Utz, & Göritz, 2011). Certain social media platforms, such as Twitter, Facebook, and individual blogs, are most frequently used for information sharing, especially in the first 12 hours of a crisis, when the most citizen-generated content appears online (Baron & Philbin, 2009; Heverin & Zach, 2010; Wigley & Fontenot, 2010).

Social media also do not adhere to the more constrained schedules of traditional media and instead allow publics to access information where and when they see fit (Procopio & Procopio, 2007; Purcell, 2011), as well as stimulate or trigger certain behavioral responses based on that information (Murdock, 2010). Publics with high involvement in crises, however, are more likely to use active media channels such as newspapers and magazines, as opposed to more passive media channels such as television, when retrieving and processing news and crisis information (Avery, 2010). Electronic word-of-mouth (eWOM) (e.g., online discussion forums, comments and reviews of products) communication also influences how individuals involve themselves with crises and can amplify organizations' crisis messages (Kozinets, de Valck, Wojnicki, & Wilner, 2010). Publics tend to adapt their desire to spread eWOM through their judgment of the appropriateness or value of information to potential recipients (Sohn, 2009). Also, as Bucher (2002) pointed out, while online communication makes information retrieval more efficient by decentralizing and accelerating the spread of information, it increases the risk of information overflow due to the huge volume of information created, transmitted, and consumed. This inevitably increases the creation and spread of rumors online during the information retrieval process.

Publics who are dissatisfied with an organization may use social media to spread negative word-of-mouth (nWOM) communication on and offline (Bailey, 2004; Richins, 1983). This can take the form of proving worth, gaining revenge, or getting others to act against the organization (Ward & Ostrom, 2006). Employers should also exercise caution with employees who blog, as they may express or expand upon nWOM (Kaplan & Haenlein, 2010). During a crisis, although blogs publish more frequently, they tend to be more opinion-based than other online media such as online newspapers (Liu, 2010). This makes transparency essential when it comes to establishing credibility and gaining influence of any blog-mediated nWOM (Burns, 2008). Publics who interact with organizations and others via social media are also more likely to engage in other communicative behaviors, such as information sharing and having a real-time dialogue about issues, both on and offline (Dutta-Bergman, 2006). In sum, social media can facilitate information sharing, opinion sharing, and emotional expression about crises (Macias et al., 2009) in ways that reach far beyond that of traditional public relations communication tactics, such as press releases or public statements (Smith, 2010). The current social media environment, therefore, has posed professional strategic communicators with unprecedented challenges in managing crisis communication and organizational reputation (Austin, Liu, & Jin, 2012, 2014). Because of these challenges, crisis communication scholars must seek to develop and hone theories that can guide practitioners' efforts to use social media to effectively manage organizational crises in our modern media ecosystem.

Dominant Research Streams

The research on social media and crisis communication is young but vibrant, with exciting, unanswered questions for scholars to explore and examine. Throughout the past decade, researchers have identified how publics consume social media during crises, the functions social media play in crisis situations, and what factors motivate publics to use (or avoid) social media in crises. Current and emerging issues regarding the unique roles social media can play in crisis communication can be summarized as the following (Fraustino et al., 2012).

- *Publics' motivations and engagement in using different types and functions of social media in crisis communication.* Whether publics' motivations to use social media in crises varies depending upon the social media type and platform functionality.
- *Primary functions of social media in crisis communication.* Whether some of the functions social media play in crises are more important than others to users as a function of crisis type and demographics.

A noticeable lack of theory-driven, social science based approaches to social media and crisis communication research limits the field's ability to expand testable knowledge and generate new ideas (Baran & Davis, 2006). Much of the extant research has included episodic case studies without a theoretical framework to guide the research design and analysis. A few notable exceptions are the situational crisis communication theory (SCCT) (Coombs & Holladay, 2012), uses and gratifications theory (UGT) (Lev-On, 2012), and channel complementarity theory (Dutta-Bergman, 2004, 2006).

SCCT, one of the most prominent crisis communication theories, posits that crisis managers should match an organization's crisis responses to the perceived crisis responsibility and level of reputational threat involved. Factors that influence publics' crisis responsibility attribution include crisis type, crisis history, and prior relationship. SCCT has been widely applied in social-mediated crisis communication research among public relations scholars.

UGT explains how and why audience members and stakeholders seek out specific information, based on the satisfaction of specific needs. According to Lev-On (2012), "the study of media uses and gratifications is particularly important in emergency and crisis situations, which magnify needs and make them more acute" (p. 101). Based upon premises of UGT, Dutta-Bergman (2004, 2006) proposed channel complementarity theory in order to address the changing media climate, which asserts that audiences select multiple forms of media, complementary to the forms they already use to fulfill functional needs (Dutta-Bergman, 2004, 2006). Channel complementarity theory helps explain congruence between traditional and social media use and has been explored in social-mediated crisis communication research in light of why audiences prefer certain forms of communication.

Based on the above theoretical foundations, as well as crisis managers' pressing need for responding appropriately to each unique crisis generation phase, researchers have started to build theoretical frameworks that address the unique challenges and opportunities social media has brought to crisis communication. Grounded in rumor psychology theory and suggested rumor-quelling strategies (DiFonzo, 2008), Jin and Liu (2010) adapted the three-stage rumor transmission model as the blog-mediated rumor cycle that communicators should manage at each level: rumor generation, rumor belief, and rumor transition. Existing crisis management literature (e.g., Coombs, 2007a, 2007b; Huang & Su, 2009; Liu, 2010; Taylor & Kent, 2007) has also been applied in understanding crisis communication practice in the social media era. Primarily based on Coombs' situational crisis communication theory (SCCT) (Coombs, 2007a, 2007b), which proposes four response categories, namely to deny, diminish, rebuild, and reinforce (Coombs, 2007a, 2007b; Heath & Coombs, 2006), Jin and Liu (2010) proposed that crisis managers should primarily treat blog-mediated crises as rumors and combine rumor-management strategies with traditional crisis-response strategies. Moving forward, researchers need to make a concerted effort to build theory so that the research findings can be better united and applied. Of particular importance is testing whether theories developed before the advent of social media can be applied to understanding new media, with modifications as needed (e.g., uses and gratifications theory and SCCT) or whether new theories are needed (e.g., channel complementarity).

In a non-crisis context, research indicates that different types of social media perform different functions for users. For instance, people tend to use YouTube for entertainment seeking and Facebook for content sharing (Liu, Austin, & Jin, 2011). Unfortunately, research on social media use in crises overwhelmingly examines one or two social media tools, specifically Twitter or Facebook, and researchers tend to generalize findings from those types to all social media. Therefore, more research is needed to understand what, if any, unique roles various social media platforms play in publics' communication activities in crisis situations. Further, to date, research has identified several reasons why publics use social media during disasters (e.g., convenience, social norms, to self-mobilize) and, conversely, shun social media during disasters (e.g., privacy fears, accuracy concerns, access issues). Yet, existing research has not provided evidence-based guidance for identifying the likely predictors of these behaviors (e.g., contextual factors, individual-level characteristics, etc.).

Areas for Special Consideration

Taking into consideration the aforementioned extant research and theories—particularly SCCT and rumor psychology theory—at least four key areas require explicit research attention in order to further understanding of social media's role in crisis communication: organizational approaches and considerations, audience-oriented approaches and considerations, characteristics of crises, and characteristics of social media.

- *Organizational approaches and considerations.* Organizational characteristics have the potential to influence how organizations respond to crisis situations and how publics receive this response. Some important organizational characteristics to understand include logistics (e.g. type and size of the organization), values, leadership, crisis planning, pre-crisis reputation, social media engagement level, and past crisis history.
- *Audience-oriented approaches and considerations.* Audience characteristics may impact crisis situations. Some notable audience characteristics include their information seeking, production, and sharing before, during, and after crises. Individuals' motivations also affect their use of social media in crisis communication, along with their use of traditional media and word-of-mouth communications.
- *Characteristics of the crisis.* Characteristics of the crisis itself also affect social media use. The crisis type (e.g. man-made vs. natural disaster), responsibility

attribution, controllability, severity, and duration all influence the role social media can play during a crisis.
- *Characteristics of social media.* Characteristics of the social media platform also impact the nature of crisis communication. Specific types of social media (e.g., Facebook, Twitter, Instagram, etc.) and sources of social media messages (e.g., organization, third party, etc.) can have varied impacts on the effectiveness of social-mediated crisis communication. The enhanced real-time visual storytelling capacity of most social media platforms, as well as their ability to stoke emotions, provide unique challenges and opportunities for organizations to address and utilize in communicating about crises.

The Social-Mediated Crisis Communication Model
Overview of the SMCC Model

The SMCC model was developed to provide evidence-based guidelines to help crisis communicators decide if, when, and how to respond to influential social media, while also acknowledging the influence of traditional media and offline word-of-mouth communication (see Figure 9.1 below). The SMCC framework highlights the importance of integrating social media into the media mix for crisis communication and issues management (Liu, Jin, Austin, & Janoske, 2012).

Origin of the BMCC Model

The SMCC model evolved from the Blog-Mediated Crisis Communication (BMCC) model (Jin & Liu, 2010), which provided guidance for crisis managers on identifying influential blogs and implementing communication response strategies for these influential blogs before, during, and after crises. The BMCC model implies that crisis communicators with limited resources must identify influential blogs to maximize resources and monitoring capabilities. Influential blogs are identified through bloggers' information authority and credibility, and through their issue- and self-involvement. According to the BMCC model, influential blogs address blog followers' informational and emotional needs during crises by providing issue-fit opinion leadership, which exerts influences by providing timely and accurate information on issues that affect and concern blog followers. The original BMCC model included a checklist matrix for evaluating the potential influence of a blog, as well as recommended response and recovery communication strategies based on a variety of organizational and crisis factors (see Jin & Liu, 2010, and Liu, Jin, Austin, & Janoske, 2012, for the matrix and communication strategies that have informed the SMCC).

The BMCC model was later enhanced to include all social media, in addition to blogs, and renamed the Social-Mediated Crisis Communication (SMCC) model (Liu, Jin, Austin, & Janoske, 2012; Liu, Jin, Briones, & Kuch, 2012). The renaming of the model and its more inclusive focus stemmed from emerging research on the influence of social media and social networks as crisis management tools (Briones, Kuch, Liu, & Jin, 2011; Liu, Jin, Briones, & Kuch, 2012), including a series of interviews with American Red Cross communicators exploring the model's propositions. The SMCC model, therefore, highlights the influence of social media platforms, in addition to influential bloggers, traditional media, and offline interactions (Jin, Liu, & Austin, 2014).

Components of the SMCC Model

The SMCC model describes the relationship between the following core concepts: an organization, key publics, social media, traditional media, and offline word-of-mouth communication before, during, and after crises (see Figure 9.1).

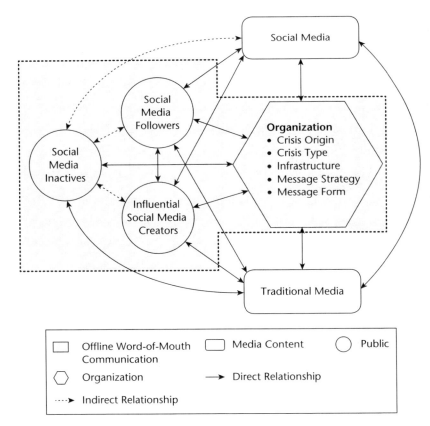

FIGURE 9.1 Social-Mediated Crisis Communication Model (Jin, Liu, & Austin, 2014)

Key Publics

First, the SMCC model identifies three key publics who seek, produce, or share information before, during, and after crises: influential social media creators, social media followers, and social media inactives (Jin, Liu, & Austin, 2014; Li, Bernoff, Fiorentino, & Glass, 2007). Influential social media creators develop and post crisis information online; social media followers consume this information from social media creators and also share this information both on and offline; and social media inactives do not participate actively in the social media, but receive this crisis information via other channels—including traditional media and word-of mouth communication—from social media followers, creators, or other inactives.

The Flow of Information

Next, as represented in Figure 9.1, solid arrows represent direct relationships in the flow of information, while dotted arrows represent indirect relationships. For example, social media inactives have an indirect relationship with social media, receiving information indirectly from followers and creators. Arrows also indicate a two-way, reciprocal flow of information. For example, social media and traditional media directly inform one another's crisis coverage with traditional media utilizing information from social media in news development and vice versa.

Forms of Information

The model also highlights three main forms of crisis communication, including social media, traditional media, and offline word-of-mouth communication. The organization responding to an issue/crisis and the key publics are situated within a gray box in the model to represent the ubiquitous nature of offline word-of-mouth communication among the organization and social media creators, followers, and inactives. Social media, which may include information from influential social media creators or the organization, has a direct relationship with key publics, the organization, and traditional media, while traditional media has a direct relationship with social media, key publics, and the organization.

Organizational Considerations

The SMCC model portrays the crisis management considerations of a single organization and situates the organization responding to an issue/crisis as the central source for crisis information. As Atkins (2010) notes, crises rarely impact only one organization and successful crisis planning should consider multiple organizational perspectives. The model can potentially be applied to multiple-organization crisis contexts, although it is important to note that SMCC researchers acknowledge that external organizations' influences on the crisis and public and media responses are beyond the scope of this model (Jin & Liu, 2010).

The SMCC model includes five criteria for organizations to consider in their response to emerging issues and crises: (1) crisis origin, (2) crisis type, (3) organizational infrastructure, (4) message strategy, and (5) message form. The crisis origin refers to the starting point of the issue, whether internal or external to the organization, which influences publics' attribution of responsibility for the crisis (Coombs, 2007b). Publics are likely to respond more negatively to crises of perceived internal organizational origin (e.g., unfair employee labor practices, corrupt leadership, or mismanagement of funds) versus crises of perceived external origin (e.g., terrorist attack or natural disaster event) (Jin, Liu, & Austin, 2014; Lee, 2004). Based upon the attribution of responsibility, varying crisis message strategies are recommended (Jin & Liu, 2010).

Second, crisis type is identifiable based on the characteristics of the crisis and may also influence attribution of responsibility (Coombs, 2007a, 2010, 2012; Jin & Liu, 2010). Based on SCCT (Coombs, 2007a), a crisis may be perceived as victim-based (i.e., the organization is also the victim of the crisis), accidental (i.e., actions leading to the crisis were unintentional, such as technical errors), or intentional (i.e., the crisis is perceived as preventable and the organization as placing people at risk). Organizations should carefully consider how the type of crisis might influence publics and adjust crisis response strategies accordingly.

Third, organizational infrastructure refers to whether a crisis should be handled in a centralized way through a unified organizational message or should be localized through tailored messages meant for specific audiences, including branches and affiliates (Jin, Liu, & Austin, 2014). Depending on the type and origin of the crisis, a centralized message, which can also be communicated by local entities, may be more effective in facilitating crisis recovery (Liu, Jin, Briones, & Kuch, 2012). For example, the American Red Cross might consider developing more centralized messages for its local chapters to disseminate to publics affected by national and/or local disasters, which would allow a consistent overarching message and localized implementation.

Fourth, crisis message strategy refers to the content of the organization's crisis communications, which helps publics respond to and make meaning of the crisis. Content may include instructing and adapting information for impacted publics (Coombs, 2012), which informs publics of the crisis and any actions they should take. It may also provide them with emotional support. Crisis response strategies for reputation management can range on a continuum from defensive to accommodative strategies (Jin & Liu, 2010; also see Table 9.1). Defensive strategies separate the blame for the crisis from the organization and often include a combination of attacking the accuser, denial, scapegoating, ignoring, excusing, justifying, and separation. Conversely, accommodative strategies emphasize image repair, which is needed as image damage increases, and include bolstering, ingratiation, victimage, endorsement, compensation, transcendence, and full apology (for a full description of these response options see, Coombs, 2012; Jin & Liu, 2010). SCCT and SMCC research (Coombs, 2007a, 2010, 2012; Jin, 2010; Jin & Liu, 2010;

TABLE 9.1 Social-Mediated Crisis Response Strategies (adapted from Liu, Jin, Austin, & Janoske, 2012)

Response Options		Strategy	Rumor Phases			Crisis Recovery
			Generation	Belief	Transmission	
Base		Instructing information	▓			
		Adjusting information: Corrective action	▓			
		Adjusting information: Emotion	▓			
Defensive	Deny	Attack the accuser		▓		
		Denial		▓		
		Scapegoat		▓		
		Ignore		▓		
	Diminish	Excuse		▓		
		Justification		▓		
		Separation		▓		
	Rebuild	Compensation				▓
		Apology				▓
		Transcendence				▓
	Reinforce	Bolstering		▓		
		Ingratiation		▓		
Accommodative		Victimage		▓		
		Endorsement				
Punish*		Legal action			▓	

*Not a recommended social media response strategy

Jin, Liu, & Austin, 2014) provide suggestions for when and how organizations should respond (see Table 9.1). Grounded in rumor psychology theory, Jin and Liu (2010) adapted the rumor-transmission process to the social-mediated rumor cycle and suggest differing communication strategies for varying stages of rumor transmission including rumor generation, rumor belief, and rumor transition.

Fifth, crisis message form refers to how the crisis is distributed or conveyed. The SMCC Model identifies varying crisis message forms including messages distributed through social media, traditional media, and/or offline word-of-mouth communication. Crisis message form has been shown to impact publics' acceptance of crisis messages (Liu, Jin, & Austin, 2013; Schultz et al., 2011). For example, one recent study found that when a crisis origin was external, participants were most likely to accept an organization's evasive responses if the crisis information was delivered through traditional media (Jin, Liu, & Austin, 2014).

Summary of Extant SMCC Research

To date, the SMCC model has been tested through interviews and experiments with crisis communicators at nonprofit organizations and strategic communications agencies, as well as through interviews and experiments with various publics of organizational crises. Previous research has explored how factors such as crisis origin (e.g., emanating from the organization or from an outside entity), crisis information form (i.e., traditional media, social/new media, or word of mouth), and crisis information source (i.e., organization or a third party) affect publics' emotional and cognitive responses to crisis information, their information seeking patterns and crisis communicative tendencies, as well as acceptance of crisis response strategies (Austin et al., 2012; Jin, Liu, & Austin, 2014; Jin, Liu, Anagondahalli, & Austin, 2014; Liu et al., 2011; Liu et al., 2013). Additionally, interviews with senior-level crisis communicators at strategic communications agencies have focused on crisis recovery in addition to crisis response, identifying factors for effective recovery from crisis (Austin, Liu, & Jin, 2014). Recently, the SMCC model has been applied not only to organizational crisis communication but also to disaster communication contexts (Liu, Jin, Briones, & Kuch, 2012). We next provide a more detailed discussion of key findings stemming from SMCC-based research.

Expanding the BMCC Model Propositions

Interviews with 40 professional communicators from the American Red Cross explored disaster communication contexts. These interviews highlighted the importance of varying types of social media during crises and illustrated how crises emerge through multiple types of media simultaneously, including social and traditional media and offline word-of-mouth communication (Briones et al., 2011; Liu, Jin, Briones, & Kuch, 2012). In the case of the Red Cross communicators, traditional blogs were not viewed as useful venues for crisis communication (Liu, Jin, Briones, & Kuch, 2012). As mentioned earlier, these

TABLE 9.2 Summary of Empirical SMCC Model Research by Model Components Examined

	Organization					Publics			Media Content			Message Source		Outcomes				
	Crisis Origin[1]	Crisis Type[2]	Organizational Infrastructure[3]	Message Strategy[4]	Message Form[5]	Social Media Inactives	Social Media Followers	Influential Social Media Creators	Traditional Media	Social Media	Offline Word-of-mouth	Organization	Third-party	Information Seeking	Information Sharing	Acceptance of Message	Crisis Emotions	Crisis Recovery
Liu, Austin, & Jin, 2011	■												■					
Briones et al., 2011			■						■	■		■					■	
Liu, Jin, Briones, & Kuch, 2012			■						■	■		■						
Austin, Liu, & Jin, 2012									■	■	■	■		■				
Liu, Jin, & Austin, 2013									■	■	■	■			■			
Jin, Liu, Anagondahalli, & Austin, 2014		■							■	■	■	■	■				■	
Jin, Liu, & Austin, 2014				■													■	
Austin, Liu, & Jin, 2014	■																	■

Notes

1 Internal vs. external
2 Victim-based, accidental, or intentional
3 Centralized vs. decentralized
4 Instructing/adapting or defensive to accommodative
5 Social media, traditional media, offline word-of-mouth communication

insights inspired expansion of the BMCC model to reflect the broader social media landscape and prompted the initial name change of the BMCC model to the SMCC model.

The Impact of Form and Source on Information Seeking

The SMCC model was further explored through interviews and an experiment with college students to examine publics' crisis information seeking behaviors and factors affecting media use (Austin et al., 2012). Findings revealed that publics used social media to obtain insider information from individuals who might have direct access to relevant information and check in with family and friends during crises. Publics, however, sought traditional media more often to obtain educational and instructive information, such as how to respond in crisis situations. Publics viewed traditional media sources as providing more credible information during crises than social media or offline word-of-mouth communication. Additionally, findings stressed the importance of third-party information in enhancing crisis information credibility.

The Impact of Form and Source on Information Sharing

A series of in-depth interviews and an experiment with college students also explored publics' crisis information sharing behaviors (Liu et al., 2013). Interview findings revealed that participants communicated about crises primarily through offline word-of-mouth communication, followed by social media (e.g., Facebook and Twitter) and texting. Participants described four major themes for their choice of media for communication, which included humor or entertainment value, the ability to share insider information, social norms, and privacy concerns. The experiment varied initial crisis communication form and source, to include messages via three forms (traditional media, social media, and word-of-mouth communication) and two sources (the organization or a third-party, such as a journalist). Findings revealed that publics were most likely to communicate positively about the organization when they initially received crisis information from the organization via traditional media. Conversely, publics were most likely to communicate negatively about the organization when they initially received crisis information through the organization's offline word-of-mouth communication. Overall, crisis communication through social media yielded more positive communication behaviors from publics, such as sharing and posting positive comments.

The Impact of Form and Source on Crisis Emotions and Acceptance of Response Strategies

An experiment with college students applied the SMCC model to study the effects of crisis information form (traditional media, social media, and offline word-of-mouth communication) and information source (organization versus third-party) on publics' emotions during crises and their acceptance of response strategies (Liu et al., 2011). Based on prior research (Austin et al., 2012: Liu et al., 2011), six salient crisis situations were selected for the experiment (see Figure 9.2). Findings revealed significant message acceptance effects, as measured by self-reported likelihood of accepting different organizational crisis responses. Specifically, (a) publics were most accepting of defensive organizational responses when these came through the organization through traditional media, (b) publics were most accepting of supportive responses when these came through a third party via traditional media, and (c) publics were most accepting of evasive responses when these came from the organization through traditional media. Findings from this experiment also revealed significant effects on attribution-independent emotions (e.g., anxiety, apprehension, and fear), external-dependent emotions, (e.g., anger, contempt, and disgust) and internal-dependent emotions (e.g., embarrassment, guilt, and shame), based on the crisis information form and source. For instance, when information about a crisis of internal origin was sent by a third party using social media, participants were likely to feel attribution-dependent emotions such as anger, contempt, and disgust. The results also highlighted the need for considering both information form and source in organizational crisis responses.

The Impact of Form, Source, and Origin on Publics' Crisis Responses

A further experiment explored the SMCC model by examining the effect of crisis information form, crisis information source, and crisis origin on publics' responses to crisis information (Jin, Liu, & Austin, 2014). Findings reflected the complex nature of crisis communication in a converging media climate and furthered the impetus for strategically matching crisis information form and source, while also considering the crisis origin. Specifically findings suggested that, when the crisis origin was internal to the organization, publics displayed more crisis emotions (e.g., anger) and were more receptive to accommodative responses. When the crisis origin was external, however, publics were more receptive to defensive responses. For a crisis with perceived internal origin, publics displayed more attribution-dependent

Scenario	*Conditions*
Bomb threat (TM + Third Party)	Campus newspaper
Riots (SM + Third Party)	Facebook update from friend
Blizzard (WOM + Third Party)	Phone call from friend
Disease outbreak (SM + Organization)	Facebook update from the University
Embezzlement (WOM + Organization)	Town hall meeting at the University
Violent partying (TM + Organization)	Press statement transcript in campus newspaper

FIGURE 9.2 Crisis Scenario Conditions

emotions (e.g., anger, contempt, and disgust) when messages came through a third party via social media. For a crisis with perceived external origin, publics seemed most likely to accept evasive responses if they were sent by the organization.

Scale Development for Measuring Crisis Emotions

Based upon the SMCC experiments measuring emotional responses to crisis, as well as attribution theory and the crisis emotions literature (Choi & Lin, 2009; Jin, 2010; Weiner, 1986), a scale was proposed and tested for measuring publics' crisis emotions (Jin, Liu, Anagondahalli, & Austin, 2014). This scale examined 13 discrete emotions: anger, anxiety, apprehension, confusion, contempt, disgust, embarrassment, fear, guilt, sadness, shame, surprise, and sympathy. In various crisis scenarios, participants were asked to indicate how the situations made them feel. Three types of crisis emotions in an organizational crisis were explicated according to the presence of attribution (whether certain feelings result from the perception of who/what causes a crisis) and the direction of such attribution, if any (whether an emotion is related to how individuals feel about themselves as associated with a crisis or toward an organization involved in the crisis).

Thus, the tested scale, which conceptualized and operationalized attribution-independent versus attribution-dependent crisis emotions, revealed three emotion clusters in experience with organizational crises: (1) attribution-independent emotions (four items of anxiety, fear, apprehension, and sympathy), (2) external-attribution-dependent emotions (four items of disgust, contempt, anger, and sadness), and (3) internal-attribution-dependent crisis emotions (three items of guilt, embarrassment, and shame). The three factors capture the domain of publics' crisis emotions in organizational crisis situations. Findings revealed that publics' emotions felt in relation to organizational crisis situations differed in structure from those felt in non-crisis situations, and the scale proved to be valid and reliable in measuring emotions in response to organizational crisis.

Crisis Recovery Definition and Factors for Effective Recovery

Most recently, the SMCC model has been explored through in-depth interviews with senior-level crisis communicators at strategic communications agencies with varying crisis management and communication experience. Twenty open-ended phone interviews were conducted using purposive, convenience, and snowball sampling strategies to recruit communicators at major strategic communication agencies across the U.S. Agency representatives were purposively selected due to their specific expertise and years of experience in crisis communication, Agency representatives are more likely to have significant, sustained, and varied experiences managing crises than their communication counterparts within single organizations (Liu & Pompper, 2012). This research expanded prior work on the

SMCC model in its exploration of crisis recovery, specifically in its identification of factors for effective recovery from crisis (Austin et al., 2014). Interview findings revealed principles for effective crisis recovery communication, including proactively addressing failures that led to the crisis, being transparent and honest while mostly positive, focusing on future directions, and rebuilding and repairing symbolic damage. Organizational best practices included tested organizational values and strong crisis leadership. Publics were important in crisis recovery for the purposes of facilitating healing, highlighting victims' voices, and providing evidence of recovery. A definition for crisis recovery was proposed based on the findings: "Crisis recovery begins when crises end, which can be determined by public perception and repair of symbolic and physical damage" (Austin et al., 2014).

In sum, findings from the aforementioned studies exploring the SMCC model have shown the significance of crisis origin, crisis type, information source and form, and crisis message strategy. Results suggest the importance of strategic approaches to matching crisis information form and source in response to crisis, which currently is not addressed in other crisis communication theories such as the SCCT.

Future Directions

Needed Areas of Research for Social Media and Crisis Communication

Our continued work with the SMCC model has revealed three broad areas for future research: (1) explicating publics' motivations for using different social media platforms in different crisis situations, (2) identifying why some social media functions are preferred over other functions during crises, and (3) exploring further how crisis type and individual-level characteristics affect social media use—and motivations for use—in response to a crisis. Tackling these areas will provide an even more theoretically detailed understanding of how individual, organizational, and media variables shape communications in the wake of organizational crises.

In line with this research direction and with an emphasis on how media professionals view social-mediated crisis communication, Austin and Jin (2015) conducted 40 in-depth interviews to study media professionals' views of organizational crisis communication and the role of social media in crisis coverage production and dissemination. Respect, objectivity/neutrality, sensitivity, empathy/compassion, accuracy, timeliness, verification of facts/sources, honesty, and transparency were identified as major ethical guidelines for crisis reporting. Interviewed media professionals also indicated that crises represent unique situations for stakeholder engagement and relationship building between media professionals and public relations professionals.

Future research should also examine applications of social media in specific crisis communication contexts, including corporate, political and government, nonprofit and philanthropic, sports, health, disasters and natural hazards, and higher education contexts. In addition, it is important to provide a global perspective on social media and crisis communication. Cultural influences, different social media landscapes in different countries and regions, and varied social media policies and regulations all are likely to play an important role in determining how organizations can optimize their crisis communication efforts using social media platforms. For example, Facebook or Twitter is not accessible in mainland China, but their counterparts, Renren and Weibo, are widely used by Internet users in China. With the advent of globalization, organizations confronted with crisis situations must now understand their audiences across multiple cultures and the types of social media platforms to which they have access.

Plans for SMCC Model Research

To address gaps in current research on social media and crisis communication, our SMCC model research will continue to focus on how the characteristics of social media, crises, organizations, and audiences influence SMCC effectiveness, individually and jointly. We are particularly interested in visual storytelling (e.g., crisis information embedded in photos, videos, and infographics) and the capacity of social media as a venue for emotional expression and support. For instance, inspired by recent work on how fast food company crises were represented on Instagram (Guidry, Messner, Jin, & Medina-Messner, 2015) and how health risks were portrayed on Pinterest (e.g., Guidry, Jin, Haddad, Zhang, & Smith, 2015), our research team is working on a new theoretical framework that defines the role and functions of visual social media (VSM) platforms in crisis and risk communication, with regard to information processing, emotion sharing, and calling for action. We plan to examine how different VSM platforms, such as Pinterest and Instagram, can be utilized strategically and managed differently compared to more textual-oriented platforms, such as Facebook and Twitter. In addition, we also plan to focus on how mobile technology can enhance the spread of crisis information and the speed of crisis communication. The SMCC model will also be applied further to varying contexts (e.g., risk and health crises), as a theoretical framework explaining how media form, message source, and audience and organization characteristics, make a difference in crisis, risk, and health information dissemination and reception. We also intend to address the following issues.

Moving From Description to Cause-and-Effect Explanation

Beyond descriptions stemming from case analyses, SMCC researchers seek a social-scientific approach to examine individual parts and linkages proposed within the model. For example, this research is needed to examine what features of social-mediated crisis messages sent by an organization—depending on the crisis type and organizational crisis history—will be most effective in communicating to and motivating social media creators, followers, and inactives. We believe these findings would help provide a map that more comprehensively explains the process of crisis communication in the modern media landscape. Critical to this effort is the need for data derived from nationally representative samples. These samples would yield more generalizable findings that could help fill a massive methodological gap that exists within the research on social media and crisis communication (Fraustino et al., 2012). Echoing this need, most recently, Liu, Fraustino, and Jin (in press, 2015) conducted an online experiment using a nationally representative sample. The study findings shed light on how publics' crisis perceptions, emotions, information seeking and sharing, and intentions to follow governmental instructions during a disaster vary as a function of crisis information form (Facebook post vs. Tweet vs. Website post) and source (local government vs. Federal government vs. local media vs. national media). Social media platforms as well as Federal government sources were found to be significant factors that led to higher disaster salience and more active communication and protective behavioral tendencies. In addition, as with many emerging communication topics, another research gap is the lack of longitudinal studies, for instance, capturing social media use prior to a crisis, during the immediate response, and into recovery. It is important to factor in not only social media platform, information source, and crisis type, but also demographic information and cultural background such as gender, race, age, and other potential contextual influencers. Future studies should seek to compare how organizations and publics use social media differently at different stages of a crisis cycle, ideally using nationally representative samples.

Developing Influence

Beyond identifying why publics use (and do not use) social media in crisis communication, more research is needed to examine what motivates specific individuals to become influential in creating and distributing crisis information (Fraustino et al., 2012). Additional empirical research is needed to develop an understanding of how an individual or groups of individuals become influential and to map the information flow among social media creators, followers, and inactives, as outlined by the SMCC model. This research could be aided by incorporating insights from established communication models, such as two-step flow, opinion leadership, and innovation diffusion (Jeffres, Neuendorf, Braken, & Atkin, 2008). Understanding the emergence of influential crisis content producers would also help researchers to evaluate what social media message features are most effective in convincing publics to take protective actions prior to, during, and after a crisis.

Classifying Media Types

As communication technologies advance, the delineations among social media, traditional media, and interpersonal communication will increasingly blur. Such blurring underscores the importance of examining social media use in the context of other communication types. The interactions among various modes of communication, if planned and managed strategically, may exert stronger, synergistic crisis communication effects to enhance crisis response acceptance and help protect and/or restore organizational image. Research should explore the information flow among various types of media and the current tendency to artificially segment and bundle certain media. Crisis media clusters—bundled according to the characteristics of crisis, organization, and primary publics—can play a significant role in classifying media types. Clusters could be used to recommend strategic media combinations that might be effective for organizations in crisis to communicate with publics in a timely and accurate fashion.

Full Cycle of Crisis Management

As mentioned earlier, existing research largely describes how publics use (and do not use) social media in crisis situations but does not provide evidence-based guidelines on how to effectively use social media to facilitate crisis recovery. Future SMCC model research needs to examine how social media monitoring helps with organizational crisis preparedness, and how social media can be used as a reputation management tool for crisis recovery.

Conclusion

Social media provide unique challenges and unprecedented communication opportunities for organizations in crises. As this burgeoning research area advances, more guidance is needed to explain how various social media, traditional media, and word-of-mouth communication forms interact in terms of crisis information and, most crucially, to what extent those crisis messages influence crisis recovery. The SMCC model is a new framework for crisis and issues management in a rapidly evolving media landscape, which aims to further understanding of the role of social media in crisis communication. Key factors, such as characteristics of crises, organizations, publics, and communication, need to be jointly taken into consideration for effective and ethical SMCC practice. The application of SMCC in different sectors and areas (e.g., health, corporate, nonprofit, political, sport, disaster, university, or other specific crises) will further provide industry-specific recommendations.

The SMCC model sets a new agenda for crisis scholars and practitioners. The model provides evidence that enriches the body of knowledge in crisis communication and provides research-based insights for crisis communication practice, for both managerial decision-making and crisis response implementation. Findings from emerging SMCC research suggest the importance of considering crisis origin, information form, information source, crisis type, and crisis message strategies when communicating during crises.

References

Austin, L., & Jin, Y. (2015). Approaching ethical crisis communication with accuracy and sensitivity: Exploring common ground and gaps between journalism and public relations. *Public Relations Journal, 8*(5), 1–26.

Austin, L., Liu, B. F., & Jin, Y. (2012). How audiences seek out crisis information: Exploring the social-mediated crisis communication model. *Journal of Applied Communication Research, 40*, 188–207.

Austin, L., Liu, B. F., & Jin, Y. (2014). Examining signs of recovery: How senior crisis communicators define organizational crisis recovery. *Public Relations Review, 40*, 844–846.

Avery, E. J. (2010). Contextual and audience moderators of channel selection and message reception of public health information in routine and crisis situations. *Journal of Public Relations Research, 22*, 378–403.

Bailey, A. A. (2004). Thiscompanysucks.com: The use of the Internet in negative consumer-to-consumer articulations. *Journal of Marketing Communications, 10*(3), 169–182.

Baran, S., & Davis, D. (2006). *Mass communication theory: Foundations, ferment, and future* (4th ed.). Belmont, CA: Wadsworth.

Baron, G., & Philbin, J. (2009, March). *Social media in crisis communication: Start with a drill*. Retrieved from http://www.prsa.org/SearchResults/view/7909/105/Social_media_in_crisis_communication_Start_with_a

Botan, C. H., & Taylor, M. (2004). Public relations: State of the field. *Journal of Communication, 54*, 645–661.

Briones, R. L., Kuch, B., Liu, B. F., & Jin, Y. (2011). Keeping up with the digital age: How the American Red Cross uses social media to build relationships. *Public Relations Review, 37*, 37–43.

Bucher, H. J. (2002). Crisis communication and the Internet: Risk and trust in a global media. *First Monday, 7*(4), Retrieved from http://131.193.153.231/www/issues/issue7_4/bucher/index.html

Burns, K. S. (2008). The misuse of social media: Reactions to and important lessons from a blog fiasco. *Journal of New Communications Research, 3*(1), 41–54.

Choi, Y., & Lin, Y-H. (2009). Consumer responses to Mattel product recalls posted on online bulletin boards: Exploring two types of emotion. *Journal of Public Relations Research, 21*(2), 198–207.

Coombs, W. T. (2007a). Attribution theory as a guide for post-crisis communication research. *Public Relations Review, 33*, 135–139.

Coombs, W. T. (2007b). Protecting organization reputation during a crisis: The development and application of Situational Crisis Communication Theory. *Corporate Reputation Review, 10*, 163–176.

Coombs, W. T. (2010). Pursuing evidence-based crisis communication. In W. T. Coombs & S. J. Holladay (Eds.), *The handbook of crisis communication* (pp. 719–725). New York, NY: Wiley-Blackwell.

Coombs, W. T. (2012). *Ongoing crisis communication: Planning, managing, and responding* (3rd ed.). Thousand Oaks, CA: Sage.

Coombs, T. W., & Holladay, S. J. (2012). Amazon.com's Orwellian nightmare: Exploring apology in an online environment. *Journal of Communication Management, 16,* 280–295.

DiFonzo, N. (2008). *The watercooler effect: A psychologist explores the extraordinary power of rumors.* New York: Avery.

Dutta-Bergman, M. J. (2004). Interpersonal communication after 9/11 via telephone and Internet: A theory of channel complementarity. *New Media & Society, 6*(5), 659–673.

Dutta-Bergman, M. J. (2006). Community participation and Internet use after September 11: Complementarity in channel consumption. *Journal of Computer-Mediated Communication, 11,* 469–484.

Fraustino, J. D., Liu, B. F., & Jin, Y. (2012, December). *Social media use during disasters.* Report submitted to the National Consortium for the Study of Terrorism and Responses to Terrorism (START), University of Maryland.

Guidry, J., Jin, Y., Haddad, L., Zhang, Y., & Smith, J. J. (2015). How health risks are pinpointed (or not) on social media: The portrayal of waterpipe smoking on Pinterest. *Health Communication, 1–9.* doi: 10.1080/10410236.2014.987468

Guidry, J., Messner, M., Jin, Y., & Medina-Messner, V. (2015). From #mcdonaldsfail to #dominossucks: An analysis of Instagram images about the 10 largest fast food companies. *Corporate Communications: An International Journal, 20*(3), 344–359.

Heath, R. L., & Coombs, W. T. (2006). *Today's public relations: An introduction.* Thousand Oaks, CA: Sage.

Heverin, T., & Zach, L. (2010). *Microblogging for crisis communication: Examination of Twitter use in response to a 2009 violent crisis in the Seattle-Tacoma, Washington area.* Paper presented at the annual meeting of the International Community on Information Systems for Crisis Response and Management, Seattle, WA.

Huang, Y.-H., & Su, S.-H. (2009). Determinants of consistent, timely, and active responses in corporate crises. *Public Relations Review, 35,* 7–17.

Jeffres, L. W., Neuendorf, K., Braken, C. C., & Atkin, D. (2008). Integrating theoretical traditions in media effects: Using third-person effects to link agenda-setting and cultivation. *Mass Communication and Society, 11,* 470–491.

Jin, Y. (2010). Making sense sensibly in crisis communication: How publics' crisis appraisals influence their negative emotions, coping strategy preferences and crisis response acceptance. *Communication Research, 37*(4), 522–552.

Jin, Y., & Liu, B. F. (2010). The blog-mediated crisis communication model: Recommendations for responding to influential external blogs. *Journal of Public Relations Research, 22*(4), 429–455.

Jin, Y., Liu, B. F., Anagondahalli, D., & Austin, L. (2014). Scale development for measuring publics' emotions in organizational crises. *Public Relations Review, 40,* 509–518.

Jin, Y., Liu, B. F., & Austin, L. L. (2014). Examining the role of social media in effective crisis management: The effects of crisis origin, information form, and source on publics' crisis responses. *Communication Research, 41,* 74–94.

Kaplan, A. M., & Haenlein, M. (2010). Users of the world, unite! The challenges and opportunities of social media. *Business Horizons, 53,* 59–68.

Kozinets, R. V., de Valck, K., Wojnicki, A., & Wilner, S. J. (2010). Networked narratives: Understanding word-of-mouth marketing in online communities. *Journal of Marketing, 74,* 71–89.

Lee, B. T. (2004). Audience-oriented approach to crisis communication: A study of Hong Kong consumers' evaluation of an organizational crisis. *Communication Research, 31*, 600–618.

Lev-On, A. (2012). Communication, community, crisis: Mapping uses and gratifications in the contemporary media environment. *New Media Society, 14*(1), 98–116.

Li, C., Bernoff, J., Fiorentino, R., & Glass, S. (2007). *Social technographics®: Mapping participation in activities forms the foundation of a social strategy*. Cambridge, MA: Forrester Research, Inc.

Liu, B. F. (2010). Distinguishing how elite newspapers and A-list blogs cover crisis: Insights for managing crises online. *Public Relations Review, 36*, 28–34.

Liu, B. F., Austin, L. L., & Jin, Y. (2011). How publics respond to crisis communication strategies: The interplay of information form and source. *Public Relations Review, 37*, 345–353.

Liu, B., Fraustino, J. D., & Jin, Y. (2015). Jumping on the social media bandwagon? How disaster information form, source, type, and prior disaster exposure affect public outcomes. *Journal of Applied Communication Research, 43*, 44–65.

Liu, B. F., Fraustino, J. D., & Jin, Y. (in press, 2015). Social media use during disasters: How information form and source influence intended behavioral responses. *Communication Research*. Published online ahead of print: doi: 10.1177/0093650214565917

Liu, B. F., Jin, Y., & Austin, L. L. (2013). The tendency to tell: Understanding publics' communicative responses to crisis information form and source. *Journal of Public Relations Research, 25*, 51–67.

Liu, B. F., Jin, Y., Austin, L. L., & Janoske, M. (2012). The Social-Mediated Crisis Communication Model: Guidelines for effective crisis management in a changing media landscape. In S. C. Duhe (Ed.), *New media and public relations* (2nd ed.), (pp. 257–266). New York: Peter Lang.

Liu, B. F., Jin, Y., Briones, R., & Kuch, B. (2012). Managing turbulence in the blogosphere: Evaluating the blog-mediated crisis communication model with the American Red Cross. *Journal of Public Relations Research, 24*, 353–370.

Liu, B. F., & Pompper, D. (2012). The crisis with no name: Defining the interplay of culture, ethnicity, and race on organizational issues and media outcomes. *Journal of Applied Communication Research, 39*, 1–20.

Macias, W., Hilyard, K., & Freimuth, V. (2009). Blog functions as risk and crisis communication during Hurricane Katrina. *Journal of Computer-Mediated Communication, 15*, 1–31.

Murdock, G. (2010). Shifting anxieties, altered media: Risk communication in networked times. *Catalan Journal of Communication & Cultural Studies, 2*, 159–176.

Procopio, C. H., & Procopio, S. T. (2007). Do you know what it means to miss New Orleans? Internet communication, geographic community, and social capital in crisis. *Journal of Applied Communication Research, 35*, 67–87.

Purcell, K. (2011, March 29). *Information 2.0 and beyond: Where are we, where are we going?* Pew Internet & American Life Project. Retrieved from http://www.pewinternet.org/Presentations/2011/Mar/APLIC.aspx

Richins, M. L. (1983). Negative word-of-mouth by dissatisfied consumers: A pilot study. *Journal of Marketing, 47*, 68–78.

Schultz, F., Utz, S., & Göritz, A. (2011). Is the medium the message? Perceptions of and reactions to crisis communication via Twitter, blogs, and traditional media. *Public Relations Review, 37*, 20–27.

Smith, B. G. (2010). Socially distributing public relations: Twitter, Haiti, and interactivity in social media. *Public Relations Review, 36*, 329–335.

Sohn, D. (2009). Disentangling the effects of social network density on electronic-word-of-mouth (eWOM) intention. *Journal of Computer-Mediated Communication, 14*, 352–367.

Stephens, K. K., & Malone, P. C. (2009). If the organizations won't give us information . . . : The use of multiple new media for crisis technical translation and dialogue. *Journal of Public Relations Research, 21*, 229–239.

Taylor, M., & Kent, M. L. (2007). Taxonomy of mediated crisis responses. *Public Relations Review, 33*, 140–146.

Ward, J. C., & Ostrom, A. L. (2006). Complaining to the masses: The role of protest framing in customer-created complaint Web sites. *The Journal of Consumer Research, 33*, 220–230.

Weiner, B. (1986). *An attribution theory of motivation and emotion*. New York: Springer-Verlag.

Wigley, S., & Fontenot, M. (2010). Crisis managers losing control of the message: A pilot study of the Virginia Tech shooting. *Public Relations Review, 36*, 187–189.

Wright, D. K., & Hinson, M. (2009). An updated look at the impact of social media on public relations practices. *Public Relations Journal, 3*(2), article 2, available at http://www.prsa.org/Intelligence/PRJournal/Spring_09.

INDEX

affective disposition 29
aggressive communication tactics xi, 91–2
aggressive discussion 85
AMA (Ask Me Anything) 66, 78, 79
America Speaks 86
Anderson, Ashley x, xi
annoyance and preference 134–5
anti-narrativists 3
assertive/non-assertive language 130–2
audience interaction 45–6
audience predispositions 79
Austin, Lucinda x, xii

Baldwin, D.A. 150, 152
Bean, Hamilton x, xi, 116, 117
behavioral economics 155–6
behavioral intention 44
Berger, J. 15
biased message processing 33
BMCC (Blog-Mediated Crisis Communication) model 169–70, 174, 176
brand promotion frequency 134
brand representation 146–7
Brock, T.C. 3–4, 25
Bruner, J. 3

Cash, S.B. 157–9
causal network model 6
causality, narrative 6–10
CCFC (Campaign for Commercial-Free Childhood) 152

Center for Strategic Counterterrorism Communications 103
character identification 24, 26, 29
Cheong, P.H. 118
children: and brand representation 146–7; CCFC (Campaign for Commercial-Free Childhood) 152; and consumer socialization 146–50; development theories xii, 142–59; drink choices and food consumption 155; executive functioning research 144–51; food branding and taste perception 153; food choices 152–8; food naming interventions 155–6; food unit pricing 157–8; health risks 142–3; healthy eating promotion 152–3; healthy food in schools 155–7; menu interventions 156–7; school menus 156–7; susceptibility to persuasion 151–2; and toy collection 154–5
climate change narratives 31
CMC (computer-mediated communication) 90
cognitive engagement, in deliberation 85, 88
collaboration, and social networks 43–4, 58
communication-as-domination 111
communicative action theory 112
Comor, Edward 116
concrete language 132
consumer socialization 146–50

consumer UGC (User Generated Content) cooperation 132–4
consumer WOM (Word of Mouth) cooperation 132–4, 136, 165
content generators 42–59
contextual model, of science communication 67–8
controversy, and strategic communication x
conversational cooperation xi; assertive/non-assertive language 130–2; contextual effects 134–5; expectations of 129–32; linguistic cooperation 125–9; linguistic expectations 133–4; persuasion knowledge 129–30; situational effects 134–5; in strategic communication 129–32; strategic/natural communication 129; in UGC (user generated content) 132–4; in WOM (word of mouth) 132–4, 136
Cornwell, T.B. 147, 154, 155, 159
crisis, *see also* SMCC model
crisis communication xii; and social media 164–9
crisis emotions 178
critical culture perspectives x, 110–11, 117–18
Critical Enquiry 2
cross-discipline approach ix–x, 2–3
CSC (Consortium for Strategic Communication) 105, 114–16, 118

Dahlstrom, Michael x, 23
Dalrymple, Kajsa x–xi
dangerous discussion 94–6
DARPA (Defense Advanced Research Projects Agency) 115
definition, strategic communication ix
deliberation 69–72, 85, 86–9; and cognitive engagement 85, 86–8; and critical thinking 88–9; democratic 113–14; of policy 87
democracy, and participation 87
democratic deliberation, and U.S. National Security 113–14
dialogic approaches: formal discussions online 69–71; formal/informal deliberation 69–72; future research direction 76–8; informal discussions online 71–2; information seeking 72–6; online activities in 69–76; in strategic communication 67–9; traditional vs. online media 72–4

diffusion of innovations 47
disagreement in discussion 85
disagreement online 89–94
discourse psychology 5–7
discussion classification 93–6
discussion networks, characteristics of 85
distributed practice 88
diverse views in discussion 94–6
Downs, A. 73
DSB (Defense Science Board) 112–13, 119
Dutta-Bergman, Mohan 112

E-ELM (Extended Elaboration Likelihood Model) 24, 25–6
ecological behavior 45
educational exchange 117
EE (entertainment education) 24, 27–8
effect studies 10
effectiveness core value 111
efficiency core value 111
ELM (Elaboration Likelihood Model) 4, 24, 25, 26, 30
engagement activities, types of 87–8
entertainment experience 28
entertainment media 27–8; constructs 28; narratives 28–9
entertainment psychology 29
environmental issues 48, 59
EROM (Entertainment Overcoming Reactance Model) 24, 26–8
ethical communication strategy 116
Eveland, W.P. 94
everyday incivility 90
executive functioning research 144–51
expertise 49–50

Fisher, W.R. 3
flaming xi, 89–93
food choices: among children *see* children; future recommendations/direction 158–9; and marketing communication 142–59; promotion 152–8; recommendations/future direction 158–9; unit pricing 157–8; value in retail settings 157–8
free agents 49
Friestad, M. 144
Furlow, R.B. 115

Gerrig, R.J. 3–4, 25
global public opinion 103
Goodale, Greg 112–13
Goodall, H.L. Jr. 114, 115

Google 74–6, 78
grassroots influentials 50
Green, M.C. 3–4, 25
Gregory, Bruce 106
Grice, H.P. 125, 126
group conformity 48

habitual behavior 145
Hallahan, K. 105, 106
Hartnett, Stephen John 112–13
health belief model 45–6, 52
healthy eating promotion 152–3
heterogeneity in discussion 94–6
heterophily 50
Hively, M.H. 94
homophily 50
Hornik, R.C. 46
Hutchens, Myiah x, xi

ICGs (influential content generators) 42–59; collaborating 54, 56–8; ethics 54; forwarding 54, 55–6; identifying 49–53; listening 53–5; online 51–8; typology category definitions 54
influentials 49, 50
interpersonal communication 46, 129
interpersonal conversation, linguistic cooperation in 125–9, 136

Jin, Yan x, xii

Kaufman, K. 22
key informants 49
Kronrod, Ann x, xi–xii, 133–5, 137
Kumar, Deepa 112

LaMarre, Heather x, 2, 3, 27, 30, 33
Landreville, K.D. 27, 30
linguistic cooperation: in interpersonal conversation 125–9, 136; online limitations 137
linguistic enquiry, future in strategic communication 136–7
linguistic expectations 133–4
Lundry, Chris 118

McAlister, Anna x, xii, 147, 150, 154, 155, 157–9
marginal innovators 49
marketing communication xii, 125–37; and food habits *see* children; food choices
marketing social good 44–8; adopting multi-way approach 46–8; drawing from theory 44–5; traditional one-way communication efforts 45–6
media engagement 29
media platforms 72–8
Melley, Timothy 112
menu interventions 156–7
Milkman, K.L. 15
Mitchell, Gordon 118
Moses, L.J. 150, 152
Moss, M. 152
motivated cognition theory 33
Moyer-Gusé, E. 27
multi-way strategic communication 42, 46–8
Mutz, D. 93

narrative: definition of 21, 22; entertainment media 28–9; as message recipient's story 22–3; as message sender's story 21–2; non-entertainment 29; political 30; structural elements 21–2
narrative causality 6–10
narrative messaging, in entertainment/emergent/hybrid media 27–8
narrative persuasion x, 1–37; accuracy 12–13; addressing normative questions 11–14; anti-narrativists 3; audience for 14–15; and communications 3, 23; in context 13, 36; cross-discipline 2–3; discipline-specific effects theory 30, 33; dominant theories 24; ethical questions 10–14; fractured research streams 2; framing tactic 11; future of 14–15; inconsistencies 5–7; internal variance 5–7; key perspectives 21–3; and new media audiences 15; normative values 1; organizational power 32–3; and perceived external realism 9–10; and psychology 3; and recall 9; sender-receiver relationship 21; setting of 2–5; specific focus 2; and strategic communication 23–7; strategic narrative 20, 30–2; strategic storytelling 20–37; Study 1 7–8; Study 2 8–9; Study 3 9–10; theoretical integration 30; theories 23–7; and time 8; traditions 2; transportation phenomenon 3–4; trends in 20–37; variables 4, 5–7
narrative quality 4–5
narrative realism 9–10
narrative/story distinction 22
narrative strategy 20, 21–3, 31

narrative transportation *see* TIM
narrative turn 2
narrative typology 32–7; agency 33–4, 36; intentionality 34–5
National Framework for Strategic Communication 103
non-entertainment narrative 29
nWOM (negative word-of-mouth) communication 166

obesity xii, 48, 142–59
O'Keefe, D.J. 3
online activities, dialogic approaches in *see* dialogic approaches
online aggression 55, 91–2
online anonymity 90, 91
online audience interaction 45–6
online communication and discussion x–xi, 42–59, 84–97
online disagreement 89–94
online flagging 93
online ICGs 51–8
online incivility 90–3, 97
online media: and behavior/attitudes 66–79; opinion leadership xi, 47, 49, 77; selective exposure 77–8; social nature of 66–79; trust/credibility 77
online media platforms 72–8
online political discussion xi, 84–97
online science communication 67–9
operationalization of network measures 97
opinion leadership xi, 47, 49, 77
optimal heterophily 50
Oregon Citizens' Initiative Review 86
organizational crisis, definition 164–5
organizational power 32–3

participation, and democracy 87
participatory media 42–59; and product marketing 42–4
Paul, C. 111–12
peer sources 50
perceived realism 9–10, 29
perceived similarity 50–1
persuasion knowledge 129–30
PEST (Public Engagement in Science and Technology) 12
Piaget, J. 144
Pierce, D.L. 22
planned behavior, theory 44–6
PLOS journal 66
policy deliberation 87

policy entrepreneurs 49
political discussion xi, 84–97
political flaming xi, 89–93
political incivility 90
political satire 31–2
polysemy 137
product marketing, and participatory media 42–4
producers 49
propaganda 106
prosocial listening studies 55
prosocial marketing 44–7, 50, 59
prosocial strategic communication 42–59
prosumers 49
prosumption 118
prototypical behavior 51
public diplomacy 106–7, 116–17
public opinion formation xi
public participation model, of science communication 68–9
PUS (Public Understanding of Science) model 12

reactance theory 26–7, 28
reddit website 66, 78, 79
rhetorical perspectives x, 110–11, 117–18
Robinson, T.N. 153
rumor psychology theory 174

safe discussion 94–6
SCCT (situational crisis communication theory) 167
science communication 67–9
SCT (Social Cognitive Theory) 24–5, 26, 46–7, 59
security themes xi
SMCC (Social-Mediated Crisis Communication) model xii, 164–83; areas for special consideration 168–9; and BMCC model 169–70, 174, 176; cause-and-effect explanations 180–1; components of 170–4; crisis characteristics 168; crisis management cycle 182; crisis recovery definition 178–9; current issues 166–7; current/emerging issues 165–6; developing influence 181; dominant research streams 166–8; effective recovery factors 178–9; form and source impact on crisis emotions 176–7; future directions 174–82; information flow 171; information forms 171; on information seeking 176; on

information sharing 176; key publics 171; media type classification 182; organizational considerations 171–4; overview of 169–74; on publics' crisis responses 177–8; research 174–82; on response strategy acceptance 176–7; response criteria 172–4; response strategies 172, 173; scale development for measuring crisis emotions 178; theories 167–8; *see also* crisis; social media

Social Learning Theory 92

social media 72–8; audience-oriented approaches/considerations 168; characteristics of 169; crisis characteristics 168; and crisis communication *see* SMCC model; definition 164; and misinformation 163; non-crisis functions 168; organizational approaches/ considerations 168, *see also* SMCC model

social media platforms 72–8, 165

social network influentials x–xi, 47–53; definitions of 49

social networks, and collaboration 43–4

stakeholders 49

Strange, J.J. 3–4

strategic communication: definition ix, 105, 106; future research direction 76–8; research academic clusters 106

strategic conversation 136

strategic informants 49

strategic narrative 20, 30–2; areas of 32; definition 31–2; terminology used 32

strategic storytelling 20–37

super influentials 50

TIM (Transportation Imagery Model) 3–4, 24, 25, 26, 29

Tirunillai, S. 137

transmediation 118

transportation theory *see* TIM

trendsetting individuals 48

true engagement 111–12

UGC (User Generated Content) cooperation 132–4

UGT (uses and gratification theory) 167

U.S. National Security: communication/ organization/security intersections 116–17; core assumptions 111–14; critical culture/rhetorical perspectives x, 110–11, 117–18; and democratic deliberation 113–14; as dysfunctional 115; key concepts and tensions 107–11; old/new agendas 111–16; security themes and overall agenda 105–7; and strategic communication 103–19

Van Laer, T. 24

VSM (visual social media) 180

Walther, W. 30

Wansink, B. 156, 159

Warnick, Barbara 110

Winseck, Dwayne 106

WOM (Word of Mouth) cooperation 132–4, 136, 165

Wright, P. 144

young people, and food marketing 142–59

Young, Rachel x–xi

Taylor & Francis eBooks

Helping you to choose the right eBooks for your Library

Add Routledge titles to your library's digital collection today. Taylor and Francis ebooks contains over 50,000 titles in the Humanities, Social Sciences, Behavioural Sciences, Built Environment and Law.

Choose from a range of subject packages or create your own!

Benefits for you
- Free MARC records
- COUNTER-compliant usage statistics
- Flexible purchase and pricing options
- All titles DRM-free.

Benefits for your user
- Off-site, anytime access via Athens or referring URL
- Print or copy pages or chapters
- Full content search
- Bookmark, highlight and annotate text
- Access to thousands of pages of quality research at the click of a button.

REQUEST YOUR FREE INSTITUTIONAL TRIAL TODAY

Free Trials Available
We offer free trials to qualifying academic, corporate and government customers.

eCollections – Choose from over 30 subject eCollections, including:

Archaeology	Language Learning
Architecture	Law
Asian Studies	Literature
Business & Management	Media & Communication
Classical Studies	Middle East Studies
Construction	Music
Creative & Media Arts	Philosophy
Criminology & Criminal Justice	Planning
Economics	Politics
Education	Psychology & Mental Health
Energy	Religion
Engineering	Security
English Language & Linguistics	Social Work
Environment & Sustainability	Sociology
Geography	Sport
Health Studies	Theatre & Performance
History	Tourism, Hospitality & Events

For more information, pricing enquiries or to order a free trial, please contact your local sales team:
www.tandfebooks.com/page/sales

Routledge
Taylor & Francis Group

The home of Routledge books

www.tandfebooks.com